War and Morality

War and Morality
Citizens' Rights and Duties

MICHAEL CAVANAGH

McFarland & Company, Inc., Publishers
Jefferson, North Carolina, and London

LIBRARY OF CONGRESS CATALOGUING-IN-PUBLICATION DATA

Cavanagh, Michael, 1937–
　　War and morality : citizens' rights and duties / Michael Cavanagh.
　　　　p.　　cm.
　　Includes bibliographical references and index.

　　ISBN 978-0-7864-6988-8
　　softcover : acid free paper ∞

　　1. War — Moral and ethical aspects.　I. Title.
U21.2.C385 2012
172'.42 — dc23　　　　　　　　　　　　　　　　2012008864

BRITISH LIBRARY CATALOGUING DATA ARE AVAILABLE

© 2012 Michael Cavanagh. All rights reserved

No part of this book may be reproduced or transmitted in any form or by any means, electronic or mechanical, including photocopying or recording, or by any information storage and retrieval system, without permission in writing from the publisher.

Front cover images © 2012 Shutterstock

Manufactured in the United States of America

McFarland & Company, Inc., Publishers
　Box 611, Jefferson, North Carolina 28640
　　www.mcfarlandpub.com

Table of Contents

Preface   1
Introduction   5

1. Conscience and Making Moral Decisions   11
2. Just War Principles: Nature and Critique   33
3. Other Perspectives on War: Pacifism and Realism   59
4. Virtue Ethics: Civilian and Military Considerations   80
5. Moral Decision-Making: The Cognitive Dimension   104
6. Propaganda, Deceit and Moral Decisions   125
7. Morality and War: Theoretical Issues   147
8. Morality and War: Practical Issues   167

Bibliography   193
Index   199

Preface

War is complicated, and morality is complicated. When the two are combined, the result is very complicated, but this does not mean war and morality are beyond a reasonable degree of comprehension. Everyday life and its constituent parts (marriage, parenthood, career) are complicated, but people generally survive and many flourish despite the challenges that life presents.

This book's main objective is to educate and empower individual citizens, the major stakeholders in war, to make informed conscience decisions about declaring, waging, and ending war. Stakeholders, as the term is used here, are individuals who can have a direct and indirect influence on their nation's decisions and who are affected directly and indirectly by these decisions and resultant actions. Stakeholders can assume one of two positions: they can actively participate in deliberating the moral aspects of their nation's wars, or they can be indifferent and dispassionate about them. Unfortunately, most stakeholders in any organization, whether it is their nation, workplace, or church, are indifferent with regard to the organization's functioning until something occurs that impacts them negatively and personally, and then it is usually too late to remedy the situation.

In pre–Christian and early Christian times, nations generally had a populace comprised of three classes: royals, ordinary citizens, and slaves. Wars were planned, initiated, waged, and ended by the royals (kings, princes, lords). Slaves were not considered "persons," so if they were recognized at all, it was only to help fight the wars. "Ordinary citizens" were individuals who had no input with respect to war because they were deemed too uninformed to take part in declaring and managing war. Their sole role was to support the sovereigns of their nation by paying in blood and treasure for the wars waged in their name. In modern times, democratic nations are comprised of many classes of citizens, most of whom have access to information and the right to make statements and cast votes that reflect their moral position on issues, including war.

Although the book is written for citizens of all nations, its primary audience is the "ordinary citizens" in democratic nations who, regardless of their status in society, often do not realize they are the major stakeholders in war because wars are fought by them and their loved ones and financed by their taxes. Ordinary citizens can realize it is within their power to significantly influence the moral worldview of their leaders.

The purpose of the book is to help today's citizens make decisions with regard to whether war in general or a specific war can be a moral enterprise based on core constitutional and humanitarian values. To this end, the book addresses the morality of war and the ways in which it differs from the political, military, legal, and economic dimensions typically considered when decisions are made regarding war. For example, all of the other dimensions may support going to war but the moral dimension — deciding whether it is the just thing to do — may not support the decision. In this case, the proposed war is immoral and all the actions that follow are morally tainted. In conjunction with addressing the nature of the morality of war, a methodology for moral decision-making is presented to bridge the void between understanding the morality of war and translating that understanding into moral action in support or non-support of a war.

The book does not present moral prescriptions or formulas for arriving at a decision regarding the morality of a war. It simply provides an updated theoretical framework comprised of just war principles that have been in existence since pre–Christian times. In addition, pacifism, realism and virtue ethics are presented as optional frames of reference. These theories are not presented as factual or perfect. Instead, the key moral concepts and positions are discussed through the prism of critical thinking in order to assess their validity in relation to modern warfare. How individuals choose to think and act within these parameters is up to them.

This book is not anti-war or pro-war, but pro-justice on issues regarding war. It presents moral foundations on which to make decisions about war and some materials for beginning the building process. Each individual may choose which design and materials to adopt in order to build a personal moral structure. In the end, individual structures may look very different from each other, but at least they will rise above moral ground zero and stimulate thinking beyond strictly political, military, economic and legal perspectives. As individual citizens become more informed about the world in general and the world of war in particular through modern media, they can move beyond simplistic statements ("I'm for the war" or "I'm against the war") based on mere moral intuition.

It is important for citizens to consider these issues because war is arguably the most devastating event that occurs worldwide. Estimating the costs of war is a complex process, but the two most quantifiable factors are the number of lives lost and dollars spent. The magnitude of these costs is seen in a research project by the Eisenhower Study Group at Brown University's Watson Institute for International Studies (2011) that brought together more than 20 academics from several disciplines to study the many cost variables with regard to the current U.S. wars in Iraq, Afghanistan and Pakistan.

With regard to human costs, the report estimates that 224,000 to 258,000 people died directly in these three wars, an additional 365,000 have been wounded and 7.8 million people have been displaced. These statistics do not include those who died indirectly in these nations due to the lack of clean drinking water, health care, and nutrition. According to the report, the final bill for the U.S. government is estimated to be $3.7 trillion to $4.4 trillion. In addition, the report estimates that health care for veterans of these wars will cost between $600 billion and $950 billion and will not peak until 2050.

These numbers are more than the simple operating costs of a war. They represent serious moral issues because they reflect the destruction of human life and the inherent right of all people to life, liberty, and the opportunity to pursue happiness.

The field of research for the book includes several academic disciplines, including philosophy, theology, psychology, law, politics, international relations, and military science. Each discipline plays a significant role in the morality of war and therefore is included in order to provide a holistic picture of the topic. The book also is organized to provide the reader with a logical sequence of topics: the nature of conscience, moral norms to be consulted by conscience, moral decision-making and the factors that interfere with it, and the theoretical and practical issues involved in acting morally in the real world of war.

While every war is horrific and reflects the worst kind of human failure on all sides, reality indicates that, in an imperfect world, war will always be with us. However, when war is deemed absolutely necessary, the challenge remains for national leaders and ordinary citizens to make every effort to wage it in a moral (just) manner. This book strives to advance and sharpen that moral deliberating process as it applies to war.

Introduction

Moral inarticulacy in the face of war is itself a moral stance—one that rejects the possibility of reason, accepts normlessness in international affairs, and capitulates to cynicism. To seek to apply objective moral reasoning to war is to defend the possibility of civil society and a world community based on justice.

—Jean Bethke Elshtain

Historically, when discussions, plans, and debates arise regarding war, the topics of thinking and acting morally seldom enter the picture. A "good war," a "popular war," is one that is being won, and a "bad war," an "unpopular war," is one that is being lost. For example, the Vietnam War was perceived by most Americans as a good war until the cost-benefit ratios began to slide in the direction of cost. As American casualties and economic costs rose and the reasons for the war became increasingly murky and suspect, a good war morphed into a bad war—a popular war into an unpopular one—a noble cause into an ignoble one—a military to be honored into a military to be dishonored.

What caused the shift? Was it that mounting human and economic costs jump-started the conscience of individual Americans, gradually causing the war to be rightly or wrongly perceived as immoral, or was it simply that the war was being lost, or was it a combination of the two? If the United States had been clearly winning, even though the human and economic costs remained the same, would morality ever have entered the picture? Would anyone have cared about how the war was declared, waged or ended?

In modern democratic societies, individual citizens are the employers of their political and military leaders and therefore are in the position of ultimately authorizing or not authorizing wars. Yet, all too frequently, the tail wags the dog. Political and military leaders act as if they are the employers—the bosses—who dictate to individual citizens when wars are to be declared, how they will be waged, and when and how they will end.

Citizens often are complicit in this arrangement because they may have a vested interest in donating their consciences to their leaders in all matters, including wars. If a war is won, "*We* won the war"; if the war is lost, "*They* lost the war." As a result, citizens can have clean hands, no matter what happens. Politicians and generals were blamed for losing the Vietnam War, yet they could have done nothing without the support of the majority of the American people, including Congress and the president. In the final analysis, wars are "owned and operated" by individual citizens who have a profound, though not total, moral (as well as political, military, and economic) responsibility for them.

As is true with many concepts that deal with complicated behaviors, several definitions of morality and war are found throughout the literature. Morality is sometimes defined as a concept that is clearly distinct from ethics, while at other times the terms are used as synonymous and interchangeable. In the following chapters, the term "morality" is used to describe both the process of analyzing what constitutes good and evil and the actions that follow the analysis, except in situations that require a distinction between morality and ethics. "War" is defined as widespread armed conflict between political communities, whether they be nations or other political groups, for the purpose of fending off a serious military threat, conquering a nation or territory for political or practical gain, or protecting third party nations or groups from unjust violence, as would occur in genocide, for example.

The concept that individual attitudes, beliefs, and values are critical in moral decision-making requires an awareness of the distinction between individualism, individuality, nationalism, and paternalism. Individualism holds that individuals are the center of the moral universe, and it is appropriate that they consider only themselves, not national or international issues, when they make moral decisions. At the other end of the scale is nationalism, which refers to the belief that the nation is the center of the moral universe and the rights of individuals are secondary or have little or no importance in the overall process of governing.

Individuality, which lies midpoint between individualism and nationalism, holds that individuals have certain inalienable moral duties and rights, which include the right to inform their consciences as thoroughly as possible, make moral judgments based on this information, and act according to their decisions. Similarly, societies have a conscience in what Socrates called "the conscience of the laws" which individuals also must respect in order to protect the well-being of the social community. For example, individuals have a duty and a right to follow their well-informed consciences, and society has a duty and right to follow its well-informed conscience. When these respective consciences conflict, as they often do, especially regarding war, open debate ought to be available to all stakeholders.

Paternalism refers to the government's assumption of the role of parents. Like authoritarian parents, national leaders often view critical thinking by ordinary soldiers and civilians as psychologically recalcitrant, politically unpatriotic, and religiously heretical. Therefore, "good citizens" are disinclined to think critically, and only those with moral courage do so in times of war. Paternalism reduces individual citizens, who may be as wise as, if not wiser than, some of their leaders, to the role of obedient, disobedient, or disinterested children. In turn, paternalistic leaders withhold important information well beyond that which is legitimately classified from the citizens, and then use their "ignorance" as a justification to make decisions for them.

A topic typically omitted in discussions of war is the collective responsibility of individual citizens for the wars they allow to be fought in their name. The last time collective guilt was seriously discussed and debated was during and immediately after World War II with the citizens of Germany in mind. Americans generally believed that all German people who knew or should have known that Germany was waging an unjust war and using unjust tactics ought to be held morally responsible or liable.

Many moral philosophers and theologians who have discussed the issue of collective guilt believe all citizens are partially, though not directly, responsible or liable for the illegal and immoral actions of their national leaders and armies during times of war, whether their nation was the victor or the vanquished. The only exceptions would be citizens who truly did not know what their leaders or armies were doing or those who actively dissented and took whatever actions they could reasonably take to stop the destruction. However, individuals who accuse the citizens of enemy nations of being complicit in immoral acts carried out in their name ought to accept the same degree of moral responsibility if their own nation commits immoral actions while declaring, waging, and ending wars.

John A. Rohr (1971) comments on the moral responsibility of individual citizens regarding war:

> We must consider the principles behind our rejection of the idea that a citizen in a democratic society has no obligation to investigate the justice of a particular war. Such a position contradicts a basic premise of sound democratic theory — the personal responsibility of all citizens to promote the common good or, more simply, civic virtue. A good citizen in a democracy cannot absolve himself from the responsibility of looking into the merits of major policy questions. One of the reasons [the medieval philosopher] Vitoria says "subjects" need not bother about whether

a war is unjust is that they cannot do anything about it anyway. In a democracy it is precisely because the citizen can do something about a war he finds unjust that he must investigate the whole question [p. 114].

In keeping with Rohr's statement, this book's basic premise is that it is morally incumbent on each individual citizen, both civilian and military, to take part in the decision process, arrive at an informed conscience decision about the morality of war in general or a specific war, and act on the decision.

There are four basic elements in the process of individual stakeholders becoming educated and empowered. They are:

- Having an intellectual, emotional and moral investment in an issue. These qualities provide the motivation, the impetus, to affect a situation in one way or another. Action requires motivation, and without action, nothing can change. Lacking sufficient motivation to change a situation can stem from three sources: not caring about the situation, caring but not having the quantity or quality of information to develop a clear position, or caring but having a pessimistic attitude about the likelihood that change will occur under any circumstances.
- Having access to informational resources that can shed light on the issue. This process includes gathering information from all sides of issues as they are discussed and debated in various media and, in particular, seeking out sources generally acknowledged to be moderate, independent, unbiased and dispassionate.
- Having a reasonably optimistic belief that the actions one takes will make some difference in the situation. For example, due primarily to the advocacy of ordinary citizens, changes have occurred in the military that would never have been envisioned a half-century ago: women and racial minorities are completely integrated into the military; homosexuals are allowed to serve openly, women are deployed to combat areas; solders with significant combat injuries are allowed to remain in the service, and there is an all-volunteer army. None of these changes "just happened." They began as grass roots movements and eventually garnered sufficient intellectual, emotional, and moral momentum to overcome the inertia of the *status quo*.
- Having the commitment and moral courage to act on their values and beliefs. Simply having a position on an issue, no matter how strong, will not lead to change if the values and beliefs are kept private or shared only with family and friends.

William F. Felice (2009) provides some practical examples of how individual citizens can translate their moral beliefs into constructive action:

In a democracy, all citizens have a duty to take responsibility for the direction of their country's domestic and foreign polices. Opinions can be expressed through voting, speaking out, writing letters to Congress and local papers, signing petitions, organizing and participating in demonstrations, civil disobedience, and so on. We have the ability to seek truth and apply moral reasoning to foreign policy. In this information age, we have the means to gather the relevant information and assess the moral case for [war]. We have the ability for moral reasoning and should apply it to decisions that the government makes in our name [p. 181].

Toward this end, the following topics will be discussed: Chapter 1: "Conscience and Making Moral Decisions" addresses the nature of individual conscience, theories of conscience, the moral decision-making process, and a critical analysis of conscience. Chapter 2: "Just War Principles: Nature and Critique" addresses the concepts underlying the just war principles, the elements of the nine just war principles, and the challenges to them. Chapter 3: "Other Perspectives on War: Pacifism and Realism" addresses pacifism and realism as they pertain to making ethical decisions regarding war and the challenges of each view, as well as their relationship to each other and to just war principles. Chapter 4: "Virtue Ethics: Civilian and Military Considerations" addresses the nature of virtue ethics, the virtues of patriotism, duty, integrity, courage, competence, and humility, and the challenges to virtue ethics. Chapter 5: "Moral Decision-Making: The Cognitive Dimension" addresses the psychological aspects of realistic and defensive thinking, the nature of responsible thinking, the development of a moral worldview, and how these factors facilitate or interfere with the decision-making process.. Chapter 6: "Propaganda, Deceit, and Moral Decisions" addresses the nature of war propaganda and its techniques, the nature of deceit in war and its consequences, and how these factors can preclude informed moral decision-making by leaders and citizens. Chapter 7: "Morality and War: Theoretical Issues" addresses military and moral theories: military necessity, double effect, and preemptive and preventive attacks, along with critiques of each theory and how they are applied to decision-making in war. Chapter 8: "Morality and War: Practical Issues" addresses the moral issues related to terrorism, unmanned aerial vehicles, cluster munitions, economic sanctions, and depleted uranium, and the implications of these issues for making conscience decisions regarding war.

1

Conscience and Making Moral Decisions

Nothing is more powerful than an individual acting out of conscience, thus helping to bring the collective conscience to life.
— Norman Cousins

This chapter deals with the awesome responsibilities of individual conscience as it relates to empowering individuals to make moral decisions and act upon them. The challenge for individuals is to determine how they can empower themselves to make moral decisions based on sound knowledge and an analytical process that goes beyond the parochial needs, perceptions, dynamics and dictates of their nation and its leaders. Furthermore, the principle of justice, as well as other moral principles, obliges individuals to arrive not only at well-informed decisions but also to act upon them in meaningful ways. This chapter will address the following issues: the nature of conscience, the decision-making process, a critical analysis of conscience, and an examination of conscience regarding war.

The Nature of Conscience

Conscience is what most separates human beings from animals, which have intellects but not consciences in the ordinary understanding of the concept. Yet, conscience does not get the respect it deserves, not even from its owners. Conscience is commonly ignored, manipulated, abandoned, or handed over to others (a conscience by-pass), especially in times of war. One of the ironies of human behavior is that individuals who would never hand over a prized possession to someone have no trouble handing over their consciences. This is especially true in institutions that have a hierarchical system of management or government — "My bosses told me to do it, so I did it — talk to them about it."

Conscience is described here as the part of the intellect that gathers knowledge from the internal and external environments, critically analyzes and judges it according to moral principles, and arrives at a moral decision. This description of conscience is developed partly as a reaction against the early, classical definitions of conscience which were legalistic (the law supersedes individual conscience), minimalist (the proper use of law and reason alone will result in right behavior), compartmentalized (conscience is located in the faculty of reason and in no other dimension of human nature), and deductive (individuals draw moral conclusions solely from analyzing external data).

No universally accepted view of conscience exists. There are, for example, Catholic, Protestant, Jewish, Muslim, and secular views and often disagreements within each of these groups. Conscience is not mentioned in Hinduism or Buddhism, and skeptics doubt its existence. However, most of the world religions and many secularists have a place for conscience, and there is a special place for it in Judeo-Christian ethics when making moral judgments about war. The following understanding is derived from various theories of conscience in order to arrive at a holistic model that would generally be acceptable to a large number of people.

One common concern about the nature of conscience is the issue of subjectivity-objectivity. On one end of the continuum is subjectivity which, in its classic form, means that it is entirely up to individuals to decide, for both themselves and others, what constitutes morally good and evil behavior. This is a common understanding of conscience in a society that encourages and rewards individuality. Young people especially are told to "just follow your conscience," "trust your intuition," or "let your conscience be your guide." This fits in nicely with the skeptics' position that there is no such thing as conscience and that the "voice of conscience" is simply the echo of an individual's own voice bouncing off the soundproof walls that keep contrary voices from entering awareness.

For subjectivists, a "well-formed conscience" weighs the positive and negative effects of past, present or future actions and their impact on the welfare of the individual. Moral good is defined as anything that helps individuals achieve their legitimate goals, and moral evil is defined as anything that prevents individuals from achieving their legitimate goals. External reality is taken into consideration but only in a self-centered way ("If I take the action I am contemplating, will I be rewarded or punished by society?"). The problem is that classic subjectivism is self-absorbed and virtually ignores the rights and duties of others. Analogously, "subjectivist" automobile drivers would have no need to know the speed limit laws in any area because they consider themselves capable of deciding the appropriate speeds based on their personal assessment of each situation.

At the opposite end of the continuum is objectivity, which, in its classic form, means that moral norms are entirely external to the individual. These norms may be gleaned from the tenets of philosophy, science, politics, law, theology, psychology, economics, and so on. For classic objectivists, a well-formed conscience discerns what specific external norms apply (the laws of the nation, the laws of war, the laws of nature, religious laws, and so on) and then applies them to a past, present, or future action. No personal, internal moral code exists for objectivists; instead, the moral code lies largely in the teachings and laws of moral authorities, and all that remains is for individuals to know and obey them. Analogously, automobile drivers need only know the speed limit laws on particular stretches of road and obey them. They need not, indeed should not, analyze each traffic situation to determine whether the general norm (55 mph) is too slow or too fast for conditions.

The paradigm presented in this chapter is holistic and includes a combination of objective, subjective, intellectual, and affective dimensions of human behavior. It is important to keep in mind that moral decision-making is related to "doing the right moral thing," or "not doing the wrong moral thing," in contrast to making decisions based on other types of "right things." In other words, the military, legal, political, or religious "right thing" may not necessarily be the moral "right thing."

Individual conscience is not a thing or a place; it is a process that considers whether an intention or act is good or evil, proceeds to gather information to shed light on the nature and possible consequences of an act, and ends by measuring this information against a set of moral principles. At this point a moral decision is made, which may or may not be put into action, depending on the individual's appraisal of the entire situation.

Conscience is not a static entity. As a part of intellect, it needs constant exercise, challenge, and development. It is important to keep current with what is happening in the world, because, all other things being equal, the more knowledge individuals have, the better prepared they will be to make sound moral decisions.

Not every theorist believes conscience exists. Some believe that decisions made on the basis of what constitutes right and wrong and good and bad behavior are simply projections of what individuals want to do in the first place and are based on personal impulses, intuitions, and desires rather than on a moral analysis of behavior. For example, a young family man may enter the military against his wife's wishes because he wants to get away from home, regain lost freedom, experience some excitement, and perhaps return a hero. He cannot realistically admit these reasons to himself, much less his family, so, subconsciously, he turns a selfish decision into a moral boast: "I can't sit home doing nothing for my country while my friends are risking their lives to keep us safe and free." On the other hand, a young woman may want to get out of the military because she hates it, feels homesick, and is afraid she will be deployed to a combat zone. Because she cannot admit these reasons to herself, much less to her company commander, she claims that, after seeing the true nature of war, in good conscience she cannot remain in the military. In other words, both of these individuals have strong self-serving motives that they artificially elevate to decisions of conscience in order to justify their actions to both themselves and others.

The fact that many individuals make decisions based solely on self-centered rather than moral reasons does not negate the existence of conscience. It only indicates that individuals can bypass conscience when making decisions that can seriously affect their lives and the lives of others, but this type of behavior is a perversion of conscience. A well-informed conscience takes into account one's own interests, the interests of others, the interests of relevant institutions, the interests of society, and universal moral principles before coming to a final, well-analyzed decision. Sometimes the decision is in line with the individual's self-interests, and sometimes it is contrary to them, and this is when having a sound conscience can be a financially, psychologically, professionally, and socially expensive possession.

In a perfect world, all individuals who perform a moral analysis of the same act at the same time would arrive at the same conclusion, such as a particular war is moral and religiously permitted, or it is immoral and religiously sacrilegious. However, as soon as imperfect human beings enter the picture, the situation changes, so that one intelligent and reasonable individual may decide a war is moral and religiously permitted, while another equally intelligent and reasonable individual concludes the opposite. These concepts will be described more concretely as they arise throughout this and other chapters in the book.

The moral analysis of a past, present, or future act does not guarantee that the resultant decision and behavior will be morally correct, any more than doing a fiscal analysis guarantees that the conclusion will be economically correct. But a moral (or fiscal) analysis is likely to render a decision closer to truth than if no analysis or a superficial, disjointed one is undertaken.

Ethical Theories

The term "ethical" will be used here to describe theories and analyses of good and evil behavior because "ethical" refers more to the science and study of good and evil than does the general term "moral" which primarily describes the actions that follow the analyses. Ethical theories provide a norm, a benchmark, against which conscience can measure whether an act is good or evil, for example, whether it is just or unjust. The most common ethical theories are natural law, deontology, and consequentialism. However, interest in virtue ethics as an ethical norm has increased over the past few years, especially in the military, so it will receive a more complete treatment in Chapter 4. Because these theories are complicated and controversial, only the basic principles and challenges of each are discussed in this chapter. Each theory will be presented as a proponent of the theory might explain it.

Natural Law Theory

Since the time of the early Greek philosophers, natural law theory has been applied to politics, law, science, war, philosophy, theology, and ethics. There have been scores of natural law theorists throughout the ages, from Heraclitus (6th century B.C.) to Aristotle (4th century B.C.), Cicero (2nd century B.C.), Aquinas (13th century), Grotius (17th century) and modern theorists such as John Finnis, Philippa Foot, and Germain Grisez in the 20th century.

Moral natural law theory is robustly discussed and debated even today in the fields of medicine, law, philosophy, theology, and military science. Like most theories in all disciplines, moral natural law has several versions from the most traditional (narrow) to the most modern (broad). The theory as developed by Thomas Aquinas will be addressed here because it often sets the stage for discussions of natural law theory, although secular versions of the theory long preceded him.

Natural law is imbedded in nature in order to help it survive and flourish in an orderly fashion. Christian natural law theorists believe that God as a guide and grace created natural law, so that the world would flourish according to God's plan, which included guiding human beings toward eternal happiness with God. Secular natural law theorists believe the law is an inherent part of nature just like other elements in nature, such as the law of gravity. Both Christian and secular natural law theorists hold that natural law is universally knowable by practical reason and absolutely binding on all human beings across centuries, cultures, and circumstances.

Moral natural law supersedes all secular laws because natural law stems from God or some greater force, while common, conventional law stems from human beings. When common law contradicts natural law, it is an illegitimate law or no law at all and, therefore, may be or ought to be disregarded.

Natural law is self-evident and engraved in the minds and hearts of all individuals and is apparent even in young children who have an instinctual understanding of right and wrong behavior even before they develop it from the environment. Knowledge of natural law is always unfolding and will never be completely known. However, it can be perverted by ignorance, passion, and an evil disposition. For example, the Nazis appealed to natural law when they classified Jews and others as being less than human, which allowed the Nazis to commit genocide "in good faith."

The first principle of natural law is that good ought to be done and evil ought to be avoided. Because these are abstract tenets, people require direction that is more concrete. Aquinas lists some moral goods: the gift of life, procreation, knowledge, reason, and community. In addition to the moral goods that ought to be sought, evils ought to be avoided, such as murder, lying, adultery, and blasphemy.

Natural law theory has been an important part of the laws of war for many centuries. In this context, natural law focuses on justice. Natural law relates to the rights and duties of sovereign nations engaged in war, the nature of legitimate authority to wage war, the justice principles regarding going to, waging, and ending war, and the just treatment of enemy soldiers, prisoners, and civilians.

However, natural law has also been used to justify gross violations of the rules of war. It was used to justify the Crusades, in which Christian soldiers invaded sovereign nations and killed their soldiers and inhabitants for being heretics and infidels. Hugo Grotius (1583–1645), a lawyer and medieval scholar, used natural law to justify enslaving the soldiers and civilians of defeated nations who surrendered their freedom as the price of survival. This justification initiated a lengthy and interesting debate as to whether it is morally permissible for people to surrender their natural law right to freedom under such circumstances.

In any case, natural law has often been an integral part of domestic (national) and international laws, treaties, and covenants and has been a basis for theories of human rights and duties. For instance, it is reflected in concepts such as human beings have an inalienable right to life, liberty and the pursuit of happiness. These inalienable rights exist not only in domestic situations during peacetime, but also are equally important considerations when nations declare, wage, and end wars.

No ethical theory is beyond criticism, so it is not surprising that some tenets of moral natural law have been challenged. Following are some questions that can be raised with regard to moral natural law theory:

- Can a secular moral natural law exist that has no religious connection? If it exists, what is its source, and how does it define good and evil?

- Can there be a moral natural law which is universal but not absolute, which binds in the vast majority of situations but does permit occasional exceptions, for example abortion, birth control, and active euthanasia?
- Can moral natural law always stand alone as an objective norm and avoid weighing the consequences of an act and using them as an integral part of the final ethical decision? For example, if a decision must be made with regard to saving the life of a pregnant woman or her fetus, on what basis can the decision be made without entering into consequentialist calculations as to which choice constitutes the greater good?
- Can the tenets of natural law, based on medieval understandings of science (medicine, law, psychology) be applied to human behavior in modern times, for example, to moral philosophy, religious doctrine, gender issues, stem cell research, homosexuality, the death penalty, war and so on?
- Can all human beings intuit, understand, and act on moral natural law principles to the same degree, or do individual differences exist based on varying degrees of intellectual, emotional, social and moral capacities that compromise the ability of some human beings to live according to the tenets of natural law?

Deontological Theory

The word "deontology" comes from the Greek and means "the study of duty." The premise underlying deontology is that all human beings have an inherent duty to follow certain moral rules that set the norm for what constitutes good and evil behavior. This duty is based on various philosophical and theological postulates, depending on the particular version of deontology being applied. These rules may be absolute (always tell the truth regardless of the situation) or conditional (always tell the truth unless more evil would come from telling the truth than from lying). For example, a prisoner of war who is fighting for a just nation may use deceit during an interrogation to protect the lives of his fellow soldiers.

In general, deontologists hold that an act and, in some versions of the theory, its intention are what define moral worth, not the consequences of the act. A morally good act could have evil consequences and a morally evil act could have good consequences, but in neither case would the consequences define the moral worthiness of the act. For example, a soldier may try to save the life of a child who was severely wounded in crossfire, but because he applied a tourniquet improperly, the child bled to death. His good act and intention led to negative consequences, but his act was entirely moral, and this is how he should judge himself and be judged by others. The fact that his good act and intention eventually led to a negative outcome does not diminish the moral worth of his act.

The reverse is also true. A morally evil act and intention (a soldier kills an unarmed prisoner as an act of revenge) may have a positive consequence — the prisoner had secreted a knife in his cell and would have used it to kill one or more guards and escape to do more killing. Despite the fact that the soldier's evil act and intention happened to result in a positive consequence (the saving of other lives) does not absolve or mitigate the evil act and intention.

Various forms of deontology are presented in the works of Charles Fried, W.D. Ross, C.D. Broad, Thomas Nagel, Thomas Scanlon and Frances Kamm. However, Immanuel Kant (1724–1804), developed a classic version of deontology, and his works are still cited and debated today. Among other constructs, Kant developed the concept of Categorical Imperative, which is a universal duty or obligation that permits no exceptions — it is absolute. Two prescriptions of the categorical imperative are:

- Always act in ways that you wish your act would become a universal law binding all human beings for all time.
- Always act so that you treat others as an end and never merely as a means.

As applied to war, the Categorical Imperatives have a good deal of meaning. The first Categorical Imperative leads to the principle of universalizability, which means that the political and military leaders of a nation as well as ordinary citizens should take no actions they would not want drafted into universal laws that would be forever binding on them. This principle is commonly referred to as the Golden Rule (treat others in the same way that you would want them to treat you in a similar situation). For example, if it is morally permissible for one nation to torture prisoners then it must be morally permissible for all nations, allied and enemy, to do so. A nation cannot legitimately claim the moral right to torture prisoners (invade sovereign nations, drop bombs on populated areas, deploy nuclear weapons), yet deny this "moral right" to the enemy. Nations cannot simply define themselves as the "just nation" and thereby claim their use of torture is moral, but the enemy's use of torture is immoral because the enemy is regarded as the "unjust nation." Torture is either moral or immoral; it cannot logically be moral in the hands of one group and immoral in the hands of a different group.

The principle of universalizability trumps the principle of exceptionalism, which holds that some nations and individuals are above the moral (and civil) law, at least in certain circumstances. Using the principle of exceptionalism, nations that perceive themselves as noble are above the laws meant to keep lesser nations in check. The principle of universalizability also transcends parochial national values: we are a nation of laws, but only with respect to fellow citizens, not with respect to any other nation or their citizens.

Kant's second imperative is often translated as "The ends do not justify all means." All individuals are to be treated justly because they are human beings, not merely instruments for attaining a desired good.

The principle that the ends do not justify all means is often relevant in international conflicts. For example, if economic sanctions directly target the innocent men, women, and children of the sanctioned nation so that they will eventually rise up and oust the enemy regime, but these sanctions deprive the innocent civilians of the necessities of life, this tactic would violate Kant's second Categorical Imperative. In other words, unjust means (harming civilians) are used to bring about a just end (the target nation complying with the sanctioning nation's demands). This action also relates to Kant's first Categorical Imperative (the Golden Rule) because it raises the question: would the citizens of the sanctioning nation find it morally acceptable to be treated in the same way if the situation were reversed?

The basic theme of Kant's deontology is that individuals have a moral duty to act according to the Categorical Imperatives, which are universal and applicable in all situations. Thus, deontologists hold that a nation's decisions regarding war ought to be predicated on treating enemy soldiers and civilians with the same care, respect and justice that one's own soldiers and civilians would expect in similar circumstances. In other words, all soldiers ought to expect that they may be killed or imprisoned in war, but no soldier ought to expect to be shot as a prisoner of war.

Some basic challenges to deontology are reflected in the following questions:

- Who decides the moral rightness or wrongness of an act and on what basis? Who decides that soldiers ought always to tell the truth, even to enemy interrogators, or to treat all enemy civilians with beneficence?
- What happens when laws (rules) conflict? What ethical means are used to resolve the conflict, if the possible consequences of the act cannot be considered?
- What is the justification for absolute laws and duties that likely will make the world morally worse? How will justice prevail if all soldiers have an absolute moral duty to tell the truth to the enemy even when doing so will lead to greater moral harm than simply telling a lie?
- How can deontologists subscribe to just war principles when some of the key ones, proportionality and discrimination, require consequentialist calculations?

- How can a just nation win a war if it conscientiously abides by absolute moral laws and rules, but enemy nations and terrorist groups do not? If we stop torturing their captured soldiers, does anyone believe that they will stop torturing our captured soldiers?

These challenges are not beyond rebuttal but are offered to provide a realistic perspective on this theory.

Consequentialism

Consequentialism holds that the moral worth of an act lies not within its nature or intention, but with its specific moral consequences. If the consequences produce more benefit (good) than harm (evil) to the greatest number of people, it is morally good. If the act produces more harm than benefit to the greatest number of people, it is morally evil. The act itself is morally irrelevant. If killing, lying, or stealing ultimately produces more benefit than harm to the greatest number of people, then these acts are moral. The theory was first developed by Jeremy Bentham and John Stuart Mill in the 18th and 19th centuries and revisited by G.E. Moore and R. M. Hare in the 20th century.

A soldier with a deontological attitude would likely say, "I shall not torture prisoners because my duty to obey the laws of war prohibits me from abusing soldiers in captivity." Soldiers with a consequentialist attitude could respond in one of two ways: "I shall not torture prisoners, because if I do, the enemy will torture our prisoners in return." In other words, the act (torture) has no intrinsic moral relevance but only consequential relevance: "If we harm them, they'll harm us in return." Another response from a consequentialist soldier might be, "I must torture this prisoner in order to obtain information to prevent the loss of many innocent lives," which makes torture in this case a moral act.

Consequentialists apply cost-benefit assessments to weigh the possible good consequences of an action against its possible harmful consequences. However, consequentialism requires a theory of good that helps define what constitutes good (and evil) consequences. For example, the definition of "benefit" in the cost-benefit assessment depends on the version of consequentialism applied and may include pleasure, power, happiness, psychological and/or spiritual development, peace, and so on. In war, "benefits" generally refer to personal survival and national victory, and "costs" generally refer to the loss of life, liberty, and property as well as military and political defeat.

Consequentialism is also referred to as situationism, universalism, and impartialism. These terms are not necessarily synonymous but refer to different yet overlapping elements in consequentialism that go beyond a narrow cost-benefit focus.

Situationalism (which differs from situational ethics) refers to the concept that there are no inherently, absolutely good acts — the same act could be morally permissible (or required) in one situation but not in another. It may be a moral good to tell the entire truth about a situation to a trusted friend, a partial truth to an associate who may or may not be trustworthy, and a lie to someone who has no right to the truth and is likely to use it to do harm. In war, national leaders may tell the truth to the public about the number of troops killed in a battle but lie about the troops losing the battle because that information might reveal a weakness in the battle plan that national leaders do not want revealed to the enemy, and this would be perceived as a morally good act.

Universalism means that whatever good consequences might result from an act, they must be good for everyone in the universe. In war, universalism means much the same as the deontologist's principle of universalizability — if the benefits of intentionally de-housing thousands of enemy civilians so that they clog the enemy's supply routes are greater than the costs, it would be morally permissible for the enemy to do the same to us, and we would have no legitimate complaint.

Impartialism means that if a cost-benefit assessment determines the consequences of an act are worth the cost and therefore good, the good act must be impartially applied to everyone in similar situations. In war, for example, if risking the lives of Medivac helicopter pilots is morally "worth it" to transport and save the lives of our wounded soldiers, we should provide the same service for enemy soldiers under similar circumstances because their lives are of equal moral worth.

Some modern consequentialists adhere to "common sense ethics," which argues that the principle of partialism is more moral than the principle of impartialism. In war, for example, partialism holds that it would be morally permissible to medically treat — be partial to — our wounded soldiers before we treat the enemy wounded, but we are still morally required to treat enemy soldiers whenever reasonably possible. In other words, neither impartialism nor partialism allows any nation to treat its own troops but ignore or mistreat enemy troops in similar circumstances.

Consequentialism has its challenges that should be considered when using it as a norm for making conscience decisions:

• Do the good consequences of an immoral act, such as murder, absolve the person performing the act of any moral responsibility?

- Is it possible to predict with any degree of accuracy what factors will evolve in an upcoming action so that a reasonably accurate cost-benefit assessment can be completed in time to render a sound moral decision?
- Who decides the costs and benefits with respect to possible events in an upcoming decision — can one expert's cost be another expert's benefit? Can an air commander and a ground commander have very different ideas as to what constitutes a cost and a benefit in an upcoming operation?
- How are cost-benefit assessments applied in situations that do not lend themselves to numerical calculations but deal with abstractions such as respect, justice, compassion, patriotism, reputation, truth, and religion as an integral part of the ethical assessment process?
- How is the line between morally acceptable costs and morally unacceptable costs established? If it is morally permissible to murder one enemy prisoner to save 100 of our soldiers, is it morally permissible to murder 1,000 enemy prisoners to save the lives of 1,001 of our soldiers?

DEONTOLOGY AND CONSEQUENTIALISM

Although deontology and consequentialism appear to be mutually exclusive, some theorists believe they sometimes can be combined to provide a more inclusive ethical norm for making conscience decisions.

Brian Orend (2006) believes that a combination of the two theories can be applied to just war theory.

> War theory is, in my view, best understood as a commonsense blending of ... deontology and consequentialism. It is a mixing of rule-based appeals to bedrock first principles — like respect for human rights, and the entitlement to resist any physical aggression that seeks to violate them — with results-based appeals to satisfying outcomes. So, for example, in *jus ad bellum*, you have the "consequentialist" appeals to last resort, probability of success, and proportionality — and those force decision-makers to consider the consequences of their actions. But you also have the justice-based, first principle appeals to just cause, right intention, and public declaration of war by a proper authority. It is an attempt to mix talk of justice and rights and proper procedure with concern for how one's actions are likely to affect the world, with the overall result being a quite comprehensive, persuasive, and commonsense approach to the ethics of war and peace [p. 473].

The thought of combining these two theories for any reason would not be welcomed by all theorists, especially "pure" deontologists and consequentialists who believe doing so would violate the nature of each theory.

Standing alone, these three ethical theories are only of academic interest. However, they are an integral part of the ethical decision-making process when it is applied to practical situations — the act of "doing ethics." After all the objective and subjective information about the factors involved in an ethically sensitive situation are gathered, the ethical theory acts as a benchmark against which individuals measure the moral worth of various elements of the situation and, finally, the situation as a whole.

The following section addresses a process that may be used in making moral decisions regarding war as well as other important matters.

The Process of Moral Decision-Making

The moral decision-making process, as described here, has five dimensions: objective reality, subjective reality, conscience, moral will, and affective reaction.

OBJECTIVE REALITY

The first dimension of moral decision-making consists of objective (empirical) reality, objective in this case meaning observable and not necessarily meaning "true." For example, when a president tells the people that another nation is planning to attack the United States, the statement is an objective event, whether or not it is true. Other related objective factors in the situation include the reactions of the president's cabinet, Congress, other nations, and media commentators, as well as information on domestic and international law and estimates of the projected casualty rates and the cost of the war. The objective dimension also includes moral norms against which these factors are measured. All these elements form part of the objective (observable) constellation of events to be considered when making a moral decision.

The objective dimension of the process demonstrates how two equally rational, intelligent, mature, experienced, and moral people can come to diametrically opposed conclusions on the same issue. One individual may have access to more or different information than the other, so each individual begins with a different foundation. As individuals are exposed to new or different information, they may modify or even reverse their original positions and decisions.

SUBJECTIVE REALITY

The second dimension in the moral decision-making process is subjective reality, which includes an individual's perception, interpretation, and emotional reaction to the objective information. Emotions play an important role both before and after conscience becomes involved. When individuals hear the president's statement regarding war, they will perceive his verbal communication (the words he chooses, his tone of voice) and non-verbal communication (facial expression, posture, gestures), and interpret them (he appears frightened, angry, confident, knowledgeable, and so on). Finally, the individual reacts emotionally, feeling worried, optimistic, confused, angry, excited, or depressed. The individual will go through the same steps (perceive, interpret, and feel) with respect to all the objective factors listed in the above example.

Emotions are as important as objective reality in the decision-making process because they can cause distortions in the perception and interpretation of objective reality. An individual's powerful feelings about a war may tilt the moral decision-making process so that it becomes a search for affirmation rather than a quest for truth. For instance, individuals who, before seriously considering the moral dimensions of a situation, confidently claim, "I'm definitely for the war," or "I'm definitely against the war," may have already taken a position without ever making a decision. A surge of strong emotions can short-circuit the moral decision-making process, causing a "conscience outage."

Even when two individuals agree on the objective details of a situation, each may perceive, interpret and feel differently about it and, thus, arrive at a very different moral position on the issue.

Conscience

The third dimension of the moral decision-making process is conscience. The word "conscience" means "with knowledge"; in this case, it means an individual's conscience makes decisions about the moral rightness or wrongness of an act with knowledge gained from the objective and subjective dimensions. Conscience is the hub of the entire moral decision-making process. The benchmarks used by conscience to judge if an action is moral are moral principles, such as justice, freedom, honesty, care and respect.

Individuals whose conscience plays a role in their decision-making will apply moral standards to the information from the objective and subjective dimensions. Depending on the complexity and importance of the situation, this examination may take seconds, days, or weeks. There may be weeks or months to consider a military strategy, for example the D-Day landings in World War II, but only minutes or seconds to consider a military tactic, as in the case of a preemptive attack. For this reason, it is important to consider and analyze possible future eventualities so that a morally based decision can be made in a timely manner when the situation arises.

Using this process will not necessarily bring individuals to a consensus on any issue, but it will introduce moral considerations into discussions that will enhance the possibility that morality will be an important part of the total decision-making process and debate.

Moral Will

The fourth dimension of a moral decision-making process is the moral will of the individuals involved, meaning how much will (courage, commitment) they have to act upon their moral judgments. This dimension draws the distinction between making a moral decision and acting upon it, which are two different behaviors. A rational, well-informed, sound conscience empowers individuals, but it is worth little if it is not acted upon in reality. It resembles a fine-turned engine in an automobile that the owner proudly displays but seldom drives. Morality is a lecture-lab course — individuals first study morality, then act morally. As John Dinneen (1971) states:

> Conscience is morally free to choose this or that good, to incarnate a certain good in this war or that, and to follow what it judges to be good upon honest investigation. When all is said, perhaps it would be more accurate to speak of the rights and duties of conscience rather than of the freedom of conscience [p. 106].

In other words, on the practical level, a sound conscience decision is like a vehicle engine; it is only as good as its performance on the road.

Internal and external obstacles can prevent individuals from acting morally. Internal obstacles reside within the individual and are motivated and maintained by fear: the fear of appearing foolish, prudish, cowardly, scrupulous, rigid, moralistic, naïve, disloyal, stupid, unsophisticated, superior, judgmental, immature, recalcitrant, or cowardly. These fears demonstrate how conscience is closely tied to the other dimensions of personality: self-confidence, self-respect, self-identity, self-integrity, and self-reliance. A sound conscience decision in an individual with self-respect and self-confidence is more likely to be actualized than that of an individual with poor self-respect and low self-confidence. For this reason, the personality of those chosen to be political and military leaders is of the utmost importance. The question is not so much can they do the job but can they do the job morally, and, more importantly, not only can they do the job morally, but *will* they do the job morally?

External obstacles to moral behavior reside in the environment. These obstacles are also grounded in fear — the fear of losing votes, jobs, promotions, and the fear of losing one's reputation as a team player, good soldier, trusted friend, loyal employee, or psychologically stable individual.

At times, putting a difficult moral decision into action can be an expensive proposition. Fears about repercussions may be appropriate. Does a high-ranking military officer tell the truth about the friendly-fire death of one of his troops against the wishes of his superiors and risk putting his career on the line, or does he go along with the cover-up and receive a promotion? At some point, individuals ought to determine their core values, those that are non-negotiable — the ones on the hill on which they are willing to die.

Affective Reaction to the Decision

The final dimension of the moral decision-making process is the affective (emotional) reaction to the moral decision. After individuals make a moral decision, they can feel peaceful, relieved, virtuous, integrated, spiritual, courageous, or proud. They naturally interpret this reaction to indicate that they made the correct decision. The problem is that, through the workings of psychological defense mechanisms, it is possible to make a deplorable moral decision and feel good about it. For example, some religious extremists feel morally ecstatic when they blow up buildings and kill dozens of innocent people.

On the other hand, individuals who make sound moral decisions can feel despondent afterward. An individual who makes the decision to report his co-worker and best friend for embezzlement may feel guilt, shame, doubt, and regret, even though he knows the decision is morally sound.

Still other individuals have little or no feelings when they act in destructive ways because they have "no conscience." For example, Adolf Eichmann, a German officer responsible for murdering thousands of innocent people during World War II, claimed he slept peacefully during all the massacres. In fact, he only slept fitfully when he felt that he had let Hitler down by not killing as many people as he should have on a particular day. Individuals with psychopathic personalities can commit the most heinous crimes and feel no remorse, at least with respect to the effect of their crime on others.

Feelings are not reliable indicators of the soundness of moral decisions and acts. In fact, no foolproof method exists to determine whether one has made a morally sound decision. However, after making a moral decision, it is generally better to go to one's intellect — to one's "rational capacity" — rather than to emotions for affirmation. Individuals can ask: Did I gather all the relevant objective and subjective information possible; did I analyze it critically and dispassionately, and did I make a decision I can justify to the people in my life that I most love and respect? The answer to this question will not be foolproof evidence of the soundness of a moral decision, but it is likely to be more accurate than an appraisal based solely on feelings and intuitions.

Depending on the importance of the issue, moral decision-making may be relatively simple because there are only a few objective and subjective factors to consider, such as a student's dilemma with regard to plagiarizing a term paper. Other issues may present a more complex set of considerations. For example, a couple may have to weigh staying together for the sake of the children or choosing divorce as a better alternative. In any situation, moral decisions ought to be based not only on feelings, desires, hopes, or intuitions, but also on sound knowledge about oneself, the environment, and the impact of the decision on others. Conscience, then, can be used to measure this information against the relevant moral principles in order to arrive at a sound decision that empowers the individual to act morally.

Critical Analysis of Conscience

Critical thought and analysis are necessary to develop a more complete understanding of conscience. The following points related to conscience are particularly important to examine.

INVOKING CONSCIENCE

The very act of "invoking conscience" raises questions. Individuals commonly treat conscience as a localized part of their being that contains moral principles and direction. When faced with situations requiring a moral decision, people often speak in terms of invoking, examining, consulting, and appealing to their conscience. This terminology may reflect a misunderstanding of the nature of conscience, which can create serious practical problems.

One problem is that this view treats conscience as a part of anatomy like a heart rather than as a process composed of a thorough analysis of the objective and subjective dimensions of a situation. As a result, individuals run the risk of making decisions based on mere moral intuitions (reflexive thoughts and feelings) rather than on sound moral analysis and discernment. When individuals speak in such terms, they are likely talking about emotionally based intuitions. They are really saying—"My heart tells me that I should do this," but hearts (emotions) are only one part of moral decision-making and not necessarily the most reliable part.

A second problem with this misunderstanding is that it allows individuals to escape responsibility for their moral decisions. They skip the objective dimension of the process, which would require them to thoroughly and dispassionately study and consult with individuals who represent all sides of the issue. They begin and end the decision-making process with the subjective dimension. For example, a soldier may state, "As a soldier committed to serving his country, I truly want to be in combat, but the voice of my conscience tells me that all killing is against God's will. Therefore, I am applying for conscientious objector status." This individual distances himself from full responsibility for his decision — he truly wants to fulfill his duty to the military and the nation, but his conscience will not go along with what he claims he would like to do. This is the reverse of "the devil made me do it" justification; it is "the angels forbid me to do it" justification.

As Kenneth Kirk (1999) counsels:

> It is dangerous even for the upright man to think or speak too much of conscience as an independent agent "commanding," "forbidding," "condemning," "acquitting," "allowing." Conscience is not something alien and external to myself; and the more I think of it as such the more I am apt to regard it as a tyrant whose rulings I must by hook or by crook evade. Conscience is just *myself*; not indeed my whole self—for (as I know only too well) I am not a unified personality, but a complex of contesting and only half-harmonized interests — but my best self, or my higher self, or my true self, or whatever other name I can employ to express the required meaning. To make conscience an *other* than myself is to identify myself with those lower motives against which my higher self is in arms; or at best to treat myself as the resultant and plaything of forces — conscience included — over which I have no control. The danger may not be a great one, but it is there [p. 56–57].

UNCONSCIOUS FACTORS

The theological and philosophical literature on conscience generally fails to address the real possibility that attempts to exercise reason in moral decision-making can be short-circuited by unconscious factors. For example, a military chaplain may believe in the recesses of his psyche that a war is immoral but, because he does not want to create problems for himself, he uses the psychological defense of rationalization to remove his uncomfortable belief from consciousness. He talks himself into sincerely believing that the war is just: "As Christians, we are called to rescue the oppressed." Therefore, while he reassures the troops that the war they are fighting is moral, he experiences a gnawing and growing sense of uneasiness but is unaware of its cause, which is his unconscious guilt for violating his conscience.

Another military chaplain about to be deployed to a combat zone believes the war is moral but may fear for his life and uses the defense of rationalization to remove this uncomfortable belief from consciousness. He talks himself into sincerely believing that the war is unjust: "Now that I've prayed about this war, I am led to believe it is unjust, and I can no longer be a part of it."

Because it is virtually impossible for individuals, including those highly trained in psychology, to realize they are using defense mechanisms to fend off conflicting thoughts and feelings, it is important for people to discuss their moral conflicts with others who may be able to detect factual and methodological flaws.

Autonomy of Conscience

No person or institution can make a conscience decision for another individual. The strong temptation, especially in today's complex world, is to delegate decisions of conscience to other individuals, groups, and institutions. The people most likely to be on the receiving end of these conscience handoffs are political, military and religious leaders, as well as educational, psychological and religious mentors. The justification is that these individuals know more about the relevant issues, and, therefore, individual civilians and soldiers should simply follow the direction of their leaders and mentors.

While it is perfectly acceptable to seek information and clarification from others regarding morally relevant issues, it is not appropriate to simply accept another person's decision as one's own. In the final analysis, individuals ought to take responsibility for their decisions based on their own moral reasoning.

Influence of Ideology

One of the more common and pernicious impediments to making sound conscience decisions is the pervasive influence of ideologues — people blindly partisan with respect to a political, military, or religious ideology.

Ideologues create a "tail wagging the dog" dynamic in which morality (if it is present at all) is the servant of an ideology, in contrast to ideology being the servant of morality. Therefore, it is important to have a healthy suspicion regarding any ideology that places an adjective before the word "values." Examples of these terms include family values, national values, Christian values, Jewish values, pacifist values, realist values, liberal values, conservative values, and so on. Individuals attempting to make a sound conscience decision regarding an issue ought to be careful not to contaminate the decision-making process with adjectives that taint the objective information upon which the analytic process is based. For example, when one group of individuals possesses "patriotic values" and another group has "pacifist values," each group's collection, perception, and interpretation of information are likely to be predetermined by their ideology before any rational moral analysis begins. The terms Christian or Jewish values, for example, are not inherently problematic, but they ought to be thoughtfully examined to see if they represent truly just values or unjust values hidden beneath the mantle of religion.

Religion can be a help or hindrance in making sound moral decisions. Individuals whose consciences are based on the dictates of religion ought to be especially careful to maintain their capacity to think independently and rationally. There is nothing wrong with having a conscience that sincerely takes into account Christian, Jewish, or Muslim teachings. However, it is important not to employ religion as a justification to act immorally. The following cautions may be kept in mind.

- Individuals are responsible for making their own decisions of conscience, for better or worse. When they think in terms of the dictates, obligations, or duties of their religion as determining factors (in contrast to one set of factors to be taken seriously), their conscience can become hijacked, which can preclude arriving at a true moral decision.
- An authentic conscience decision is based primarily on doing the right (just, honest, caring) thing and not on self-serving motives. It is acceptable for self-serving motives to be incidental to, but they ought not to be an essential part of, a sound conscience decision. If individuals with religious-based consciences do the right thing primarily to earn eternal salvation and avoid eternal damnation, the essence of their decision is based on self-serving considerations, which may preclude a sound conscience decision.
- It is possible to make conscience decisions that are religiously correct but morally wrong. For example, throughout history, both the Christian and Muslim faiths have been used by some believers to murder hundreds of thousands of innocent "infidels," clearly a heinous, immoral endeavor.
- When appeals to religious authority are the sole basis for a decision, it can legitimately be called a "religious decision" but not a "moral decision." Individuals who make decisions about issues based solely on what the Bible, the church, the Koran, or the Torah supposedly teach are performing a "conscience bypass" rather than a "conscience decision." If a "divine command" were the only standard needed to live a moral life, human beings would not need a conscience.
- If a religious term such as "Christian" precedes the word "conscience," it connotes a monolithic theoretical position held by a monolithic group of believers. In fact, a "Christian conscience" has many different versions. Christians whose basic moral principle is charity may vehemently disagree whether invading a nation or not invading it is the more charitable (loving) act. Christians can be pacifists, general conscientious objectors, selective conscientious objectors, just war advocates, or realists. Therefore, while religion may be an

important dimension to consult when making a conscience decision, it ought not to be the only one.

An Examination of Conscience Regarding War

The decision-making process described above provides a framework for making moral decisions in all areas of life. The following format provides questions that individuals may ask themselves as a final check on their decision-making process before they take action. While these questions are relevant to all types of situations, the focus here is on decisions that relate to declaring, waging, and ending wars.

1. What moral standards (norms, principles, criteria, benchmarks) am I using as a frame of reference? For example, am I using justice, love, peace, respect, freedom, compassion, retribution, and so on? Or, are my feelings the main or sole standard ("I don't know — I just *feel* it's the right thing to do, and I trust my feelings.").

2. Have I gathered a sufficient number of facts and theories from all sides of the issue, so I can attempt to make a truly objective decision? Or, have I cherry picked facts and theories to fit my needs and listened only to those individuals who I know would support my position?

3. Am I genuinely in the process of trying to make an important moral decision, even though I have some preliminary thoughts and feelings about where I hope it will lead? Or, have I already made my decision and am shaping the process to arrive at the decision I have already made?

4. Are my emotions helping or hindering the process of looking at the facts and theories objectively? Or, are my emotions so strong that they are tinting the lenses I am looking through?

5. Is the judgment I am using to analyze all the factors rational (reasonable), or is my judgment irrational (unreasonable) in that it ignores or exaggerates the importance of key issues? In other words, does my moral arithmetic add up correctly and render a sum that coincides with reality, or do my strong needs and emotions short-circuit my judgment so that my moral arithmetic adds up to a sum I want but that has little relationship to the moral reality of the situation?

6. Am I willing and able to act on my final decision — to take a moral stand that may bring admiration or ridicule? Or, does my final decision not matter because there is no way I am going to act on it?

7. Contrary to the moral platitude that holds truth always wins in the end,

do I realize that if I act on my decision, I may be perceived as disloyal, ungrateful, untrustworthy, stupid, or as a "whistleblower" for the rest of my life? Or, am I acting under the rather dubious expectation that while my decision may make me very unpopular now, it will be vindicated in the future and those who criticize me will later apologize?

While these questions will not guarantee sound conscience decisions about war, they may at least serve as basic points to consider. Future chapters will provide material to concretize and refine the decision-making process with respect to many war-related issues. This knowledge will help ordinary citizens become empowered to resist the emotional undertow, personally and publically, which often sweeps nations into ill-advised and possibly immoral wars. Consequently, they may be able to prevent these wars or at least diminish their horror and end them more quickly. Knowing how to develop one's conscience in order to make moral decisions about war is a first step in this process, and this theme will be developed in different ways throughout the remainder of the book.

2

Just War Principles: Nature and Critique

> *One of our beliefs about political morality is that ordinary citizens have a stake in just-war doctrines during times of war or rumors of war ... [Just-war tenets] enable citizens to ask about war's cause, authority, aims, timing, and risks, along with the war's proper and improper methods. For citizens who concern themselves with the morality and prudence of military action, just-war tenets provide a basis for analysis, criticism, and approval or dissent.*
>
> — *Richard B. Miller*

Chapter 1 addresses moral principles that give individuals a general framework within which to make moral decisions. This chapter addresses moral principles that focus specifically on war and offer a second story to the moral structure described in the first chapter.

The history of just war principles spans over 2,000 years and includes the writings of some of history's better-known philosophers, theologians, and lawyers. In times of war, just war principles are frequently alluded to, directly or indirectly, in diplomatic negotiations, political decisions, moral assessments, legal analyses, military planning, and religious considerations. Those who discuss war, including national and military leaders, often use just war principles to bolster their position for or against war.

In several instances, just war principles have been codified and have influenced the United Nations Charter, the Geneva Conventions, the World Court, the Nuremberg Trials, and many international treaties. However, as is true for any set of abstract principles, it is difficult to measure their effectiveness on the practical plain. Over the centuries, how many wars have been prevented or restricted by the application of just war principles, and how many wars, both just and unjust, have been waged appealing to these principles as justifications? Clearly, there is no way to know the answer to these questions. Whatever actual influence they have had on war, just war principles remain sufficiently respected and useful in 21st century discussions of war.

Those who espouse just war principles are far from being a monolithic group of theorists and practitioners. The one issue that most distinguishes them is their understanding of the moral nature of war. One group perceives war as an *inherent evil*. This belief can be based on natural law, humanitarian values, or religious principles that arrive at the same conclusion from different perspectives: war is inherently evil because it destroys life, nature, and all things that cause life and nature to flourish. War is always evil, and even when a just war is waged, it still is a lesser of evils and a cause for remorse and certainly not celebration. War is permissible only as a true last resort in the face of a clear and imminent threat to the security of a just nation. A basic concern is that war will be waged prematurely, based on irrational fears, misplaced nationalism, unfettered greed, erroneous information, ethnic prejudices, imperialistic designs, or pure revenge.

On the other side of the issue are individuals who believe that war is, in itself, *morally neutral*. If a war is declared or waged unjustly, it is a moral evil. However, if it is justly declared and waged, it is a moral good because its cause and intention are to protect life, nature and all the elements that cause life and nature to flourish. Just as good parents can punish their children out of love and to return them to a state of peace and order, just wars are employed to protect the peace and order of the world. The parents mentioned above should be proud of themselves for manifesting tough love with their children and restoring peace and order to the family. They have done nothing for which to feel defensive or ashamed. With regard to war, the presumption of this position is always for military intervention in situations in which a belligerent nation poses what is deemed to be a credible and serious threat to an innocent nation, whether the threat is imminent or in the near future. In other words, while it is problematic for a nation to go to war too soon, before a true last resort has been reached, an equally serious problem is going to war too late, after the belligerent nation has fully prepared itself for war and is close to launching an attack.

The debate between the "presumption against war" and "presumption for war" schools is robust and has practical consequences in terms of what constitutes just cause, right intention, and last resort with respect to declaring war. These opposing positions will enter discussions directly or indirectly as different aspects of war are addressed. This chapter addresses some fundamental concepts regarding the development and application of just war principles followed by a discussion of the specific *jus ad bellum, jus in bello, and jus post bellum* principles, as well as a critique of these principles.

Concepts Underlying Just War Principles

The term *just war principles* will be used in this book in contrast to other terms employed throughout the centuries—just war tradition, just war theory, and just war doctrine. Each of these terms has a different meaning that can cause confusion and controversy. The term *just war principles* provides the simplest, least controversial framework for discussing justice in war.

DEVELOPMENT OF JUST WAR PRINCIPLES

The moral attitude toward war has changed dramatically since the early days of Christianity, when war was perceived as an absolute evil for several reasons, the most fundamental one being that it required killing, which was clearly against God's commandment. However, after barbarian tribes that attempted to abolish Christianity overran the Roman Empire, force was deemed necessary to preserve and restore peace and order in the world so that Christianity could flourish once again. Therefore, it was decided by the Catholic hierarchy that the evil of threatening forces had to be held at bay by the evil of waging war, just as firefighters intentionally set backfires to defeat approaching forest fires. So, while the *objective evil* of war could never be mitigated—lessened by some acts or circumstances—the *subjective guilt* of the soldiers who fought the wars could be mitigated in the sight of God if the war was based on a just cause, brought about by just means, and responded to with remorse followed by confession, forgiveness, and penance.

John Howard Yoder (1996) summarizes this situation:

> The patterns of governmental decision-making before democratic times did not include that kind of openness about how decisions are made and why. Just war thinking was done in the confessional, and in the studies of the priests who developed canon law. The criteria were needed when a knight or soldier returned from battle, and the question was whether he could be admitted to the Eucharist, and what difference it made in that connection whether the war in which he had killed was "just" or not. The point at which the detailed just war rules were worked out the most thoroughly was thus the determination of the form and type of penance called for after killing.
>
> Even for killing in a just cause some period of penance was demanded; even for killing in a just cause a candidate for the priesthood could be rendered ineligible to receive orders. In fact, those restrictions applied to those whose participation in killing went no farther than serving on a jury that condemned someone to death [p. 11–12].

This early Christian attitude toward war was different from today's view because there was no sanitization of the concept of "killing." It was viewed as a terrible moral evil, even when it was done in the name of a just cause.

In the modern era, war has been euphemized by many people, though certainly not all. Our soldiers do not "kill the enemy," they "neutralize" them; they do not torture prisoners, they employ "enhanced interrogation methods"; they do not kill civilians but cause them to become "collateral damage." The media often portrays war as exciting, romantic, patriotic, heroic, god-approved and sometimes even fun. The thought of receiving cash bonuses for enlisting in the military, holding welcome home parades, and awarding medals would have been a sacrilege to early Christians.

While just war principles tend to be perceived as a Christian concept, albeit based on pre–Christian foundations, it is rarely seen as inclusive of Jewish teachings on permissible and impermissible wars. Although Judaism does not delineate just war principles as such, the Old Testament often speaks of war, and the Mishneh Torah, a systematic code of all Jewish law written by Maimonides, divides war into mandatory and discretionary wars and details what is forbidden in war. For example Chapter 6, Law 7 of the code indicates that an army that invades a city must leave at least one escape route so that those who wish to flee can save their lives. Everett E. Gendler (1968) writes:

> It seems evident ... that Judaism cannot be characterized, in the strict sense of the term, as a "pacifist" tradition. It seems equally evident that Judaism does not regard every war as permissible, nor does it regard every means of prosecuting war as permissible. It is further evident that while Judaism is highly respectful of duly constituted authority, this does not absolve the individuals from the duty of making responsible moral decisions. Neither of these moral decisions nor their bases are delegated to human authority in any unchallengeable way [p. 100].

Islam, through the Quran, also considers situations in which wars are and are not permissible. Wars are permissible when a nation is unjustly attacked and may continue as long as the response to the attack promotes peace, the destruction is limited to that which is necessary to win, every attempt is made to protect women and children, the elderly, infirmed, disabled, and prisoners are allowed to live comfortably and are released immediately when the war ends. The Quran does not permit war when the intention is to gain worldly power and glorification or to persecute the enemy on religious grounds. During a war, holy places may not be damaged, nor may prisoners be mistreated, and further battle is not permissible if the enemy reaches out in peace to discontinue the war.

As is true of many philosophical principles, just war principles have had vibrant periods and times when they lay dormant. They were not a recognizable part of deliberations in World War I, World War II, or the Korean War, and only became resurrected in the last few years of the United States' participation in the Vietnam War (1965–1973). With regard to World War II,

John Courtney Murray (1964) writes: "I think it is true to say that the traditional doctrine was disregarded during World War II. This is no argument against the traditional doctrine. The Ten Commandments do not lose their imperative relevance by reason of the fact that they are violated. But there is a place for an indictment of all of us who failed to make the tradition relevant" (p. 253).

The most pressing question regarding the validity of just war principles today is whether principles dating back over 2000 years to Cicero are still viable, especially in the modern world of nuclear weapons and terrorist attacks. George Weigel (2003) addresses the issue:

> Some have suggested, in recent months, that the just war tradition is obsolete. To which I would reply: to suggest that the just war tradition is obsolete is to suggest that politics — the organization of human life into purposeful political communities — is obsolete. To reduce the just war tradition to an algebraic casuistry is to deny the tradition its capacity to shed light on the irreducible moral component of all political action. What we must do, in this generation, is to retrieve and develop the just war tradition to take account of the new political and technological realities of the twenty-first century. September 11, what has followed, and what lies ahead, have demonstrated just how urgent that task is [p. 14].

Just war principles morally permit war to be declared and waged under certain limited circumstances, which should be re-evaluated continually throughout a war to ensure that they are not eroded by the many vicissitudes of politics and conflict. A just cause can gradually morph into an unjust cause without anyone realizing it or, in some cases, wanting to realize it.

Because these principles are necessarily general in nature, they are not meant to be a moral checklist to be completed before war is declared. However, as Paul Ramsey (2002) states: "This does not mean these tests laid down by the just-war doctrine on the uses of force are of no more avail. Nor does it mean that they are addressed only to the topmost magistrates or political leaders of the nations. In modern democratic society they are addressed to every man who must say whether war is justified or unjustified in these terms" (p. 132).

Just war principles as described here are divided into three categories: *jus ad bellum* (the reasons for declaring war), *jus in bello* (the means by which the war is waged), and *jus post bellum* (the manner in which the victorious nation treats the defeated nation). It is generally held that each of the following principles should be met in the order they are presented. A war may not be considered just if even one principle is lacking. It ought to be kept in mind that just war principles, as all principles, are vulnerable to misinterpretation and manipulation. To add to this complexity, the world of war is constantly and rapidly changing so that some modification of the traditional interpretations of the principles may be necessary in order not only to wage a just war but also to win it.

To use a legal analogy, the United States Constitution is a set of political principles that, on their face, are clearly stated. However, the more these principles are applied to modern challenges, the more their simplicity is replaced by complexity. Individuals with competing interests can interpret the Constitution in diametrically opposite ways, just as they can, and do, in the case of just war principles. However, one must start somewhere, so the following presentation will be an introduction to just war principles rather than anything resembling a thorough treatise.

Jus ad Bellum (Conduct Before War)

The principles involved in *jus ad bellum* are competent authority, just cause, right intention, proportionality, probability of success, and last resort.

Competent (legitimate) authority: Declaring war may be permitted as long as a nation's leadership has been lawfully appointed or elected and the intent to wage war is declared publicly.

In moral terms and specifically in just war terms, the declaration of war requires more than a nation declaring war in a document, speech, or press conference. A declaration of war is not solely a legal and military act but, more importantly, a political and moral one. It requires a nation to communicate openly not only its intention to wage war, but the political and moral reasons and evidence that justify going to war.

These reasons and their supporting evidence ought to be honest, correct, documented, logical, rational, and thorough. When possible, all sides of the political and moral spectrum ought to be allowed to debate the issues publicly before a final war declaration is made. Simply offering one side of the issue with evidence that is weak, equivocal or suspect does not constitute a political and moral act — it is simply a legal formality to be gotten out of the way and is not in keeping with the spirit of just war principles.

Francisco Suarez (1548–1617), one of the most notable teachers of just war principles, pointed out that it is the moral duty of military and political counselors to speak the truth and to voice whatever reservations they have about a pending war. This action represents the opposite of political groupthink and the pep rally mentality that often accompany declarations of war.

Even today, it is not clear who is authorized to declare war. For example, the United States Constitution authorizes only Congress to declare war, but, in reality, Congress has not declared war since 1941, despite the fact that the

United States has initiated armed aggression against several nations. This issue begs to be clarified once and for all, so that an unambiguous understanding will exist with respect to who has the authority to declare war for the United States and who does not. The fact that domestic law permits a nation to declare war does not mean international law gives the same permission, and the fact that domestic law and international law grant permission does not necessarily mean that the act of declaring a war is a moral one.

The issue of moral authority is especially complex in a democratic society in which only one person (the president, prime minister) or a handful of people (Congress, Parliament) actually make the decision to go to war. The fact that a majority or large minority of the citizens of the nation may be against going to war may not be ignored in making the decision, based on a "what do they know?" rationalization. A morally virulent vicious cycle often results in nations that claim to be democratic but whose leaders fail to provide their citizens with the information necessary to make a moral decision about going to war. The issue needs to be addressed, not only by national leaders but by individual citizens as well, because failure to address it creates a nebulous area of moral responsibility and readily casts suspicion on a nation's true motives for going to war.

The concepts of legitimate authority and competent authority are not synonymous. *Legitimate* refers to the legal aspect of authority and is a simpler concept to define. *Competent* refers to a psychological competency, the ability to collect, grasp, and assimilate information sufficient in breadth, depth, and objectivity to make an informed moral decision (as discussed in Chapter 1). This competency requires several essential personality characteristics, which include the ability:

- To think abstractly, in contrast to thinking only concretely
- To critically analyze information, in contrast to taking it at face value
- To truly hear what others have to say, in contrast to perfunctorily listening to them
- To be reasonably resolute, in contrast to becoming swept up by the undertow of groupthink
- To seek the counsel of contrarians, in contrast to sycophants
- To be intellectually humble, in contrast to being intellectually arrogant
- To be reasonably steadfast, in contrast to being malleable or stubborn
- To give weight to moral factors, in contrast to weighing only political and military ones
- To assess, respect, and consider the will of the people, in contrast to discounting it

Therefore, citizens ought to keep these qualities in mind when choosing leaders, especially in modern times when decisions to go to war often occur within months of each other, in contrast to the "war every quarter of a century" schedule of the past.

Just cause: Declaring war may be permitted to prevent or respond to an unjust attack on one's own nation (self-defense) or on a just third party nation (just aggression) or to respond to a gross violation of human rights in another nation.

Without just cause, everything a nation does in war, no matter how just or benevolent it appears, will lack a necessary moral foundation. Analogously, when a man enters a bank with the intention of robbing it, shoots a teller in the process, and then calls an ambulance for her, his final action does not morally excuse or even mitigate his original unwarranted act of aggression — entering the bank with the purpose of robbing it.

Contemporary theory generally holds that just cause can exist under four circumstances. The first situation occurs when a nation is actually under armed attack by another nation. A nation has a moral right and obligation to protect the humanitarian rights of its citizens.

The second just cause for war exists when a just nation has clear and convincing evidence, if not moral certitude, that an unjust nation is about to launch an imminent and existential attack against it or against a just third party nation. However, new challenges arise: Does just cause include the right to launch a preemptive attack, one aimed at neutralizing an imminent attack before it begins, or a preventive attack, one aimed at striking a nation that is bellicose but does not pose an imminent threat? These concepts are morally and legally controversial and are discussed in more detail in Chapter 7.

The third just cause for war occurs when a just third party nation is unjustly attacked. A nation may have just cause to intercede with armed force to protect an innocent nation, especially when international laws or covenants require nations to protect other nations under siege.

The fourth just cause for war is to prevent or correct an egregious and massive violation of human rights in a nation after all reasonable means of accomplishing this objective peacefully are exhausted.

In summary, war is permissible only to defend against a real and certain danger, to protect life and conditions necessary for survival, and to stop the wanton violation of human rights. The following causes for going to war are likely to be considered just, all other factors remaining equal:

- Protecting innocent life
- Securing a peaceful, just order

- Preventing forced exile of innocent people
- Rendering humanitarian aid in dire circumstances
- Regaining territory wrongfully seized in the recent past
- Assisting people in overthrowing an egregiously repressive and violent regime
- Supporting a legally sanctioned cease fire
- Preventing or stopping ethnic cleansing
- Protecting another nation in the face of unlawful attack
- Preventing a clearly imminent attack

All other factors remaining the same, the following are unlikely to be considered just causes for going to war:

- "Sending a message" that an offensive behavior must stop
- Seeking to expand power, territory, or wealth
- Exacting revenge for past acts
- Enforcing the authority of an illegal or immoral regime
- Changing regimes solely for political reasons
- Spreading political or religious ideologies

The moral justifications that underwrite just cause are not the same as legal justifications. International law is quite complex with respect to initiating hostilities, and the interpretation of these laws can be even more complex because political as well as legal considerations typically enter the deliberations. If a nation firmly believes it has just cause to declare war but international treaties and courts do not agree, the nation has to address a second important moral issue — whether it has a sound moral basis for ignoring international laws and treaties. A decision to go to war under these circumstances would likely have serious negative consequences, both nationally and internationally, short and long term, intended and unintended, but could be morally justified in rare circumstances.

The fact that just cause appears to be present at the beginning of a war does not necessarily mean it will endure throughout the war. A war can begin morally but rapidly or gradually decompensate into an immoral war — one that is prosecuted with immoral means. Therefore, just cause is not a fixed entity but a dynamic one that ought to be continually reevaluated as the war progresses and ends.

If a nation goes to war solely to spread a political or religious ideology, this does not constitute just cause. Just cause principles were created because over the span of history, rogue nations were attacking just nations, often in barbaric ways. Moreover, some nations waged holy wars to spread their religion and attempt to convert, under threat of death, the "heathens" and "infidels" residing in other sovereign nations.

In addition to religious holy wars, ideological ones based on philosophies such as democracy, capitalism, socialism, communism and Nazism often become secular holy wars. Wars are seen as "religious" when politicians believe their ideology is necessary for the salvation of the world and therefore must be forced on other nations. When this occurs, a dangerous mixture of legitimate religion, fanatical religion, secular religion, legitimate moral values, and specious moral values combine and, given a superheated political and military environment, may well ignite wars that continue to be unjust and unnecessary throughout their duration.

Therefore, individuals would do well to suspect the concept of "spreading" a political doctrine to other nations or "nation building," especially by armed force. True moral values such as justice need not be clothed in a political or theological ideology for justification or support.

After a war is launched based on just cause, a nation may discover that its claim of just cause was in error. In this case, the question is: Does the aggressor nation have a moral obligation to stop its aggressive acts as soon as reasonably practical and make restitution? On the other hand, can the nation continue to prosecute the war as if it had just cause, conjuring new "just causes" along the way? A war unjustly entered into is permanently unjust, and no discoveries during the war can rehabilitate its first cause.

Right intention: Declaring war may be permitted if the intentions for doing so are strictly limited to the protection of life, liberty, sustenance, and the peace of a nation's populace.

Right intention can be distinguished from just cause in that just cause includes the reasons for going to war, while right intention addresses the intentions for doing so. For example, a nation may have a just reason for declaring war (to free oppressed people), but have an unjust intention (to free them so that they can participate in capitalistic ventures which will provide needed resources for the nation declaring war). As with just cause, right intention must be present at the beginning and throughout the war.

A war may be declared with right intentions but as it progresses, wrong intentions can gradually or suddenly surface. Often the justification for this modification is "As long as we've spent so much blood and treasure on this war, we deserve to help ourselves to this nation's resources." The reverse can also occur. A nation may begin a war with the unjust intent to capture the natural resources of the invaded nation. However, as the war progresses new information may indicate that the invaded nation is stockpiling weapons of mass destruction. This newly discovered information cannot be used to absolve the unjust invasion. In other words, right intentions cannot be morally retroactive. Only the intentions clearly present before war is declared can be employed to justify it.

A nation's intentions are not always conscious. It is important to recognize that national leaders and even nations at large can have unconscious intentions for going to war. On a conscious level, nations may sincerely believe their intentions for going to war are just, honest, and compassionate. However, below this level of consciousness may lay a collective unconscious composed of unacceptable intentions, for example, to punish a nation that is openly defiant, bellicose, and corrupt but not a serious, imminent threat. Unconscious intentions generally become clear if the war is won and can be seen in what the victors do with the vanquished — its citizens, politics, wealth, treasures, and natural resources.

"Good intentions" and "good faith" are not synonymous with right intention. A largely subliminal sentiment exists that good intentions and good faith are all that can be expected when making difficult moral decisions. In fact, nothing could be further from the truth. It is not enough for individuals and nations to have their heart in the right place; they also ought to have their head and consciences in the right place and make sound moral decisions based on empirical evidence, especially when deciding to go to war. Good intentions and good faith may mitigate culpability in court or in a confessional, but they fail to lessen the objective evil consequences that result from bad acts.

Proportionality: Declaring war may be permitted as long as the harm done to the people and infrastructure of the nations involved is limited only to that amount necessary to accomplish the military and moral objectives of the war.

The principle of proportionality considers whether the moral good that comes from a war is likely to outweigh the moral evil. Proportionality has a place in three parts of just war analysis: *jus ad bellum, jus in bello* and *jus post bellum*. This section addresses the principle as it applies to the decision process that considers whether going to war is just.

The principle of proportionality is dynamic — it begins in pre-war (*ad bellum*) moral deliberations and ends when the victorious nation leaves the defeated nation, hopefully forever (*post bellum*). In other words, considering proportional response is a daily exercise rather than one that occurs only when specific issues arise and addresses one basic question: Will this war (or battle) be worth it in the end?

The following theoretical construct of a proportional cost-benefit assessment of a war can be considered. Some variables can be quantified, such as the number of casualties and the cost of the war, but others require a qualitative assessment, for example the political, psychological, and moral cost and benefits of the war. The following are a few variables that ought to be assessed:

- Number of our soldiers and civilians killed and wounded
- Number of enemy soldiers and civilians killed and wounded
- Economic cost to our nation and the enemy nation
- Political and moral damage to our reputation
- Political and moral damage to the enemy nation
- Ecological damage to our nation, the enemy and third party nations

The results of this cost-benefit assessment can be examined through three prisms: political, military, and moral. It is important to keep in mind the difference between a largely political, military, and economic cost-benefit assessment and a moral cost-benefit assessment. A political, military, and economic analysis of a war may yield a low cost–high benefit result, yet the moral analysis may show a high cost–low benefit ratio.

The difference between a general cost-benefit assessment and a moral one is twofold: the moral assessment takes into account the losses of the enemy nation as well as our nation because morality is universal, not parochial, and the norm for assessment is based on good and evil (justice-injustice) rather than on solely material issues.

Probability of success: Declaring war may be permitted if there is a reasonable expectation that the war will be decisively won.

This principle assumes that the moral analysis going into the decision to fight a war will be rational, thorough, and objective, considering what could go wrong as well as what could go right. It raises the question: How will the probability of success be defined and measured? To answer this general question, several specific questions may be asked:

- What constitutes a military victory? Would a conditional surrender suffice, or would an unconditional surrender be required?
- What constitutes a political victory? Would effecting a regime change be a political victory, even if it would incur international disdain?
- What constitutes a psychological victory? Can nations win a war militarily, politically, and morally and yet lose it psychologically because their citizens did not believe the war should have been declared in the first place, lost faith in their leaders, or believe the economic cost, casualty rates, and postwar commitments were not worth whatever good resulted from the war?
- What constitutes a moral victory? Would the victorious nation maintain its moral authority if it wages a war based strictly on political pragmatism with little regard for just war principles?

There is more than one definition of success in war, and all of them ought to be considered and weighed against each other before launching a war.

Nations that perceive the principle of probability of success as valid ought to continue to see it as valid if the likelihood of success clearly turns into the likelihood of failure, as occurred six years before the end of the Vietnam War. In other words, if probability of success is perceived as a viable prewar principle that justifies going to war, its viability must remain intact during the war, requiring nations to discontinue the war as soon as it becomes reasonably clear to knowledgeable, objective observers that the war cannot be won.

Can a war be just if the probability of success is equivocal or even poor? Hopefully, this question will remain theoretical, but, as more nations attain nuclear capability, it may become a practical issue as well. Religious martyrs knew they were going to be killed if they refused to denounce their faith, yet they chose to die because their religious values were worth dying for. Can there be a moral equivalent with respect to war? Are all the individuals who declare they would die for their nation's values willing to do so, even in a losing effort? Finally, would it be a moral act?

Last resort: Declaring war may be permitted after all reasonable economic, diplomatic, and political interventions have been exhausted, and the only realistic option is to wage war.

Last resort is the "trigger principle"— by the time it enters the moral calculus, the prior criteria presumably have been met. In other words, the gun is fully loaded and aimed at the target. Problems can arise because those who strongly believe the declaration of war is necessary may prematurely pull the trigger ("let's get this over with now"), and those who are deeply resistant to declaring war may wait too long to pull the trigger ("let's give them just one more chance"). Significant harm can result from pulling the trigger too early or too late.

The decision that last resort has been reached should not be the sole domain of national leaders. Whenever possible, input ought to be solicited from many sources. Input from the government's opposition party should be seriously considered. The nation's secular and religious institutions may provide information that would be helpful in the decision-making process. Other nations, preferably neutral ones, but also friendly and unfriendly nations, may provide information with respect to whether last resort has been, or is close to being, reached.

Obviously, decisions to go to war cannot be based on a democratic vote, nor can they be debated for a prolonged period. However, with the exception of 9/11 types of attack, national leaders and citizens have a reasonable idea whether war appears to be on the horizon. During this period, national leaders have sufficient time to solicit and seriously consider the information necessary to make a truly informed decision.

The decision as to whether last resort is just around the corner ought to be shared with world bodies, including the target nation. Making this process public, which is not the same as making specific political and military strategies public, serves three purposes:

- To send a "last chance to change" ultimatum to the target nation, as was done during the Cuban Missile Crisis
- To invite other nations to "talk sense into" the target nation and offer mediation services to the nations involved
- To provide input to the nation deciding about war that may help it make the best decision possible

When nations have an attitude that reflects "This is nobody else's business but ours" or worse, "We don't need a permission slip to go to war," they make suspect the seriousness of the claim that they are doing everything possible to avoid war.

As part of last resort, the peaceful means often pursued to solve international tensions are not always as benign as they are portrayed. In addition to diplomacy, three strategies often are employed as last resorts before declaring war: sanctions, embargoes, and blockades. The stated purpose of these actions is to force an offending nation to comply with the nation imposing the sanctions, which may or may not be just. The rationale is that when the citizens of that nation are no longer able to live with the deprivation and illnesses caused by these tactics, they will rise up against their government, in armed or political rebellion, and oust the offending regime.

However, when sanctions, embargoes, and blockades are casually mentioned as "peaceful means" of resolving conflicts, this concept should at least be questioned. In many cases, sanctions are referred to as "the gateway to war," because the serious deprivation imposed on the sanctioned nation causes death and resentment that may significantly increase rather than decrease the likelihood of war. Chapter 8 presents a more detailed discussion of sanctions.

Jus in Bello (Conduct in War)

The principles involved in *jus in bello* are proportionality and noncombatant immunity.

Proportionality: The principle of proportionality remains the same as it was in *jus ad bellum* principles. In other words, excessive force, unnecessary force, unbridled force, wanton force and unnecessarily prolonged force ought not to be used in a just war.

In waging war, proportionality is not easily measured. In business, a cost-benefit analysis can be used which renders a ratio which may indicate, for example, that the cost of a business decision clearly outweighs the benefits. This type of analysis can be done because the variables being analyzed are largely quantitative. However, in war, although quantitative analysis can be performed on some variables, the more important variables are qualitative. Will the cost of having twenty-five soldiers of the just nation killed trying to destroy a power station outweigh the benefit derived from destroying the power station? At first, this sounds like an easy question to answer — the lives of the soldiers are more important than a power station. However, if the power station supplies electricity and clean water to all the civilians in the area, including schools and hospitals, and, without these resources, a large number of civilians are likely to die, then the answer to the question becomes more difficult morally. The ratio becomes 25 lost soldiers to 100 lost innocent children and adults. The situation can become even more difficult if the loss of the power station cripples all of the enemy's electrical communication and weapons systems, saving the lives of 250 soldiers of the just nation who would have died in future battles compared to the 25 soldiers of the just nation who were killed in the attack on the power station.

It is somewhat easier to measure proportionate (reasonable) force in law enforcement than in war. Typically, law enforcement officers have a fairly accurate idea how many armed suspects are hiding in a building and can factor that number into their strategy and tactics so they use just enough force, plus a little more to allow for a margin of error. Troops in battle often have little or no idea how many enemy soldiers are hiding in a village, how many enemy soldiers will converge on the village when they hear gunshots, how many civilians will be helping the enemy and how many civilians will be innocent bystanders.

The most used justification for violating proportionality is the claim "They did it first," meaning that the enemy is using disproportionate means in battle, so it is morally permissible to retaliate with disproportionate force "to even the score." While this attitude is understandable emotionally, it is questionable and morally complicated. May the principle of proportionality be violated if the enemy violates it first (an eye for an eye), or should punishment, in contrast to necessary force, be deferred until after the war?

Noncombatant immunity (discrimination): Waging war may be permitted as long as every reasonable attempt is made to protect noncombatants from displacement, injury, and death.

This principle includes three elements: intentionality (what constitutes intended and unintended damage?), the definition of noncombatants (who qualifies as a noncombatant?), and military responsibility (what constitutes "the military" and the various kinds of harm to noncombatants?). Michael Walzer (1977) describes the importance of noncombatant immunity:

> The structure of rights stands independently of political allegiance; it establishes obligations that are owed, so to speak, to humanity itself and to particular human beings and not merely to one's fellow citizens. The rights of German civilians — who did no fighting and were not engaged in supplying the armed forces with the means of fighting — were no different from those of their French counterparts, just as the war rights of German soldiers were no different from those of French soldiers, whatever we think of their war [p. 158].

Intentional attacks are consciously planned, such as an attack on a section of the noncombatant population or on a non-military structure, in order to lower civilian morale and put pressure on the target nation to cease hostilities. In contrast, unintentional attacks occur by truly unforeseen and unpreventable accident.

There is an important moral and legal space between purely intentional and purely unintentional damage, which can be filled by introducing the legal concept of a "reckless attack." This concept means that while the direct attack on noncombatants and their structures is not formally written into the battle plans, it is foreseeable or ought to be foreseeable to competent planners that noncombatants are likely to suffer unnecessary casualties and property damage. The principle of reciprocity may be applied here: "Would you consider it moral and legal for the enemy to attack the city in which your family lives under the same circumstances?"

Noncombatants are civilians who do not aid their nation in any material way that would endanger the lives or property of the just nation's soldiers. Civilians may or may not be noncombatants. Civilian combatants are those who, although they do not formally belong to a military organization, nevertheless participate in military activities, such as making explosives, acting as lookouts, transmitting messages, hiding soldiers, transporting supplies, recruiting soldiers, revealing enemy positions, and performing acts of sabotage. The "noncombatants by day, combatants by night" Viet Cong soldiers in the Vietnam War did great damage to coalition forces and could not legitimately claim noncombatant immunity based on the fact that they were also part-time farmers.

The military includes all individuals directly involved in the aggressive waging of war. This includes not only soldiers, but also paramilitary personnel: intelligence agents, contract soldiers, and personnel from third nations who interrogate and torture prisoners to extract information to help one nation against the other.

Harming noncombatants is not limited to directly targeting them, but also includes harming them by employing cluster munitions, land mines, incendiary devices, and chemical agents. Moreover, the destruction of power stations, which provide electricity to keep food, water, and medical supplies fresh, can cause far more noncombatant casualties than does the collateral damage of routine, contained military attacks.

Using the term "collateral damage" to justify all noncombatant deaths in all battles is almost surely overreaching. When large expanses of a nation are carpet bombed or "strategically bombed," the deaths of noncombatants cannot plausibly be unintended and unexpected. If a hostile nation carpet bombed or even precision bombed New York City or London causing the deaths of hundreds or thousands of civilians, would the United States and England agree that the deaths were morally permissible?

Jus Post Bellum (Conduct at the End and After the War)

Jus post bellum: Waging war may be permitted as long as the victorious nation has a serious commitment to help the defeated nation, or the nation about to be defeated, restore itself so that it can rebuild on a foundation of justice and stability for all its citizens.

Concern about how victorious nations ought to act when the war is in its final stages and after armed hostilities cease is not new. It was discussed by philosophers in passing ways throughout the Middle Ages, but was not considered an important part of the morality of war until Kant addressed it at some length. The following concepts are representative of those currently under discussion: just conditions of surrender, just termination, establishing a just civil order, restoration of vital resources, allowing a just sovereign state to develop, making the environment safe, mutual legal and moral accountability, attitude toward the defeated nation, establishing war crimes tribunals, and employing a just exit strategy.

JUST CONDITIONS OF SURRENDER

This principle addresses the conditions of surrender placed on the nation that is nearing ultimate defeat. In World War II, the United States and its allies called for the unconditional surrender of both Germany and Japan. In other words, these nations were to totally capitulate and hand over all power and resources to the conquering nations. However, demands for unconditional surrender can be morally problematic for three reasons.

- They can force the enemy nation to prolong the war unnecessarily, fighting until the last man (and woman and child) dies. This may be necessary, but only in rare cases. When the continuance of a war is based solely or mostly on revenge — a "We'll teach them a lesson they'll never forget" mentality — hundreds of thousands of innocent civilians may be killed and dislocated for no other reason than to punish them for "geographic immorality."
- The unnecessary extension of a war can cause the death and dislocation of thousands and possibly hundreds of thousands of innocent civilians after the war due to exposure to toxins, accidents, and fires, as well as a continuing lack of electricity, water, sanitation, and medical supplies.
- The long-term hardships and humiliation caused by unjust conditions of surrender are likely to percolate over time. The result is a political atmosphere in which these hardships and humiliation propel a regime into power that capitalizes on these resentments and embarks on a war of reclamation of lost territories and revenge for years of hardship and humiliation, as happened with the rise of Nazi party in Germany immediately after World War I.

Just Termination

Nations ought to terminate a war as soon as it becomes convincingly clear that one nation will prevail over the other. Just cause and just intention play a major role in just termination. For example, if the sole or primary reason for entering the war was to stop oppression, once that goal has been reasonably achieved, the war ought to stop and other troublesome issues can be handled during the occupation process. To continue a war after this point casts doubt on the veracity of the victorious nation's original intentions.

Two problems can arise as wars wind down. "Right intention creep" can begin in which new "right intentions" are discovered in order to continue the war. For example, a nation's oppressive regime is ousted but a strong anti-democratic sentiment arises from the ashes that "poses a serious threat to our national security." This situation is used to justify another prolonged phase of the war when, in fact, the actual threat is no more than exists in a score of other nations which are not deemed to be a serious, imminent threat.

A second problem has arisen in modern wars because many political and military leaders are not certain about what defines success in war on the practical level. Confusion has existed on this point since the Vietnam War era. Increasingly, there seems to be an attitude among many national leaders, ordinary citizens and soldiers that is reflected in the suggestion "Let's just declare victory and get the hell out of that godforsaken country." This view is problematic for a number of reasons. One is that if the war was justly declared and justly waged, on what moral basis can the country be abandoned and victory declared when the fundamental objectives of the war were never close to being accomplished? Certainly, at some time, it may become abundantly clear that the war, just or unjust, is being lost as more people on both sides are killed, with no end in sight. In cases like this, withdrawal may be the only morally right thing to do. There is something morally and psychologically redemptive in admitting defeat, assessing where serious mistakes were made, and making certain that the same mistakes are never made again in similar circumstances. However, when victory is declared and the war is quickly relegated to a place where all painful memories go, the same mistakes are, and have been, repeated in future wars.

Establishing Civil Order

Establishing order is the first objective of postwar justice after a just conditional surrender is achieved. Without order, none of the remaining objectives can be actualized. Establishing order means making the defeated nation safe, so that citizens can go about their daily affairs without fear. Laws are enforced, transportation is operative, civil conflicts are controlled, and the streets and buildings are safe and sanitary.

Unfortunately, establishing order is likely to be more difficult today than it was in the occupation of Axis (enemy) nations after World War II. The difference is that Germany and Japan were largely monolithic nations and not bitterly fractured by insurgency groups with intra- and international political, military and religious agendas. Germany had been a democracy for many years before Hitler came to power, so democracy was not a new or foreign concept. Japan had an orderly civil society governed by an emperor the people considered divine. As such, despite massive destruction and millions of casualties during the war, both nations recovered in a remarkably orderly fashion. Moreover, peace treaties were signed between nations and when they were signed, hostilities generally stopped within weeks, if not days. However, in an era of terrorism, with many sects, tribes, cultures, and religions involved, no one individual or group functionally represents the defeated nation or can sign an enforceable peace treaty or cooperate in reconstruction. Therefore, the occupation of Germany and Japan after World War II is not likely to be a legitimate model for any current or future occupations.

Restoration of the Defeated Nation

Restoration encompasses three areas. First, the human rights of the citizens ought to be restored or granted for the first time. Second, the infrastructure ought to be restored, at least to the point at which it is functional, ensuring shelter, power, electricity, water, sanitation, and medical care to the citizens of the defeated nation. Third, the economy should be restored, which includes creating opportunities for financial viability and growth.

The goal of returning the defeated nation to its pre-war state is not necessarily desirable because the quality of its pre-war state was likely a direct or indirect cause of the war in the first place. Restoration can be measured by how closely it resembles the victorious nation's standard of life. Caution ought to be exercised in this endeavor because a thin line exists between legitimate restoration and nation building, the latter not being part of right intention and postwar justice.

Allowing Sovereignty

The defeated nation should be allowed sovereignty only after it earns this right by meeting certain conditions. Examples of these conditions may include:

- The promise to compensate all parties, including all nations, that suffered loses directly related to the war
- The relinquishment of all instrumentalities of war except those needed to maintain order on the law enforcement level
- The promise to release all prisoners of war
- The promise that its citizens will be allowed to exercise their human rights to the fullest
- The promise that no citizens will be punished for aiding the victorious nation
- The promise to prosecute their war criminals who are not being prosecuted by other legal tribunals
- The agreement that the victorious nation or an international organization will be allowed to monitor compliance with these conditions

Allowing sovereignty means creating an environment in which qualified candidates chosen by the people are the future leaders of the nation in contrast to a victorious nation rigging an election or appointment so that the defeated nation's leadership will continue to pay homage to the victorious nation. Failure to allow true sovereignty is likely to create more tension within the population and more suspiciousness of the victorious nation, thus prolonging the occupation process.

Providing a Healthy and Safe Environment

The effect of war on a defeated nation causes extensive human and environmental damage. For example, Nicholas Wheeler (2001) discusses the fact that 100,000 civilians died in the aftermath of the Persian Gulf War due to malnutrition, disease and maltreatment by Iraqi oppressors. Ecologically, every possible type of pollution occurs in war — the air, water, trees, and ground contain toxins that can last for many decades. In addition, armaments are left behind after hostilities cease — unexploded bombs, shells, and land mines. Although it is impossible to clear up all the pollution and locate all the armaments during an occupation, the victorious nation has a moral obligation to help the defeated nation make the environment as safe as possible during and after the occupation.

Accountability

The citizens (military and civilian) of the defeated nation who committed egregious war crimes will be prosecuted and punished proportionately by the victorious nation or an international court. However, reciprocal morality ought to be an integral part of any punishment for war crimes to ensure universal principles of justice are followed and not simply "victor's justice." This means that the victorious nation will take accusations of war crimes committed by their own military and civilians seriously and prosecute these individuals or hand them over to a neutral court, such as a world criminal court, for prosecution.

Attitude Toward the Defeated Nation

The victorious nation's attitude toward the defeated nation is critical, not only for setting the stage for restoration but for future relations with that nation. A respectful and helpful attitude is both morally and pragmatically appropriate. It is morally appropriate because the defeated soldiers and civilians are human beings with human rights, which include respect, if not compassion and care. A healthy respect is pragmatically appropriate because, over time, it evokes respect rather than revenge on the part of the defeated nation.

Just Exit Strategy

The victorious nation ought to commit itself to remain in the defeated nation as long as it takes to meet the stated objectives of restoration but no longer. For example, to leave the nation while it is in the midst of civil disorder diminishes the justice that was promised. On the other hand, remaining in the defeated nation longer than necessary may retard its attempts to fully develop into a sovereign nation.

An important distinction should be made between premature withdrawal from a defeated nation simply because the task of maintaining order has become burdensome and strategic withdrawal because continuing hostilities are causing high casualty rates disproportionate to the amount of good the victorious nation can accomplish under the circumstances. As with all things in war, this distinction is easier to draw in theory than in practice. In the final analysis, however, if the victorious nation knew, or should have known, that hostility within factions of the defeated nation would continue after the war ended, moral culpability is attached to a strategic withdrawal in that the victorious nation failed in its duty to bring about and maintain order and stability. Strategic withdrawal in this case may be a necessary evil, but it is likely to be an evil, nevertheless.

Finally, it can be argued that postwar considerations ought to be included as a principle in *jus ad bellum*. In other words, before a war is launched, nations ought to have a reasonably clear plan, as well as contingency plans, for restoring order after the war should they be the victorious nation. It is unrealistic and unacceptable to begin making postwar plans in the final months or weeks of a war. As Eric Patterson (2007) states:

> In sum, *jus post bellum* is essential to a comprehensive just war theory. Durable postwar settlements that promote order, justice, and when possible, reconciliation, restrain future conflicts from breaking out over unresolved disputes and old grievances. Moreover, *jus post bellum* provides a new venue for scholarship by philosophers and practitioners of politics in elucidating specific mechanisms and structures for a just and lasting peace [p. 49].

Challenges to Just War Principles

No theory of philosophy (or morality, psychology, theology, and sociology) is beyond being challenged. Theories of philosophy that came into being thousands of years ago are still robustly debated today. This is a healthy and necessary activity because it forces theorists to continually refine their beliefs and hone them to a sharper point.

Each challenge has lengthy rebuttals but to discuss them here would go beyond the purposes of this chapter. The following challenges to just war principles have been made by both proponents and objectors.

The first challenge is that just war principles begin with an implicit presumption for war. They are seen as a recipe for declaring a just war, not for maintaining a just peace. It is unlikely that, in the history of warfare, just war principles were ever a force for intercepting a political-military trajectory toward war and deflecting it toward peace. This is especially true when national and military leaders invite their own moralists as "expert witnesses for the prosecution" to offer "ultimate opinion" testimony. Until "just peace principles" exist to counterbalance just war principles and moralists to argue for them at the highest levels of government, just war principles are more likely to justify war than keep the peace.

Second, an opposite challenge to just war principles is that they begin with an implicit presumption against war. The principles and theory underlying just war thinking are viewed as unrealistic and make a just war virtually impossible. In the real world, it is difficult to meet even one of the just war principles in any meaningful and lasting way, much less all of the principles. Just war principles are not only impractical but also dangerous in that, if scrupulously followed, they may cause nations to wait too long to launch an attack, which may cause them to suffer a major defeat if not annihilation.

Proponents of these first two challenges can find evidence in the literature to underwrite their claims, and both claims have some validity in that the principles are merely intellectual instruments that can cut in opposite directions, depending on the predispositions of those who interpret them and the situations to which they are applied.

A third challenge to just war principles is that just war vocabulary can lead ordinary citizens and soldiers to believe the war being planned or waged is a just one: "Our cause is just, our intentions are pure, our actions proportionate to the threat. We will take all precautions to protect civilians, and we have exhausted all reasonable attempts to avoid taking this regrettable step." What more could good, patriotic citizens and soldiers want from their political and military leadership? As James Standish (2001) states:

> The just war tradition sounds very good in theory; they are very good principles, but they are very malleable. We can think back to the First World War, for example, where we have very Christian nations on both sides getting their guns blessed by priests, and so forth. So my question is, can this theory be applied in a principled manner in a real world? Is there a danger, in fact, in applying this principle, because it gives a sort of infallible God-sanctioned type of war?

A fourth challenge is that just war principles are relative and indeterminate — they can be used to justify even the most unjust wars when the subjectivity of the interpreters overrides the objectivity of the situations surrounding war. This challenge points out the problem most moral theories face when they are put into practice. The moral principles ought to strike a balance between being so narrow that they are barely useful and so broad that they can be used to justify anything.

A fifth challenge is that, like all principles, just war principles can be set aside, even by those who are most well versed in them, when the lust for war gathers momentum. For example, world-renowned German philosophers and theologians, who were certainly well versed in just war principles, set them aside as the lust for war gained momentum in Germany from 1935 to 1939. Gordon C. Zahn (1962) writes regarding the German Catholic leadership's role prior to and during World War II:

> Nowhere in these episcopal statements does one encounter the question, or even a hint of any question, of whether or not the Hitler war effort met the conditions set for a "just war." This silence on what one might expect to be a bishop's first and most troubling concern is crucial to our analysis. The German Catholic who listened to or read these messages could only conclude that either the war was "just" or, if not that the "just war" question held little or no immediate behavioral relevance for him; that the mere fact that the war was in progress obligated him *as a Christian* to give it his fullest support, even to the point of offering up the ultimate sacrifice of his own life. Unquestioning service to *Volk* and *Vaterland* and the protection of the *Heimat* emerge as virtually the only two standards for determining the individual Catholic's obligations with regard to the war [p. 68].

While Zahn restricted his study to the Catholic Church and its moral role in Germany, the same observations could apply as well to the Protestant churches.

When judging the relevance of just war principles, it is necessary to distinguish between the principles themselves and their deployment, just as a distinction ought to be made between a knife used for saving a life and one used to take a life. A serious challenge of just war principles is not so much that the principles themselves are deficient but their application in certain circumstances may violate the very principles the acts are supposed to be protecting. Daniel C. Maguire (2007) states: "The mischief of the 'just war theory' was that by putting the word *war* alongside the word *just*, it baptized war, making it seem rational, and moral, and good as long as certain rules were observed. It helped to rationalize war" (p. 21).

A final challenge to just war principles is that adhering to them places just nations in a dangerously vulnerable position in an era of asymmetrical warfare and morality. This situation may occur in a war against terrorists and terrorist nations that use wholesale murder and destruction to achieve their goals. Their aim is not simply to win a war but to annihilate every person and nation that does not share their beliefs. They are not interested in diplomacy, compromise, social contracts, rules of engagement, public opinion or moral constraints. Moreover, they view their enemy's threats of destruction as proving the evilness of the enemy and view being killed in war as a way to earn eternal happiness. Nations that play according to the moral and legal rules of warfare when they fight terrorists bring a knife to a gunfight and will pay a dear price for doing so.

Of all the challenges leveled against just war principles, this is arguably the most valid because it thoroughly tests the moral commitment and perseverance of those who espouse them. Questions can be asked, such as: In the final analysis, is justice worth dying for individually and as a nation? Is it better to be dead but moral, or alive but immoral? Alternatively, as Bertrand Russell said during the Cold War with the Soviet Union; "I'd rather be red [a communist] than dead."

Principles are like tools, they can be used correctly to bring about good effects, incorrectly to bring about damaging effects, or not used at all to the betterment or detriment to all concerned. This is the heart of any discussion regarding just war principles. Maguire (2007) adds:

> The need is not to jettison these rules but to update them and insist on their morally binding necessity. When fleshed out with an eye to the psychology, history, and science of war today, they can still serve the peacemaking agenda. They can stand as an obstacle to the facile resort to violence. They can place a massive burden of proof on the heads of war-makers [p. 25].

However, Maguire also sees great merit in just war principles:

> The main merit of just-war theory is its recognition that war is a horror and any defense of it bears the burden of proof. So the theory sets up tests that must be met for a war to be "just." Nothing could be more serious because if the war is not justifiable, the killing it involves is murder and those waging and fighting the war are murderers. *Murder, by definition, is killing for no justifiable reason* [p. 25–26].

Individual citizens have always been the silent partners in war. They pay for the war; leave their families and go off to war; are killed in war, or may return from war maimed, traumatized or both. Yet, they are treated as if they are intellectually incapable of making moral decisions about war and are cast into the role of mere functionaries.

However, the emerging view of the role of individual citizens in times of war is reflected in the thoughts of Uwe Steinhoff (2007):

> The "key criteria" of "last resort, proportionality and prospects of success" are hardly quantum physics; they are concepts which ordinary citizens use to make all kinds of decisions on a daily basis, and which they could therefore use also in deciding on war or peace. To do so, of course they will require the necessary information. In particular, people will need information about specific difficulties and particular aspects that must be kept in mind when applying these concepts to questions of war and peace ... [These concepts] certainly require a certain level of concentration, persistence, and preparedness for discussion (and contradiction) in order to be profitably read. To be understood, they may even require a dictionary, but certainly not a Ph.D. They do not present average citizens with an insurmountable obstacle [p. 69–70].

This position sets the stage for individual citizens to assume their proper role as important stakeholders with respect to war. It calls for a marked change in the way political and military leaders view individual citizens. Leaders would do well to replace disrespect with respect and propaganda with truth, and help empower citizens to become the ultimate war deciders. The framework for helping citizens judge the moral worth of declaring, waging, and ending war presented in this chapter is complemented by the next chapter, which addresses two other theoretical perspectives on war: pacifism and realism.

3

Other Perspectives on War: Pacifism and Realism

I object to violence because when it appears to do good, the good is only temporary; the evil it does is permanent.
—Mahatma Gandhi

While we should never give up our principles, we must also realize that we cannot maintain our principles unless we survive.
—Henry Kissinger

As Chapter 1 states, conscience is the hub of moral decision-making. A spoke for deciding the morality of war consists of moral norms for judging the justice of declaring, waging, and ending wars. Chapter 2 addresses just war principles as one moral norm. This chapter describes two other norms—pacifism and realism, both of which differ substantively from just war principles. A fourth norm, virtue ethics, is addressed in the following chapter. These four perspectives provide a holistic presentation upon which individuals can build an ethical framework for making informed decisions about war.

This chapter addresses the basic principles of pacifism and realism, their relationship to just war principles, and challenges to each perspective. The point is not necessarily to choose one theory over the other but to understand the specific elements of each in order to construct a reasonable and defensible set of norms.

Pacifism and War

Although many versions of pacifism exist, this section addresses two basic types: absolute (principled) and selective (conditional). Absolute pacifists believe all war is morally wrong — their belief is exceptionless. Selective pacifists believe war is not inherently immoral but can be a lesser of evils if it is fought to protect order and peace in the world.

Absolute Pacifism

Absolute pacifists hold that peace is a superlative value because it provides an environment in which nature, including human nature, has an infinitely better chance to survive and flourish than it does in times of war. A peaceful environment permits moral virtues such as justice, truth, honesty, freedom, compassion, security and care to become actualized. Therefore, pacifism is not primarily an anti-war but a pro-peace position.

Absolute pacifism views war as morally wrong in principle because it physically, psychologically, socially, and morally ravages the peaceful environment that protects fundamental moral virtues. Resisting evil with aggression only compounds and spreads evil. Therefore, war is inherently and always wrong.

Absolute pacifists believe morality has no national boundaries. There should be no difference between private and public morals — if it is immoral to kill your next-door neighbor, it is equally immoral to kill your neighbor in another nation. Moreover, all human beings are of equal worth, whoever they are, wherever they live, whatever they do. This does not mean that all human acts are morally equal, only that killing people who act immorally is not a step in the direction of removing evil from the world.

Pacifists also believe war is morally wrong in practice because it fails to meet its purported goal — to maintain order and peace. War is violent and employing violence to stop violence is not only logically but also materially circular. War may temporarily stop violence but, like a virus, war will eventually return to nations that were involved in it and spread to other nations that previously had been war-free. War can have a pernicious effect on defeated nations. They often learn from their mistakes and strive to become more effective warriors in order to exact revenge for their defeat. In addition, war often has a virulent effect on victorious nations because it bolsters their confidence as warrior nations and whets their appetite for future wars. War can even infect third-party nations, especially if their immune systems are weakened by internal stressors (civil war, political and religious conflicts, and economic pressures) which lead them to start wars as a distraction from, if not a cure for, their problems.

Finally, absolute pacifists believe that no war can ever be justified and consider terms such as just war, Christian war, and good war to be oxymorons. Modern warfare with its nuclear capability, gas attacks, carpet bombing, firebombing, land mines, and terrorist attacks places the thought of a moral war beyond any serious consideration.

Absolute pacifists believe no nation ever "wins" a war, except in the narrowest political and military terms. In every other sense — moral, humanitarian, religious, ecological, sociological, economic, and psychological — war is a catastrophe for humankind and the world. In World War II, "the last good war," approximately 72 million individuals were killed, 47 million of whom were innocent civilians. The Allied nations (the "winners") had 61 million individuals killed and the Axis nations (the "losers") had 11 million individuals killed. The Soviet Union (one of the "winners") suffered 23.6 million fatalities (13.4 percent of its population). In other words, the "winning nations" had 5.5 times more fatalities than did the "losing nations," giving tragic meaning to the concept of victory.

The concept of just war principles is unacceptable to pacifists because, by definition, the principles may be used to justify war, which pacifists believe is intrinsically evil, and moralize something that cannot be moralized. The principles are so spongy that any war can be justified by any nation given the right tweaking of the criteria. Absolute pacifists view just war principles not as a justification for war but merely an excuse for it, blessing violence instead of condemning it. Mahatma Gandhi speaks to the issue of the moral permissiveness of just war thinking: "What difference does it make to the dead, the orphans, and the homeless, whether the mad destruction is wrought under the name of totalitarianism or the holy name of liberty and democracy?"

Stanley Hauerwas (2001) challenges just war proponents to think more closely about the practical ramifications of their position.

> I want to raise a question to the people who are committed to just war perspectives. Prior to a violent outbreak, how do you form people to be just warriors? Would the American people be ready to invade the beaches of Japan rather than drop the bomb on Hiroshima and Nagasaki? More lives would have been lost that way than Hiroshima and Nagasaki, but it would have been just. Are the American people ready to sacrifice lives to fight a war justly? What would the United States military forces look like if they were structured on just war grounds? Is the institutionalization of the military — in terms of the kinds of weapons it uses, how it is trained to use those weapons — just war training? It's too late if you just get to a situation and then say, "How do we fight it justly?" You have to prepare to fight wars in a just way.

Selective Pacifism

Selective (conditional) pacifism holds that peace is the ultimate value of a nation and should be fostered and protected at every turn. However, selective pacifism also recognizes that evil exists in the world and that not all individuals or nations are peace loving. When a nation clearly and certainly threatens the security of another nation, the targeted nation not only has a moral right but a moral duty to defend itself according to the principles of justice. In other words, the war ought to rest on just causes and intentions, to be a last resort, and to be fought according to the principles of proportionality and discrimination.

Both absolute pacifism and selective pacifism are serious philosophical and ethical positions and their adoption ought not to be based on a moral intuition or whim. Each has its independent elements that require careful thought, study, and discussion. The next section briefly describes the moral and legal standings of each as they relate to conscience decisions regarding war.

CONSCIENTIOUS OBJECTION AND SELECTIVE CONSCIENTIOUS OBJECTION

The concepts of conscientious objection and selective conscientious objection are basic elements of pacifism. Although the terms are generally used in relation to petitioning for dispensation from serving in the military, their moral, philosophical, psychological and theological bases are of significant interest to anyone attempting to relate moral decision-making to the subject of war. Therefore, the basic concepts of conscientious objection and selective conscientious objection will be discussed in some detail since they pertain not only to soldiers but to civilians.

In a time where there is no military draft, conscientious objection is seldom an issue because it is unlikely that an individual who believes all war is immoral would volunteer to enter the military. However, when some soldiers witness the ravages of war first hand, they may decide that no war could ever be moral. What is more likely today is that soldiers who fought in wars they considered just are later faced with a war they firmly believe is unjust or is being fought in an unjust manner and arrive at a point of selective conscientious objection. In other words, they come to believe the war they are fighting is unjust, but maintain their original position that just war can exist in certain circumstances. In general, conscientious objection is easier to claim and justify in that it has a long history, legal standing, and a categorical opposition to all war, which is easier to substantiate than selective conscientious objection.

Conscientious objection in the United States is not simply of historical interest for two reasons. First, although it was invoked primarily during the era of the military draft, which was last rescinded in 1973, it continues to be petitioned by those in the military who, largely based on their first-hand, real-life experience of war, decide that they can no longer, in good conscience, participate in war, either at all or in a combat position. Second, although the term "conscientious objector" has applied only to individuals who are in the military or facing military service, it has a broader and important application, namely, to all citizens of a nation that is facing or waging war. In other words, when applied to the civilian populace, the question becomes not, "How can I remove myself from actively engaging in matters of war?" but "How can I become educated and involved in matters of war so that I can make an informed conscientious decision about war?" Civilians, as well as soldiers, philosophically can be conscientious objectors or selective conscientious objectors and act on their beliefs in ways they deem appropriate.

The history of conscientious objection highlights the relationships between ordinary citizens and their obligation to serve their nation. Briefly stated, one premise upon which this relationship is based is social contract theory, which holds that ordinary citizens and their national leaders have mutual obligations to each other. National leaders have a moral obligation to protect their citizens from harm, while citizens have a complementary duty to help leaders meet this obligation, even if citizens loose their lives in times of war. In light of this contract, it is helpful to understand the political and legal basis for the current concept of conscientious objection in the United States.

PETITIONING FOR CONSCIENTIOUS OBJECTOR STATUS

The basic moral conflict with regard to conscientious objection to war is between the legitimate claims of personal conscience and those of the national common good. Socrates wrote at length about "the conscience of the laws." The following points offer guidance to citizens on what the "laws of the land" say about conscientious objection.

1. Conscientious objection is a statutory right — one based on law legislated by Congress — but not a constitutional right. Conscientious objection is often referred to as not a right but "a grace from Congress." The belief that conscientious objection is not a constitutional right is continuously debated based on the "freedom of religion" clause in the Constitution.

2. A conscientious objector must believe that all war is morally or religiously wrong, not just a particular war. There is no legal provision for selective conscientious objection, meaning that conscientious objection to a particular war in contrast to all war is not recognized as a legal exemption from serving in the military.

3. In the original submittal of a conscientious objection claim, the burden of proof lies with petitioners who must prove that they are sincere and that their position is based on articulated, deeply held, and documented moral or religious beliefs. However, once petitioners present their formal claim, the

burden of proof shifts to the government to demonstrate a basis in fact to deny the application.

4. The basis for a conscientious objector claim must be solely on a demonstrable history of deeply held moral, ethical, or religious beliefs. It cannot be based merely on a personal code, or on political, sociological, philosophical, psychological, or pragmatic reasons.

5. Individuals already in the service may petition for conscientious objector status if their beliefs crystallized after entering the service. However, the conscientious objection must be to all wars, not just the one in which the service member is enlisted.

Perhaps the legal decision most directly applicable to ordinary civilians is the distinction the courts have consistently made between moral, ethical or religious beliefs and those based on political, sociological, philosophical, psychological, and pragmatic reasons. Although there is often some subjective and even objective overlap within these reasons, none of them is redundant. A political belief for objecting to war could be that a war would benefit the opposition party; an economical one could be that the money wasted on war could be better used at home for education and other social services; a sociological belief could be that war mostly hurts minorities and the poor; a philosophical one could be that war violates humanitarian values; a psychological one could be that war seriously impacts the psychological welfare of both combatants and civilians, and a religious one could be that war violates certain religious principles.

Petitioning for Selective Conscientious Objector Status

Selective conscientious objection has a shorter history, becoming a noticeable issue on a practical level during the Vietnam War. Selective conscientious objection is a more difficult position to defend because it stands in contradiction to the U.S. government's position that any war it declares and prosecutes is moral. It also runs into difficulties in that opposition to a specific war requires a great deal of knowledge about that war in order to substantiate a claim for selective conscientious objector status, knowledge that most soldiers and civilians lack.

Because each selective conscientious objector's situation is different, as are those of the people judging the validity of a selective conscientious objection claim, it is not possible to make universal statements about what would be viewed as a valid or invalid claim. However, court decisions regarding selective conscientious objection indicate that appeals to "the anatomy of one's conscience" (in other words, personal moral intuition) alone is not compelling.

Decisions as to whether selective conscientious objector status will be granted take into account not only the moral obligations of the petitioner but also the moral obligations of national leaders to protect their citizens. While religious and philosophical claims for selective conscientious objector status may be theoretically legitimate, they are not likely to be compelling, unless everyone who subscribes to the religious or philosophical principles morally opposes the same war. For example, petitioners cannot legitimately make a claim predicated on the fact they are Christians because there are as many biblical passages and theologies that support the moral necessity of war as there are those that oppose war.

The burden is on soldiers claiming selective conscientious objection to prove the legitimacy of their position; the burden is not on the government to prove that the war it is declaring or waging is moral. In cases of uncertainty, the benefit of the doubt goes to military and civil authorities. The operative principle is that a war should be regarded as just "unless or until" it is clearly demonstrated to be unjust.

The basis of a petition for selective conscientious objector status cannot be personal moral codes, which generally are based on moral intuition: "I just feel this war is immoral with all the people getting killed and all." The moral code must be based on generally accepted principles of justice held up against the perceived violation of justice in a particular war.

It is important to distinguish between disagreements with a nation's political, military, philosophical, and economic reasons for declaring and waging war and having deeply rooted and clearly articulated moral principles that were present before a war was declared and which would be seriously violated if an individual participated in the war. Almost everyone engaged in declaring and waging war has some disagreement with the way the war is planned or waged. For example, members of Congress, the Senate, the president's cabinet, the generals managing the war, and religious leaders often disagree even among themselves about different facets of war. Even just wars fought for a nation's survival could not be waged if unanimous agreement that the war was moral and necessary were required before arms were taken up.

Political platforms and polls do not determine the morality of a war. To be for or against a war based on political ideology ("I support my party's position on the war") is not a moral position. Similarly, the fact that 80 percent of a nation is for or against the war is morally meaningless. If public opinion polls had been taken of the German people in 1939 and 1940, it is likely that support for their wars would have been nearly unanimous.

The number of people (soldiers and civilians) killed in a war and the cost of a war are not in themselves moral issues in the sense that they can be used to morally object to a war. It is a sad fact that people are killed in war, including just wars. The morality of the war is determined not by the sheer number of deaths or dollars spent, but rather by the *reasons* for those losses, the method used to bring them about, and the chances for a clear victory.

The fact that injustices are occurring in the waging of a war does not justify selective conscientious objector status. For example, the fact that some soldiers are torturing enemy combatants is not reason, in itself, to classify a war as immoral. Isolated immoral acts do not reflect the moral tenor of an entire war. It is only when a nation's war strategy (policy) and tactics are perceived to be generally and continually unjust and in violation of an individual's conscience that a legitimate moral claim for selective conscientious objection could be invoked. If the claim were accepted by the military and political authorities, this would not mean that the authorities agreed that they were waging an unjust war, only that the petitioner met the criteria for having made a serious conscience decision.

As can be seen, conscientious objection is not a concept reserved solely for those in the military; it is even more applicable to ordinary citizens who attempt to understand the relationship between their personal consciences and the "conscience of the laws" as much as possible. Richard Reilly (2003) analyzes this relationship:

> Surely one owes much to one's state, especially if it is justly ordered, safeguards individual rights, and promotes the common good. Both out of gratitude and a sense of fair play, one should do one's "public duty"—including upholding the war, paying taxes, voting, and otherwise participating in the political life of the community, and so on. We might say, as Jesus said, "render unto Caesar what is Caesar's and render unto God what is God's." What does not belong to Caesar is the nature, meaning and destiny of one's life, or to put it otherwise, what does not belong to Caesar is the allegiance or fidelity of one's conscience [p. 118].

CHALLENGES TO PACIFISM

The basic concepts of pacifism are challenged for various reasons. Those who espouse just war principles perceive pacifism as offering no protection for justice and abandoning it in hostile territory. Turning the other cheek is exactly what enemy nations and groups want — a swift and bloodless victory.

The foundations of pacifism are also criticized as being built on disputable claims. For example, pacifism is hard pressed to demonstrate by logic or empiricism that nations at peace thrive while those at war flounder. During World War II, the United States not only remained stable, but also flourished in many areas — national cohesion, the economy, employment, morale, pride, religion, and altruistic, even heroic, behavior. On the other end of the spectrum, the Soviet Union was at peace after World War II and progressively decompensated to a point where civil unrest, abject poverty, organized and unorganized crime, collective depression and despair were rampant.

It is also difficult for pacifists to argue that wars never work to bring stability and peace to the world. At least a few wars in recent history seem to have done so. For example, World War II put an end to the Nazi reign, which included total war against sovereign nations, forced labor, rape, torture, and the incarceration and murder of over 12 million innocent people. The Korean War saved South Korea from being overrun and oppressed by the Chinese and North Korean Communists and allowed it to remain a free democracy.

Many non-pacifists believe that pacifists are wrong to claim moral purity and clean hands while their fellow citizens kill and are killed to protect the very peace that pacifists prize so highly. In other words, pacifists reap the benefits their nation provides without paying the price for them. This unwillingness to do their fair share for their nation is viewed as a violation of the social contract, which holds that in return for their nation protecting them, citizens must serve their nation in ways their nation most needs them, especially in times of national emergency.

Finally, pacifism is criticized for failing to take into account the evil in the world that has an insatiable appetite for the annihilation of all good things. Just as forest fires sometimes are successfully fought by setting backfires, evil sometimes must be fought with the instruments of evil so that good can eventually triumph. When this is the case, pacifism is not a virtue but a vice in that it allows evil to triumph with little or no resistance.

Whatever the validity of these challenges, pacifists believe that their martyrs throughout history have made an important difference in world affairs. These martyrs were murdered because they challenged the pernicious political or religious systems of their times, but did so in non-violent ways. For example, Oscar Romero, Archbishop of San Salvador, embraced non-violent liberation theology, dedicated most of his life to helping the poor, and was murdered for his efforts while celebrating Mass in 1986. His death caused an international outcry for human rights reform in San Salvador. Martin Luther King, Jr., (1967), another pacifist martyr, sums up the theory of pacifism:

> Returning violence for violence multiplies violence, adding deeper darkness to a night already devoid of stars. Darkness cannot drive out darkness: only light can do that. Hate cannot drive out hate: only love can do that. Hate multiplies hate, violence multiplies violence, and toughness multiplies toughness in a descending

spiral of destruction.... The chain reaction of evil — hate begetting hate, wars producing more wars — must be broken, or we shall be plunged into the dark abyss of annihilation [p. 62–63].

The spirit embodied in these words was instrumental in passing the Civil Rights Act and all the justice that flowed from it over the following decades.

Realism and War

Realism is a reaction against other theories, especially pacifism and just war principles, which are perceived as predicated on idealism, ideology, moralism, and legalism, which serve only to distort perceptions of reality and lead to foolish wars or foolish appeasement. While the philosophy of realism applies to all kinds of national and international issues, this discussion will be limited to how it relates to war. Historically, Thucydides, Carl von Clausewitz, Niccolò Machiavelli and Thomas Hobbes are some of the better-known promulgators of realism, and modern realists include Hans Morgenthau, George F. Kennan, Reinhold Niebuhr, E.H. Carr, and Henry Kissinger. Three types of realism will be addressed in this section: classical realism, absolute Machiavellianism, and neorealism.

CLASSICAL REALISM

This section describes the basic tenets of classical realism.

1. Realism's sole purpose is to protect the essential interests, security, and survival of a nation because nations are the bedrock of human existence and civilization. Humanity unattached to a political community to protect and nourish it cannot exist in a world of unfettered evil, which is an overriding dimension of the human condition. Realism is particularistic — its sole concern is the continued existence of one's own nation and, in general, the welfare of other nations to the degree that they will not become unstable and pose a threat to one's own nation.

This attitude appears selfish and egocentric, but no more so than the attitude of a family that must take care of its own needs, development, and survival before it can afford the luxury of considering the needs of other families. Even more important, the family must strengthen itself in ways that allow it to protect its interests and existence against the threats of belligerent families in the neighborhood. The family has no need to purloin goods from others, except in dire situations of existential threat when the ethic becomes survival of the fittest. The lack of aggression toward other families is not necessarily based on moral principles but on realist ones. Attacking another family would elicit the wrath of the entire neighborhood as well as law enforcement, and this could constitute a direct threat to the security and possibly the existence of the aggressor family.

2. Politics is a predominant and autonomous sphere in international relations and should not be diluted by philosophical, military, economic, legal, ideological, or moral considerations. Pure power politics is the engine of international relations and adding any other consideration throws off the timing and balance of the enterprise.

However, politics in this sense does not refer to the common understanding of the word. It is not related to the parochial politics of nations — political parties, platforms, and programs. Politics in the philosophical sense refers to the community of individuals in a nation — their voice, values, needs, motives, culture, religion, community, and overall well-being.

The fact that realists view politics as the most important element in making decisions about war does not mean that other elements are not considered. No realist war can be waged without prudence, which demands that other elements such as economics, law, and morality be taken into consideration, albeit at the lower levels of the pyramid. To ignore these elements is to ignore the citizens for whom the war is being waged, which could diminish support for the war, and, in turn, threaten the survival of the nation.

3. Power is the essence of effective politics. The best foreign relations policy is impotent if it lacks the power to put its policies into action. Power is based largely on military might — armies that are deployed only when necessary for national survival but when deployed, fight with overwhelming force. They finish the job they set out to accomplish in a minimal amount of time, with a minimal amount of loss in blood and treasure, and a minimal amount of distraction from issues that at first glance appear to be relevant but under further scrutiny are, in fact, superfluous.

Like any power, political power can be used for constructive or destructive purposes. Three kinds of political power exist: soft, hard, and ultimate. Soft power is manifested in low-key discussions, negotiations, economic deals, trade enticements, and the persuasion of allied nations. Hard power is evident in heated discussions, hard-nosed negotiations, economic sanctions, exclusion from the world community, and serious and real threats of military intervention. Ultimate power is manifested in armed attacks meant to force the offending nation into removing its sources of threat that are endangering one's own and other nations.

Power should be used prudently. It should be strong enough to neutralize a threat once and for all, but not so devastating as to engender the wrath of the world community, which could turn against the powerful nation. The fact that political and military power is misused in politics and war is regrettable, but it should not be automatically assumed that realists are necessarily responsible for the abuses of power. The carpet bombing and atom bombing of World War II was supported by many just war proponents as well as other non-realists.

4. Human nature has good and evil dimensions but, in the arena of international competition and conflict, evil often trumps good, and to believe otherwise is both intellectually deficient and materially dangerous. Good seldom has a chance against evil — evil must be countered with evil in order to eventually bring about good and ensure national security and survival. International conflicts are never between good and evil because both exist in all nations. War, for example, is always between the greater, equal, and lesser of evils.

In practice, the leaders of other nations, even friendly nations, can never be trusted. Sometimes even the leaders of one's own nation are suspect because they share in the same evil (wickedness, ignorance, delusions) as other leaders. Therefore, when a nation faces an existential threat, its leaders must sometimes violate not only international laws, conventions, and treaties but also their own nation's laws and moral norms in order to fight fire with fire. This is not a unique situation domestically or internationally. For example, in the midst of natural disasters and civil disturbance, state and federal laws are often suspended until the crisis ends. The question is not so much whether such suspensions of law should be permitted but whether the suspensions are legitimate and proportionate to the crisis.

5. National self-interest is the driving force of international politics. If one's nation fails to survive and flourish, it will cease to exist in any meaningful way. Not only will it be destroyed militarily and materially, but socially, culturally, morally and religiously as well. However, national self-interest has limits because an unfettered "hunter-gatherer" approach to other nations will eventually cause other, weaker nations to align with each other and eventually destroy the predatory nation. Therefore, it is important to distinguish between prudent and marauding self-interest.

Prudence is a cardinal virtue in realism, not necessarily as moral ballast but as a pragmatic one. Moderation is always important — employ sufficient force to get the job done. Too little force is dangerous because it gives the enemy the opportunity to gather its own forces and overcome the attacking nation. Too much force elicits resentment from the rest of the world, which could eventually work against national self-interests. In other words, overwhelming force does not mean overreaching force.

6. Nations are autonomous — they rely on no political body or legal or moral laws for assistance or authority. One reason for this autonomy is that anarchy exists in the world — a lawlessness which requires every nation to stand up for itself. Domestic and international law, Congress or Parliament, the United Nations, and the World Court are seldom to be trusted, at least in their current state, because they can be infected with the same corruption as everything and everyone else. While it may be prudent and even beneficial to seek authority and support from others, in cases of existential threat (the very existence of the nation is seriously threatened), nations must act alone. To seek and rely on the authority and support of others is a fool's mission that will cause only delay, distraction, and possible annihilation.

7. Balance of power is essential in international relations. This means that the world is better off with a bipolar power structure in which the two strongest nations have equal power and the opportunity to destroy each other. Both nations recognize this equality and choose co-existence over mutual annihilation. All nations are safer because of this standoff. Other nations dare not attack the two superpowers, and the superpowers do not allow other nations to attack each other if it would threaten the superpowers' security and survival.

The balance of power ethic was responsible for keeping the world safe during the Cold War years (1945–1991) when the two superpowers, the United States and the Soviet Union, were evenly matched in nuclear weapons and the capacity to use them. This containment and deterrence strategy motivated both nations to take war off the table and live in peace — albeit a nervous peace. However, by 1991, the Soviet Union self-imploded, which left the United States the sole superpower.

Unipolar power is not good because it means one superpower can lord over all other nations and do whatever it wishes with them. Multipolar power also is not good because it presents a situation in which several nations can exploit weaker nations, which eventually threatens world peace and in turn the welfare of all nations.

8. Realists are reluctant to go to war because they believe that most wars are waged for reasons other than national security and survival and, therefore, place a nation in situations in which its well-being and security are more at risk than if it had not gone to war.

Most wars are fought to spread an ideology, send a message, acquire resources, build nations, punish contempt, exact revenge, intimidate recalcitrant nations, change political or religious attitudes, stop oppression not related to national survival, and distract from domestic problems, such as unemployment or an ailing economy. In a sentence, initiating war for non-realist reasons is the most dangerous step a nation can take to weaken itself politically, psychologically, militarily, economically, and morally.

Hans Morgenthau (1967), a staunch realist, severely criticized the United States involvement in both Cuba and Vietnam. With respect to the unsuccessful invasion of Cuba, Morgenthau writes: "The United States failed thrice. The intervention did not succeed; in the attempt we suffered the temporary impairment of our standing among the new and emerging nations; and we lost much prestige as a great nation able to use its power successfully on behalf of its interests" (p. 431).

With respect to intervention in Vietnam, Morgenthau's prediction of April 1965 and those of the realists to which he alludes all came true eight years later:

> Physical conquest would require the deployment of millions of American soldiers on the mainland of Asia. No American military leader has ever advocated a course of action so fraught with incalculable risks, so uncertain of outcome, requiring sacrifices so out of proportion to the interests at stake and the benefits to be expected. President Eisenhower declared on February 10, 1954, that he "could conceive of no greater tragedy than for the United States to become involved in an all-out war in Indochina." General MacArthur, in the Congressional hearings concerning his dismissal and in personal conversation with President Kennedy, emphatically warned against sending American foot soldiers to the Asian mainland to fight China [p. 87].

9. Morality cannot be the determinative factor in decisions regarding international relations, especially in times of war. Traditional morality presents two problems. The fundamental one is that morality is largely, if not entirely, subjective and relative. Morals are spawned from the mores, myths, customs, and narratives indigenous to particular psychologies, religions, cultures, and social milieus. It would be practically impossible to decide which morality ought to be the predominant reason for going to war. For example, Christians may be pacifist or militant, as well as capitalists, socialists, or communists. Christian moral theologies may be liberal, moderate, or conservative, and the pope may condemn a war that conservative Christian theologians support. To add the moralities of Judaism and Islam only compounds the problem of declaring war based on moral reasons.

The point is that each individual in each group can have a moral view of declaring, waging, and ending wars, which raises the question: Which "morality" will guide which war in which part of the world? National leaders cannot allow themselves to be placed in the position of deciding this question because it is an impossible task. Moreover, national leaders cannot allow themselves to be placed in the position of making decisions that will result in asking their soldiers to die for a particular group's set of moral norms regarding war, a set of beliefs to which few, if any, soldiers might subscribe. Moreover, moral restraints on tactics may well place soldiers and the nation they have sworn to protect in serious danger.

The second problem with traditional morality is that it is dangerously idealistic and narrow. It is idealistic because it assumes everyone in the world perceives morality as something to be respected and even to be emulated. When moral individuals turn the other cheek to accept a second slap, they consider it a good example for the assailants. In fact, for many aggressive nations, turning the other cheek is a welcome invitation to move in for the kill.

Traditional morality is too narrow — too circumscribed. To employ an analogy, the laws of chivalry codified in college fencing rules may serve to protect the fencers from harm. However, if the same fencers play by the same rules in the hand-to-hand combat of war, they are likely to meet with sudden death. In these cases, a broader understanding of morality must be applied — an objective, universal morality derived from natural law, which places life, liberty and equality above all other values and applies to all people in all nations. This morality holds that evil acts are permitted because they may be the "lesser of evils" in relationship to the overall good they achieve — the protection and survival of a nation's citizens.

However, while realists do not believe morality ought to be a determinative, overarching factor in decision-making, they do not necessarily eschew morality as having any influence in the calculations realists make. For example, Hans Morgenthau (1978) believes that morality based on natural law, in contrast to denominational morality, has a place in realism because political actions often have moral consequences that must be considered. To support a political or military regime that oppresses and tortures its people may be temporarily expedient but politically unwise and damaging in the long term. Reinhold Niebuhr (1943), a prominent Christian realist, believed morality ought to play a critical role in the decision-making of realists largely because, among other reasons, political decisions cannot be made in a moral vacuum.

Absolute Machiavellian Realism

This radical type of realism has its roots in Niccolò Machiavelli's (1469–1527) *The Prince*. This treatise was written for princes in the Middle Ages when principalities frequently were at war to defend their territory and citizens. Machiavelli was chancellor of Florence, Italy, for 14 years during which time he tried to broker peace between warring parities on several occasions. When talking failed, he counseled that princes should employ overwhelming force that included as much cruelty as necessary to nip wars in the bud. This cruelty included publicly torturing, assassinating and hanging people in the most excruciating ways in order to obtain information, executing the malcontents, and setting a clear example for other potential adversaries. Such actions were acknowledged as evil but necessary. Machiavelli's treatise gives a theoretical rationale and justification for cruelty, ruthlessness, and mercilessness in war that was always present but seldom admitted and authorized as an acceptable tactic.

This treatise not only allowed but required murder, plunder, rape, kidnap, torture, burning, and the devastation of houses, schools, hospitals, farms, monasteries, castles, and churches during times of war. These are the ingredients of a "scorched earth" policy that leaves nothing alive or standing in its wake. The purpose of these acts is not only to decimate the enemy but to discourage other potential aggressors from even thinking of attacking in the future. This policy is not a part of classical realism, which views excessive force and wanton cruelty as counterproductive, especially in modern war when the weapons of revenge are nuclear and intercontinental.

Machiavelli justifies cruelty based on what today would be considered humanitarian and consequentialist principles. It is better to publicly torture, maim, burn, and hang a relatively small number of adversaries at the beginning of hostilities and end them quickly than to suffer the cruelty of unnecessary war for several more years. As Machiavelli notes:

> Therefore a prince, so long as he keeps his subjects united and loyal, ought not to mind the reproach of cruelty; because with a few examples he will be more merciful than those who, through too much mercy, allow disorders to arise, from which follow murders or robberies; for these are wont to injure the whole people, whilst those executions which originate with a prince offend the individual only [Chapter 17].

However, Machiavelli indicates that the cruelty must not appear in its naked form because the people the prince rules would not tolerate it. The cruelty must be disguised in order to be palatable to one's own subjects. Scott Erb (2005) paraphrases Machiavelli:

> Yet you cannot be so brutal and obscene as to turn the people against you. You should be feared, but not hated. Keep your word when you can — it is good to be considered trustworthy, but understand when you should lie or deceive. Don't execute innocent people if you don't have to, but know that at times it might be necessary. Create the illusion that you are virtuous and noble, but in reality break from that when you must [p. 5].

The disguises to be used follow a time-honored pattern: tell the public outlandish lies, inflame their patriotic emotions, present the enemy as evil incarnate, describe the threat as existential, and "legalize and moralize" the cruelty. The cruelty can take many forms: moral and legal malfeasance, extreme torture, weapons that cause excruciating wounds and death, and carpet and incendiary bombing of populated areas. In summary, Erb stresses that absolute Machiavellian realism is not merely an historical artifact. He warns:

> One thing is certain, though: Machiavelli's ideas can't be ignored or dismissed simply because we do not wish them to be true. He captures an aspect of politics that existed in Italy in the 16th century, and exists yet today. The challenge to idealists and humanists is to not simply deny or reject Machiavelli, but confront what gives his ideas power centuries after they were written, and think seriously about what it might take to have a world where political expediency does not require amorality [p. 9].

Classical and absolute Machiavellian realism are not completely separate and distinct entities and have been evident in all wars, past, present, and future. An army might capture a town using the strategy and tactics of classical realism, then capture a neighboring town using the strategy and tactics of absolute Machiavellian realism, depending on the frenzy of the warriors and leadership that cannot or does not want to control them. Therefore, while a thin theoretical line exists between the two philosophies and tactics, it is ambiguous and movable in the "fog of war," which is sometimes artificially manufactured to cloud reality to justify illegal and immoral activities.

Neorealism

Neorealism attempts to bring the tenets of classic realism into the 21st century by recognizing that a superpower no longer can treat other nations as means to an end but must regard them as ends in themselves. Simply put, neorealism asserts that superpowers must change their worldview from a dictatorial one ("You will do what we tell you to do or else") to a cosmopolitan one ("We're all in this together, so we need to work harmoniously to maintain world peace").

Neorealism holds that individual nations are important in themselves, but other entities can be equally important. International organizations such as human rights groups, the International Red Cross, the United Nations, domestic and world courts and national and international political bodies can be important factors in war-related situations and be facilitators of order and peace.

To neorealists, power does not derive primarily from military might, which is only appropriate as a truly last resort. In fact, sometimes military might or even the threat of military might may be highly inappropriate and damaging to a nation's self-interests. Several other options can be employed before launching war, including treating all nations, even "evil" ones, with respect, along with a willingness to negotiate and compromise with them.

Nations that operate in the real world must be realistic. They must be open to striking compromises, which, by definition, means they must give up something of value to receive something of equal or greater value up to the point at which national interest will be compromised. Mutually beneficial trade agreements can be struck and political and material support offered to ease the tensions, resentments, and insecurities of other nations. It is folly to assume the attitude that a nation should only negotiate or aid friendly nations because, by definition, they are unlikely to harbor the resentment, insecurities, prejudices, and helplessness that often lead to military conflict.

Other nations, their leaders and citizens may have histories and cultures that have shaped very different perceptions of reality for centuries. Nations that ignore these differences or ridicule them do so at their own peril. The days are past when small, backward nations can be mistreated with impunity. Terrorism and nuclear weapons are the great equalizers of power and destruction in today's world.

The day has also passed in which entire nations can be diagnosed as "evil,"—terroristic, primitive, fanatical, bellicose. When a "good nation" bombs an "evil nation," in contrast to going after the evil individuals in a generally good nation, the vast majority of the casualties are innocent civilians, good individuals and families that may only "turn evil" as a result of the devastation leveled against them by the "good nation."

Neorealism is not a "one size fits all," "my way or the highway" theory, but adapts to the times, persons, and places involved in conflicts. In other words, neorealism calls for more analytical, critical, interpretive, and dispassionate thinking than classical or Machiavellian realism. Neorealism is more self-aware and self-critical. It calls for nations to monitor the cause and effect relationships between the actions and reactions they evoke from the leaders and citizens of other nations. They apply an ethic of reciprocity: "If the leaders of other nations treated us with the same disrespect as we treat them, I would be just as resentful of them as they are of us."

Finally, neorealism does not perceive morality, law, values, and religion as inherently distracting but sees a place for them in decision-making. These elements can be important and sometimes the most important factor in some international relations. This largely transcendent framework often reveals that what at first glance appears to be solely political polemics are, in reality, moral conflicts involving justice, respect, compassion, accountability and care.

REALIST VIEWS OF OTHER THEORIES

Adherents to each of the realist theories addressed above believe that to focus on just war principles is to miss the point in war. These principles indicate how to wage a just war but do not address the concerns of realists. For example, spreading democracy to a totalitarian nation could be considered a just cause driven by a right intention but realists may well consider such a war unrealistic, unnecessary, unwise, costly in terms of blood, treasure and international approbation and, most importantly, one that might ignite aggression that would seriously threaten a nation's self-interests, if not its survival.

Realists also believe those who subscribe to just war principles have a marked tendency to declare wars on principle that are not necessary to declare in reality, to wage "moral wars" and "legal wars" in ways that ultimately cause more harm than good, and to allow wars to go on longer than necessary simply to make an ideological point. Realists are more likely to wage "in and out wars"—get in quickly when it is clear a war is absolutely necessary, fight with overwhelming force, and get out as soon as the basic job is done. In other words, principles of morality, politics and law may have a place in some low intensity wars, but they have no place in wars that pose an existential threat. In fact, in those cases, these principles are likely to be not only counterproductive but also outright dangerous.

To realists, just war principles are a hindrance in the prosecution of war because their moral ideology (justice) is so abstract, relative, and subjective that it actually interferes with the prosecution of war because it clouds the core reality of protecting a nation's security interests. In the parlance of realism, self-interest alludes to the safety and survival of a nation and is not innately selfish, although it can be selfish in certain cases. For example, most realists would agree that the decision of the United States to go to war against Japan was predicated on legitimate self-interest, whereas going to war against North Korea was not.

Realists also disagree with the presupposition of just war principles that there is as much, if not more, good in the world as evil, so when nations go to war good will eventually conquer evil. However, the history of war dating back to pre–Christian times clearly demonstrates that evil can triumph over good, both in the short-term and the long-term. Moreover, while what constitutes "reality" for realists is always open to interpretation, the just war principles are exponentially open to interpretations which can be used to justify virtually any war and every act in war.

While realists are open to the idea that morality may play some role in war, they believe it must be more far-sighted and transcendent than the self-defeating morality of just war principles. Just war thinking counsels that it is more moral for a just nation to allow itself to be defeated than to use any means necessary to protect itself in order to survive and continue to protect and spread justice to the world. Realism holds that a nation's existential survival is the highest ethic, one which allows "lesser evil" tactics in a world permeated by evil. Realism's retort to just war principles is "I would rather be perceived as immoral but be alive than perceived as moral but be dead."

Realism also has no room for pacifism and views it as political and material suicide during war. Pacifists become political and ideological martyrs even before the first shot is fired. In addition, they are not available to defend their nation in any meaningful way. Perhaps most importantly, their presence conveys that something is profoundly wrong with defending the interests and very survival of their nation.

Challenges to Realism

As is true of pacifism and just war principles, realism is not beyond criticism, as the following discussion indicates. This section will be limited to challenges to classical realism for purposes of brevity.

Classical realism presupposes that national political and military leaders have the capacity to perceive reality in its objective, pure form and thus fails to be truly realistic. As long as human beings are involved in perceiving and interpreting reality, a consensus regarding what constitutes objective reality is unlikely to be reached.

Classical realists also fail to realize that a "balance of power" can also be a "balance of terror" in which superpowers (which today includes any nation with long-range nuclear weapons) own warehouses filled with weapons of mass destruction. Moreover, the balance of power concept presupposes that all nations included in the balance have equally strong needs to remain alive. In an era of terrorism, militant forces exist in some nations that seek martyrdom through war in order to earn eternal happiness.

It is a myth that a "balance of power" between superpowers maintains order and peace in the world. During the Cold War between the United States and the Soviet Union (1945–1991), both nations fought proxy wars against each other in Korea and Vietnam. In total, these wars spanned 13 years and killed over 2.5 million people, the vast majority of whom were civilians. Therefore, while a balance of power may prevent a nuclear holocaust, it clearly does not bring world order and peace.

Realists claim that national leaders have a duty to protect their nation's security interests and well-being. However, this claim raises some questions:

- What is the basis of this duty if it is not moral or at least partially moral?

- Does this duty extend to all national leaders, including those of belligerent nations? If it does not, is this exception based on a moral or partially moral foundation? If morality is not the foundation, what is the principled foundation for this exception?

These questions raise the specter that realism actually may rely on moral principles for its very existence.

Finally, realists claim that they go to war only when national security interests are threatened. However, deciding what constitutes a national security interest is a source of debate, even among realists. For example, the vast majority of prominent realists at the time did not support the Vietnam War, whereas Henry Kissinger, a leading realist statesman and U.S. secretary of state, supported and politically managed the war based on his realist beliefs. Kissinger believed the war failed to achieve its objectives, not because it was unjust, but because political and military leaders were dissuaded from using overwhelming force due to increasing dissent from soldiers and civilians.

When making moral decisions about war, individuals can address some practical concepts and questions regarding pacifism and realism, but it may also be helpful to address some practical concepts and questions regarding these theories:

- Pacifism views peace as the overarching moral virtue and addresses questions such as: How many resources do nations and their individual citizens spend on "waging peace"? How often are individuals who actively seek peace perceived as conscientious citizens who not only love their country but humankind, or are derisively viewed as communists, radicals, cowards, or peaceniks?
- Classical realism holds that if a nation goes to war, it ought to make a decision on the basis of reality rather than on naïve presumptions (what is good for our nation will be good for all nations); messianic moralism (we are the good nation and always fight justly, and they are the evil nation and always fight unjustly); or virulent nationalism (our nation and our leaders are right on all issues and even if they are wrong, our nation is worth killing and dying for simply because it is our nation).

It is important for individuals attempting to make informed ethical decisions about war to possess at least a basic grasp of more than one moral norm. While just war principles are important, so are pacifism and realism, as well as virtue ethics, which are addressed in the next chapter. Theories are windows through which individuals view and make sense of reality. The more windows that individuals possess, the more easily they can view a wide expanse of reality and gradually develop a better understanding of it, which, in turn, allows them to make more fulsome moral decisions.

4

Virtue Ethics: Civilian and Military Considerations

All virtue is summed up in dealing justly.

—*Aristotle*

Moral decisions cannot occur without a moral norm, a set of principles against which to measure and judge the morality of an act. The previous two chapters addressed three perspectives on moral norms: just war principles, pacifism, and realism. This chapter discusses a fourth norm, virtue ethics.

As partners in deliberations about going to, waging, and ending war, civilians and those in the military need to be familiar with virtue ethics. Like partners in any enterprise, civilians and the military need to be mindful of their own and each other's behavior as it affects the moral tenor of their nation's decisions and actions regarding war. This chapter addresses virtue ethics because many in the military, especially instructors in the service academies and advanced training schools, use virtue ethics as a moral paradigm and complement to just war principles. Civilians also may use virtue ethics in their search for a framework in which to base informed moral decisions. To this end, this chapter will discuss the nature of virtue ethics and the virtues of patriotism, duty, integrity, courage, competence, and humility.

The Nature of Virtue Ethics

Virtue ethics holds that simply applying classic moral theories and principles to specific moral dilemmas is not an adequate means of deciding what constitutes moral behavior. Virtue ethics proposes that if individuals develop a moral character, their built-in moral compass will direct them to do the right thing without applying complicated moral principles to every dilemma.

4. Virtue Ethics

Aristotle taught that a virtuous life may lead to a sense of *eudaimonia*, which loosely means "flourishing" or "happiness." In modern terms, flourishing refers to developing fully as a human being (continually striving for holistic excellence). For Aristotle, flourishing is the ultimate good that all human beings desire and aim to achieve, whether or not they realize it. Flourishing is based on knowledge of good and evil and making rational choices to do good and avoid evil, resulting in virtuous behavior. For example, if individuals are faced with choosing between telling the truth (good) or lying (evil) and they choose truth, they have acted honestly. The more they act honestly, the more they develop a habit of honesty and eventually develop an honest character. However, Aristotle makes two things clear. First, Aristotle states that virtuous behavior is not a habit in the normal sense, as seen in an individual who has a habit of placing money on a collection plate each Sunday at church. Virtuous action requires rational deliberation governed by wisdom. This is what differentiates habitual, reflexive action, as in reaching for one's wallet when the collection plate is passed, from deliberate moral action based on an ongoing awareness of the plight of the poor and putting aside much needed money each week to help them.

Second, Aristotle makes clear that living a virtuous life does not always lead to flourishing (happiness) because it can include great anguish in an imperfect world. For example, honesty can result in the failure to be promoted or to keep one's job in both the military and civilian worlds.

Throughout the centuries, some elements of Aristotle's tenets were dropped and replaced by concepts scholars believed were more in keeping with the knowledge and wisdom of the times. Interest in virtue ethics lay dormant throughout much of the 19th century and the first half of the twentieth century until G.E.M. Anscombe (1958) wrote a paper criticizing the two traditional ethical theories, deontology and consequentialism, as being too legalistic, technical, and impersonal. Anscombe describes these theories as emphasizing duties, obligations and rules rather than the human beings whose behavior is the subject of these moral norms. Later theorists such as Alasdair MacIntyre and Rosalind Hursthouse further developed a theory of modern virtue ethics that informs much of virtue ethics today.

ELEMENTS OF VIRTUE ETHICS

The following discussion, while academic, is necessary to understand the subsequent topics and takes on practical importance as the chapter evolves. Although no universally accepted definition of ethics, much less virtue ethics, exists, the following discussion is generally in keeping with the tenets of Aristotle, Aquinas, and most contemporary theorists. While there are many kinds of virtues, the type described here is moral virtue. Historically, virtues were believed to fall into neat and distinct categories: intellectual virtues, moral virtues, theological virtues, cardinal virtues, and so on. However, modern psychology clearly demonstrates that human behavior does not fall into neat categories but, in fact, is holistic, meaning that various dimensions of behavior are intricately interrelated and inseparable. It is still acceptable to speak of "moral virtues" as long as it is understood that they are comprised of physical, intellectual, emotional, and social elements.

The following compilation of the characteristics of virtue ethics brings together an understanding of virtue in the light of modern psychology and moral theory. Because virtue ethics has many versions and theories, these elements represent the tenets of many, but not all, contemporary virtue ethicists.

It is important to understand that moral virtues and moral values are not synonymous. The differences are not merely semantic.

Moral virtues are dispositional. They are an integral part of an individual's personality and stem from a combination of genetic predispositions and early bonding with individuals who teach virtuous behavior through consistent modeling. Virtuous behavior is "second nature." For example, individuals with the virtue of integrity reflexively act with integrity; they do not have to decide whether to act with integrity on a case-by-case basis.

In contrast, values are more superficial. They are learned off and on throughout childhood and adolescence through teaching, lecturing, scolding, and punishment rather than being instilled by continued role modeling throughout childhood and adolescence. For example, a soldier who possesses the virtue of integrity will not think twice about refusing to participate in the cover-up of a war crime, but a soldier who possesses the value of integrity might value his career more than the moral principle of integrity. He agrees to the cover-up — he "just follows orders."

Eric Ash (2001) addresses the critical difference between virtues and values in the military: "Core values do not promote the moral factor necessary in military ethics. Virtues do. Values simply do not go deep enough because they are focused on means rather than ends" (p. 35). Ash describes virtue as an end in itself. One acts with integrity in all situations because it is the right thing to do. Virtue is its own reward. Values are means to an end. We ought not to bomb their civilians not because it is morally wrong, but because if we do, they will bomb our civilians. Virtue ethicists who believe that intentionally killing civilians is innately wrong would forbid the bombing of civilians whether or not the enemy responds in kind.

Virtues Related to War

All the moral virtues relate to both military and civilian life, but four virtues are perceived as "military virtues" worthy of great attention by not only the military but the civilian world as well. These moral virtues are patriotism, duty, integrity, and courage. However, other moral virtues ought to be included in the concept of "military virtue," including competence and humility, which will be addressed as well. The failure to include these moral virtues in the concept of military virtues is unfortunate because the lack of competence (incompetence) and humility (hubris) can cause more political and military problems than a lack of any one or perhaps all of the four major virtues.

THE VIRTUE OF PATRIOTISM

Patriotism for both civilians and the military is defined as the love of one's country and the willingness to support its values, decisions, and actions. Patriotism is often differentiated from nationalism in the moral literature. For instance, the term "Devotion to the Fatherland" evoked deep patriotic passion in the German people between 1933 and 1945 and was packaged in the motto "Deutschland Uber Alles"—Germany above all other nations. Pope John Paul II (2005) distinguishes patriotism from nationalism: "Whereas nationalism involves recognizing and pursuing the good of one's own nation alone, without regard for the rights of others, patriotism, on the other hand, is a love for one's native land that accords rights to all other nations equal to those claimed for one's own. Patriotism, in other words, leads to a properly ordered social love" (p. 67).

Democracy brings a critical component to the concept of patriotism. Pope John Paul II (1995) cautions against inappropriately extolling the virtues of democracy:

> Democracy cannot be idolized to the point of making it a substitute for morality or a panacea for immorality. Fundamentally, democracy is a "system" and as such is a means and not an end. Its "moral" value is not automatic, but depends on conformity to the moral law to which I, like every other form of human behavior, must be subject: in other words, its morality depends on the morality of the ends which it pursues and of the means which it employs [p. 70].

Patriotism with respect to one's nation can be distinguished from patriotism with respect to the government of one's nation. Howard Zinn (2003), who was a bombardier in World War II and later became a pacifist, expands on this difference.

The distinction between dying for our country and dying for your government is crucial in understanding what I believe to be the definition of patriotism in a democracy. According to the Declaration of Independence — the fundamental document of democracy — governments are artificial creations, established by the people, "deriving their just powers from the consent of the governed," and charged by the people to ensure the equal right of all to "life, liberty, and the pursuit of happiness." Furthermore, as the Declaration says, "Whenever any form of government becomes destructive of these ends, it is the right of the people to alter or abolish it" [p. 1].

THE VIRTUE OF DUTY

Both civilians and those in the military possess critically important duties and rights, especially in times of war. Civilians generally have a duty to support their soldiers fighting a war both materially and psychologically, and they have a right to be informed with respect to the war's financial cost, its estimated length, and the number of civilian and military lives that may be, or are being, lost on both sides. On the other hand, soldiers generally have duties to the military and the nation at large and the right to know specifically what they are fighting and dying for and to receive the material, medical and mental health resources required to fight the war in the safest and most efficient, orderly, legal, and moral way possible.

Duties of soldiers. An examination of the virtue of duty in the military requires knowledge of the prescribed duties of soldiers, and in particular, those of officers. The officer's oath of office and the officer's commissioning letter declare that the basic duty of soldiers is to support and defend the Constitution of the United States. At first reading, these duties appear straightforward, supported, and defended by the Supreme Court, the civilian leadership, and the military command. However, history is replete with examples that demonstrate this synchrony of interpretation and action does not always occur.

Conflicts regarding duty arise primarily in wartime, which, unfortunately, is the most problematic time for basic disagreements in principle and practice to occur. Laura DiSilverio and Stephan Laushine (2002) describe the common dilemmas in deciding where one's loyalties and duties lie:

> So where does the officer owe his loyalty? Does service come before the President because lives could be at stake, or because the service or profession could suffer irreparable damage?
>
> Does loyalty belong to the President because he is Commander in Chief? Or does loyalty go to the Congress as the embodiment of the people? What if Congress seems to be pursuing an agenda that undermines the security of the "people" it is supposed to represent? Do the values enshrined in the Constitution demand that

an officer subordinate good judgment to the agendas of zealous Congresspersons? Clearly, legal boundaries alone cannot form the basis for the officer's decision. Ethical considerations must also play a substantial part [p. 7].

Duty, as it is commonly defined in the military and civilian world, cannot reasonably be absolute and unconditional. Because duty is conditional, as both the Nuremberg trials and the U.S. Military Code of Justice state (there is no duty to obey clearly illegal or immoral orders), responsible thinking leads to the following questions:

- When are duties legitimate and illegitimate?
- What are the duties and rights of soldiers?
- Do soldiers have a moral duty to themselves to obey their consciences?
- Do soldiers have a moral duty to follow clearly incompetent and foolishly dangerous orders, even though they are technically legal?
- Can an order be legal but immoral?
- Is disobedience ever obligatory?

With respect to the military, an academic course in ethics is likely to be a safe harbor to ask and discuss such questions. However, asking them outside of a classroom, especially as one rises in the chain of command, can be risky in the presence of insecure superiors. For example, officers may confront and discuss these questions with colleagues behind closed doors but would consider it unwise, if not suicidal, to discuss them at a staff meeting, especially when those in higher authority would perceive such discussions as subversive to their authority.

On the practical level, the duty of soldiers is to obey instructions and orders. Obeying orders has only one legal exception — soldiers have a legal right to disobey clearly illegal orders. However, they also have a moral duty to disobey orders that are clearly immoral, especially when they countermand the moral codes, virtues, and rules of the military.

Anthony E. Hartle (2004) states that because war is a most violent enterprise, moral awareness is especially important. War is never an excuse to put morality on hold, but is a reason to take concrete steps to heighten and strengthen the warrior's moral code so that it can be recalled immediately in the spontaneous and rapidly changing situations that occur in battle. In the final analysis, individuals must make their own moral decisions and not simply follow the leader whose moral compass may be highly accurate or inaccurate. Hartle summarizes his belief: "For a military professional, moral decisions are unavoidable. American soldiers, sailors, and airmen cannot evade or reject moral responsibility" (p. 181).

Duties to soldiers. Nations that send their soldiers to war have a moral duty to help them remain as safe and sane as possible. While this sentiment is self-evident on one level (support the troops), it becomes less so on the practical level. Simply stated, supporting the troops requires far more than sending "care packages" to soldiers, tying yellow ribbons around trees, and holding homecoming events for troops returning from combat, as important as these events may be. The major part of the moral duty to soldiers falls first on the political and military leadership, but it also falls on the civilian population in whose name the war is being fought.

The first moral duty of national leaders is to declare, wage, and end wars according to just war principles: the war is duly declared, the cause is clearly just, the intentions are obviously pure, the benefits will greatly outweigh the costs, success is highly likely, and the war is absolutely necessary to protect national security. These elements not only ought to be clearly and convincingly present, they ought to be communicated on a regular basis to the troops who risk their lives daily.

Soldiers who find themselves in battles and wars that are not going well, that is, not as promised by their leaders, typically begin to ask the following questions:

- What are we really doing here?
- Why are we employing these particular strategies and tactics?
- Why is what we are doing, or not doing, worth the cost?
- What exactly will it take to declare victory and go home?

All soldiers, from privates to generals, have a moral right to receive honest answers to these questions. Soldiers may receive state-of-the-art equipment and encouragement from home everyday, but if a war simply does not make moral sense, soldiers lack the most basic support a nation can offer: the knowledge and feeling that they are absolutely doing the right thing, no matter what the cost. As one severely wounded soldier said, "There is only one thing worse than seeing friends die or suffering life-altering wounds, and that is to feel the deaths and injuries served no good purpose."

National leaders have a second moral duty — to provide at least adequate, if not state-of-the-art, medical and psychological care to the troops and their families.

In 2010, the Army issued a report entitled *Health Promotion, Risk Reduction, and Suicide Prevention*. It is a well-researched and starkly honest account of failure throughout the Army command structure to address the psychological issues of the current generation of soldiers, with a focus on suicide. The report addresses several disturbing trends for fiscal year 2009 (October 1, 2008–September 30, 2009), including the following:

- In fiscal year 2009, there were 239 Army suicides (160 active duty) and 1,713 known attempted suicides. The Army suicide rate was 20.2 per 100,000 troops, compared to the civilian rate of 19.2 suicides per 100,000 individuals, both rates adjusted to compare individuals in the same age ranges. For the first time since the early 1980s when the Army began keeping these statistics, the Army suicide rates were higher than those in the civilian population.
- During the same period, the Marines reported the highest suicide rate in the military at 24 per 100,000 troops. The Air Force suicide rate was 15.5 per 100,000, the highest for this service since 1995. The Navy's suicide rate was the lowest in the military at 13.3 per 100,000 personnel. Eighty percent of Army suicides occurred in the United States while soldiers were on garrison duty — stationed on bases in the United States.
- "High risk behaviors," such as drinking and driving and drug overdoses, claimed the lives of 146 active duty soldiers. Together, suicides and high risk behavior killed more soldiers during the year than died in combat.
- Approximately 106,000 soldiers were prescribed psychoactive medications for pain, depression, or anxiety.
- Soldiers committed 74,646 criminal offenses, including 16,997 drug and alcohol related offenses. Since fiscal year 2004, misdemeanor criminal cases by soldiers have risen approximately 5,000 per year.
- One thousand two hundred twenty-four soldiers were discharged for mental disorders, such as post-traumatic stress disorder.

The report also notes that from January 1, 2010, to June 30, 2010, there were 120 active duty suicides and 787 active duty attempted suicides. In summation, the report states these statistics present a stark reality: "Simply stated, we are often more dangerous to ourselves than the enemy" (p. 11).

The report summarizes the basic cause of the high number of serious mental health and behavioral issues:

> [The army is currently facing] gaps in the Army's surveillance, detection and intervention process and systems.... Leaders have lost situational awareness; signs and symptoms are being ignored, soldiers are taking more and more risks, and gaps in policies are allowing it to happen. Ultimately, it poses the question: "Where has the Army's leadership in garrison gone?" [p. 45].

As General George Casey stated while testifying before the Senate in March 2010, "... We were shooting behind the target trying to prevent suicides after they happened" (Thompson, 2010).

Supporting the troops is not fulfilled unless the military also supports the families of its troops, especially those who are deployed. The following study highlights the importance and timeliness of this issue. Mansfield, Kaufman, Marshall, Gaynes, Morrissey, and Engel (2010) studied the medical records of 250,626 wives of active duty soldiers to determine the effect of their husband's deployment on their mental health. The researchers found that the longer husbands were deployed, the more their wives were diagnosed with increasingly significant psychological impairments in contrast to a control group of wives whose husbands never deployed. The psychological diagnoses included disorders related to depression, sleep, anxiety, and acute stress.

This study as well as other studies clearly indicate that the military is lagging significantly in its attempts to reach its "achievable vision," the theme of the Defense Health Board Task Force on Mental Health report (2007) which set goals to be reached in helping troops retain and regain their mental health.

The Virtue of Integrity

The word "integrity" means "to integrate, to make complete"—to pull various parts together and make them into a whole. Integrity connotes acting in a morally steady, strong, and synchronous manner. Analogously, an aircraft is said to have integrity when it is reliable, sturdy, and its moving parts work in harmony. Integrity in individuals is reflected in three basic aspects: what they believe is the right thing, what they communicate as being the right thing, and how their actions reflect what they believe and communicate. These different parts work in harmony and often effortlessly and even subconsciously after much practice.

Air Force Major W.H. Margerum (1983) writes:

> Integrity is a primary element of military professionalism and the hallmark of the professional officer. Without it, the profession loses the trust of the society it serves, and lack of public trust ultimately threatens the nation's ability to maintain the force levels necessary for peace and security. In other words, a lack or perceived lack of integrity can have a devastating effect on the military profession and its relationship with civilian society [p.1].

Integrity starts from within. It is not simply a professional façade meant to evoke respect and inspire confidence. Individuals with integrity stand up for their virtues and support individuals under their command who possess the same virtues, even when it is personally inconvenient if not risky. Perhaps the decisive test of whether integrity is authentic is that individuals who possess it and act upon it say and do things that make others uncomfortable by challenging the status quo when it is maintained by compromises of core military and civilian virtues.

It is one thing to declare integrity to be a military virtue but it is quite another to have a clear understanding of the proximate and ultimate practical ramifications of what this assertion means in practice.

Obstacles to integrity. Three basic obstacles prevent individuals from possessing and acting with integrity as it relates to the military or any other institution. First, acting with integrity is not possible if individuals are not integrated themselves. Some individuals may never have developed an appreciation for integrity because it never was a compelling virtue in their development. If anything, integrity may be perceived as a liability. When these individuals enter the military, they react to the concept of virtue as a foreign language that they are unable to comprehend.

Second, the value of a career can interfere with the virtue of integrity. Some individuals have great integrity until its expression might compromise their career aspirations. At this point, the value of success may trump the virtue of integrity.

Third, organizations may punish integrity when it threatens the organization's culture of moral trade-offs during stressful times. In some instances, an organization may not directly punish integrity which it has always trumpeted as a hallmark virtue, but will quietly replace or retire the offender who is deemed not to be a "team player."

When these situations occur, moral codes and lists of virtues cannot survive in a moral atmosphere that at times negates the very virtues it espouses. U.S. Army Col. James A. Muskopf (2006) describes the situation as it relates to military leadership:

> The leader has to set the proper command climate that allows subordinates to not feel compelled to compromise their own integrity. We need to train leaders that while we give credit to subordinates for all the great things the unit does, we take the personal blame for all the things the unit fails to do. When leaders stand up and say to their leaders, "It's my fault," then they have gone a long way toward keeping the values we should be subscribing to. When we stand up and give credit to the company commander and platoon leaders for doing the right thing in the right way, we have gone a long way toward subscribing to the values we should be striving for. Command climate is so much more than subscribing to the "consideration of others" policy and the "equal opportunity" policy and the "prevention of sexual harassment policy." All of those are part of the climate, but the underlying theme is to simply do what's right, legally and morally. We write those policies to reinforce the philosophy of the integrity value because it's the right thing to do. If we don't carry it forth to all aspects of what we do then we set ourselves up for confusion and allow subordinates to decide for themselves what they should do [p. 9].

Civilian integrity. The virtue of integrity plays a central role for civilians in times of war. In fact, since most civilians are not on the political and military front lines of war, they are often in a good position to view integrity issues dispassionately and express their views freely. The combination of honesty, responsibility, justice and respect can lead to productive self-reflection when it comes to making decisions about the morality of a war. The following are some examples of such questions:

- Would I volunteer to fight in this war or, if I were not eligible, would I donate ten percent of my salary in support of the war effort?
- Would I encourage my family members and other loved ones to volunteer to fight in the war or join the war effort in some direct way?
- Would I volunteer to help returning soldiers, especially those who are hospitalized for medical or psychological reasons, and to help other veterans find decent employment?
- Would I join an organization whose purpose is to help military families survive psychologically and financially while their service member is deployed?
- If my soldier spouse, son, or daughter were killed or maimed in the war, would I believe the sacrifice was worthwhile?

An honest answer to these questions regarding integrity will not necessarily lead to a sound conscience decision about the morality of the war, but may help start the decision-making process and give it some direction.

The Virtue of Moral Courage

William Ian Miller (2000) defines moral courage as "the capacity to overcome fear of shame and humiliation in order to admit one's mistakes, to confess a wrong, to reject evil conformity, to denounce injustice, and also to defy immoral or imprudent orders" (p. 254).

Moral courage is required to be a good citizen, especially in times of war. An important way in which ordinary civilians can demonstrate moral courage is by publicly presenting their position on a war that may be very unpopular in their social circle. For example, pacifists may exercise moral courage by publicly espousing their morally based beliefs when their family, friends, co-workers, and the majority of their fellow citizens are passionate about going to war. In these superheated circumstances, pacifists may be perceived as cowards, traitors, freeloaders, socialists, communists, or "nut cases." To stand up against this onslaught of personal ridicule, if not hatred, requires great moral courage and can be socially and occupationally costly.

Politicians demonstrate moral courage when they do or do not support a war in the face of great opposition, as long as their position is based on sound moral principles and not for political, economic, or imperialist reasons.

Military leaders can exhibit moral courage when they take a stand for or against a war or the means of waging it despite great opposition from other military and civilian leaders.

U.S. Marine Corps General (Ret.) James L. Jones (Stooksbury, 2002) makes this point when he writes of physical threats in battle where courage is required but also focuses on moral threats:

> It may also be an intangible threat where you are told your career may be ruined if, for example, you reveal that you are witness to impropriety or illegal activity by a senior or a peer. Somehow we always have courage with subordinates. In these instances, physical and moral courage respectively will lead you to taking the right actions; to assisting your buddy and revealing the impropriety or illegality. In one case you may suffer grave physical harm; in the other, a setback in your career, but either way you will retain your honor for having done the right thing [p. 45].

A U.S. Army white paper (*The Bedrock of Our Profession*, 1986) summarizes how moral courage pertains to both soldiers and civilians.

> Courage, however, goes beyond the physical dimension. Moral courage, the courage of one's convictions, is equally important. It takes a different kind of courage to stand up for what you believe is right, particularly when it is contrary to what others around you believe. Each of us must persevere in what we know is right and not make it easy for friends, peers, comrades, or superiors to do the wrong thing. Our moral principles must not be compromised because of the situation or circumstances. This does not mean that every order or policy must be questioned, but if soldiers or civilians truly believe that something is not right, they have the responsibility to make their views known [p. 3].

Moral courage can exact a high price. Therefore, it must be tempered with prudence and wisdom. Moral courage can be inhibited by both external and internal factors that may cause individuals to question whether they should speak out or act in a particular situation.

External inhibitors to moral courage include:

- Authoritarianism. An organization makes it abundantly clear that obeying authority is a core value and trumps all others. Indoctrination on the importance of unquestioned obedience creates an atmosphere in which members do not even consider questioning policies, much less actually do it.
- Retribution. The organization has a history of punishing members who speak out against wrongdoing. The clear message to anyone inclined to stand up against unethical behavior is that retribution can be immediate and obvious or delayed and subtle.
- Disrespect. These organizations do not truly respect their members, despite protestations to the contrary. Members who are "respected" as long as

their actions please executives are destroyed and discarded as soon as they raise institutional anxiety. Members who were "shining stars" for years become "falling stars" in a nanosecond, not because they gave an honest report but because they provided an honest report that did not reflect the executives' position.

- Circumspection. There is a saying in the military: Watch your lane — and watch your lane only. Originally, this admonition applied to the firing range to remind soldiers not to stray from their firing lane and risk being shot. It has come to have a broader meaning: Mind your own business and don't worry about what those around you are doing. This caution precludes reporting wrongdoing by one's comrades, especially if they are of a higher rank, or not members of one's unit or branch of service.

Internal inhibitors of moral courage. There is only one basic internal inhibitor of moral courage, fear of retribution for acting with moral courage. Although both civilian and military society claim moral courage as a preeminent moral virtue and place it at the top of their codes of ethics, it is also the most feared virtue in some organizations. Organizational cultures and subcultures can have something to hide — something they do not want to acknowledge and certainly do not want "the outside world" to discover. The secret is usually two-layered: the conduct that is at least morally questionable if not immoral and illegal and the cover-up of that conduct. This two-tiered dynamic is protected by a code of silence that trumps all other codes, including ethical codes because it protects the reputations and livelihoods of those involved in the misconduct and cover-up, as well as their families and the organization itself.

Individuals who dare to violate this code of silence are at high risk and may become the target of organizational force protection that aims to personally, professionally, and, in some cases, physically neutralize the violator. Ethical employees may be subjected to the loss of respect, advancement, privacy, peace, employment, and income. Even one of these fears can be a powerful inhibitor to individuals contemplating a morally courageous act, but a combination of two, four, or six can be paralyzing and preclude action on the part of many individuals.

THE VIRTUE OF COMPETENCE

Competence refers to the ability to accomplish a task successfully. In the study of morality and war, two kinds of competence are important: ordinary competence — the ability to complete a war-related task successfully, and moral competence — the ability to make sound moral decisions in various circumstances.

Ordinary competence. Ordinary competence refers to military and political leaders possessing the physical, intellectual, emotional and social skills to complete their assigned duties successfully. They must not only possess these skill sets, they must also be motivated to use them to their fullest capacity and have the motivation and resources to carry them out. For example, the fact that Sergeant Jones is promoted to platoon leader or Colonel Smith is promoted to general does not make Jones a platoon leader and Smith a general in any functional meaning of the terms.

It is almost axiomatic that, especially in times of war, individuals are assigned to tasks and roles that they have little chance to complete successfully, either because they lack the personal skills, the motivation, or the material and personnel to do so. In this case, "ordinary competence" can have serious moral ramifications even though the skill itself is not a moral one.

This lack of competence can be seen in the U.S. Army report (2010), referred to in the previous discussion of the virtue of duty, which presents a discouraging portrait of a lack of professional skills, motivation, or resources to offer even adequate mental health care to troops in the midst of battle or returning from combat. Yet, it is likely that many military and political leaders perceive this ongoing situation not as a moral failure, but as a professional, logistical, educational and financial "issue."

Several factors can lead to this lack of competence. A shortage of fully trained personnel may be due to the necessity of accepting recruits with minimal life and work experience, a lack of sufficient time to train them due to rapid deployment, and a lack of adequate funding to requisition needed materials. The Peter Principle also may be operative in which soldiers are promoted to leadership positions because they perform at least adequately at their previous position, despite the fact that they do not have the competencies to meet the many challenges of their new position. While these situations reflect "organizational and budgetary" problems, at their heart they reflect a serious moral problem because the areas of incompetence place troops in harm's way by eventually causing unnecessary casualties, prolonged wars, and defeats.

A similar "diagnostic work-up" could be performed in the political area, but would be largely redundant to that presented with regard to the military.

Moral competence. Moral competence is the ability to understand, identify, assess, decide and act on one's moral values. Moral competence is the moral equivalent of any other competence from flying aircraft to learning languages to playing music. Individuals with competencies in these areas have internalized the "working parts" of each of the endeavors, so that their behavior is second nature, in contrast to performing each task by the numbers. They are pilots, linguists, and musicians; they do not simply act as if they are. Just as accomplished pilots have an aptitude for flying, individuals with moral competence have an aptitude for sensing the presence of moral issues.

Moral competence entails much more than a well-articulated set of moral values, core values, military, political or religious values. In fact, research indicates that there is little correlation between religious values and moral competence. Modern research indicates that the moral lessons that develop from simply memorizing catechisms, codes of ethics, and moral manuals evaporate soon after these didactic methods cease. Air Force Major John F. Price, Jr. (2006), believes that the U.S. military is suffering from an insidious internal decay. He describes the reasons for this situation: "The Core Values revolution of the 1900s has failed to have any significant impact on this institutional malaise and now only serves to create a false sense of security regarding the institution's moral condition.... This institutional abdication of moral responsibility and failures to correct cultural problems directly undermines the moral competence of the joint warrior (Abstract).

Price also points out that moral concern and confusion in the military do not begin in the military but carry over from the civilian world. "America's warriors continue to be challenged with a morally corrosive culture, long before they ever get to the battlefield" (p. 18). This statement highlights the fact that today's warriors need more than lectures and manuals that address moral competence. They need leaders who first understand what moral competence is and then develop it in themselves in order to teach it, primarily by role modeling. The military leadership needs to understand that moral education is not limited to classroom lectures and visits to chaplains. Price summarizes this concept: "Moral considerations are fundamental to every human interaction and, therefore, must be included in every facet of military leadership, planning, and mission execution" (p. 11).

There are many ways to discuss the basic elements in moral competence, but the following method generally reflects those mentioned in the literature. Moral competence entails:

- Defining the moral question. Usually moral questions are presented as dilemmas: "Do we do X, Y, or Z considering all the variables and consequences?"
- Developing a clear picture of the reality situation. This includes obtaining as much firsthand information as possible and relying on "hearsay evidence" as little as possible, even when it comes from ordinarily reliable sources.
- Establishing the moral norms to be applied. Usually justice is the basic moral norm used as a benchmark for action in war, but there are other moral principles such as the ethics of caring and responsibility.

- Determining the exact moral issues to be addressed. It is important to distinguish between basic moral issues and other kinds of issues—political, legal, social, religious.
- Maintaining a multidimensional focus. Moral claims not only belong to the just nation in war, but also to the unjust nation(s), as well as coalition nations and nations directly or indirectly affected by the war.
- Initiating fulsome discussions with well-informed individuals. Individuals who are equally competent and reasonable ought to be involved in the discussion to represent all sides of the issue, including the enemy's side.
- Realizing that moral discernment and judgment are multifaceted. In addition to an intellectual (cognitive) dimension, these processes also have an emotional (affective) dimension as well as conscious and unconscious, overt and hidden agendas.
- Recognizing the mental mechanisms that short-circuit moral reasoning. These mechanisms include euphemistic language ("there was a good deal of 'collateral damage' when referring to civilians killed"); moral exclusion ("the enemy lost the right to be treated justly"); compartmentalization ("we killed a fair number of civilians, but we are also building hospitals and schools"); and moral exceptionalism ("we don't need to follow the legal and moral rules of war because we are the greatest country in the world and have the truth on our side").
- Exercising personal and national self-awareness: "Beneath the patriotic and moral protestations, what is my personal psychological and political investment in this war, and what are the deeper motives of my nation in terms of planning, waging, and ending the war?"
- Developing a moral action plan and making it operational: "If we go public with our moral conclusions, how can we best communicate them, and are we willing to accept the reactions to our decisions?"

The Virtue of Humility

Individuals who possess the virtue of humility accurately understand and serenely accept their strengths and weaknesses and relate with themselves and others accordingly. They do not overplay their strengths or underplay their weaknesses and are interpersonally cooperative more often than they are competitive. They are comfortable with themselves, which allows them to feel comfortable with others, and others to feel comfortable with them. When competition is appropriate, they are fair and respectful in their actions.

Both Augustine and Aquinas perceive humility as a virtue. Augustine listed humility (modesty) among his moral virtues and writes: "Do you wish to rise? Begin by descending. Do you plan a tower that will pierce the clouds? Lay a foundation of humility." Aquinas writes, "After the theological virtues, after the intellectual virtues which regard reason itself, and often justice — humility stands before all the others."

Humility is often described as the opposite of pride. However, as used here, it is important to distinguish between pride and hubris. Pride is a healthy sense of well-being that results when individuals feel good about themselves because they have acted in a genuinely laudable way. An example of pride is seen in the student who works hard and at great personal sacrifice to get through college and succeeds. No reasonable individual would criticize this student for being proud of his accomplishments.

Hubris, on the other hand, has little if anything to do with healthy pride. In fact, in most cases hubris is likely to be overcompensation for feelings of fear and insecurity. Truly courageous and secure people feel no need to make statements such as "Look how brave and intelligent I am!" Hubris is manifested in arrogance — feelings of entitlement, delusions of grandeur, disdain for limits, and imperviousness to the feelings and reactions of others. It is often demonstrated in hostility — acts that belittle, disrespect, discount, disparage, exploit, and humiliate others. It precludes honest self-reflection, admission of imperfection, accountability for mistakes, and compassion for others.

In today's world, especially in the Western world, humility is suspect on a number of fronts. The word itself denotes a lack of worth: "He's a very humble man, and he has a lot to be humble about." The notion of humility also has a ring of hypocrisy to it — a "false humility" meant to gain some advantage. Rather than being perceived as a virtue, humility is often seen as a symptom of a deficient personality — low self-confidence, self-respect, and self-efficacy. In other words, "humble" would rarely be found in a letter of recommendation or performance report to describe a brilliant student, employee, or soldier. For these and other reasons, the word "humble" has largely disappeared from modern parlance, with the exception of some religious tracts and sermons. As Kate Davies (2008) writes: "Humility is a scarce commodity in the U.S. Perhaps it's because this country was born in violent revolution against colonial overlords. Perhaps our fierce individualism leaves us with a tendency to put personal rights above collective well-being. Whatever the reason, humility has always been in short supply. No one even talks about it — least of all the presidential candidates who seem hell-bent on promoting themselves and attacking each other."

Some bright spots exist, however. The U.S. Air Force lists humility as part of its core value of integrity, but states only that "a person of integrity grasps and is sobered by the awesome task of defending the Constitution of the United States of America." While this is a step in the right direction, a more fulsome explanation would be helpful. Although none of the other military services refers to humility as part of their core values, it is discussed on rare occasions as a leadership skill. For example, Joseph Doty and Dan Gerdes (2002) write: "The humble teacher lacks arrogance, not aggressiveness. The will to serve others eclipses any drive to promote self. Many lists of leadership characteristics overlook the essential component or components that meld the leader's attributes with the leader's techniques. One such component is humility" (p. 89).

Much of the confusion and ambivalence about the nature of humility is caused by failing to appreciate that it is not one monolithic entity, but that different sub-sets of humility exist, just as there are different sub-sets of intelligence and emotions. The specific humility relevant to virtue ethics is what Mark Button (2005) calls "democratic humility." Button introduces his treatise with the following question: "Whatever happened to humility? Once held as a cardinal virtue in the ethical life of the individual, humility seems to have undergone a quiet but steady diminution in value. While philosophers and political theorists have shown a renewed interest in a wide range of virtues of late, the concept of humility has not enjoyed any similar renaissance, nor has it been referenced within the general 'return' to the virtues" (p. 840).

Button describes democratic humility as a positive, practical ethic that addresses how the virtue of humility can provide an important facilitative and salutary influence on national and international politics. "Politics" in the sense referred to here means discussing domestic and foreign policy with regard to all important world matters, including going to, waging, and ending wars. This theory has moral ramifications for ordinary citizens, ordinary soldiers, and political and military leaders because it addresses the importance of the virtue of humility in pre-war and wartime diplomatic and military deliberations and negotiations.

Political humility is the opposite of political hubris and exceptionalism — the belief and its component feelings that one's nation is superior to all others; its political and military leaders are wiser than their counterparts; its political and moral values are superior to those of other nations; its military might makes the nation right. All these beliefs give individuals and nations permission to treat the people and leaders of other nations with disrespect and, in some cases, with outright mockery.

The theory of democratic humility presupposes that its opposite, political hubris, places an abyss between nations, their people, and their leaders which causes a fight-flight response. "Fight" means that nations assume a belligerent aggressive and defensive attitude toward nations whose foreign policy is promulgated with hubris. This attitude can lead to all kinds of problems, including war. "Flight" means that nations, their people and leaders, withdraw from any meaningful relations with the hubric nation, causing many serious problems, including a refusal to support allied nations when war enters the picture. Democratic humility includes the following elements:

- Critically reflecting on self and acknowledgement of human incompetencies and imperfections that plague all individuals and political communities.
- Publicly acknowledging these imperfections as well as virtues in appropriate ways, at appropriate times, and with the appropriate people.
- Sharing not only thoughts and feelings but also humility — an attitude which reflects, "We're all in this together, so let's work with each other and not against each other."
- Taking a place next to other nations, not above them — "How can we help each other meet our shared needs for survival, security, freedom, and opportunity?"
- Assuming that all nations, their people and leaders, have gifts to share and evils that need to be exorcised.

The theory of democratic humility also presupposes its practice will create an environment in which trust replaces mistrust, security replaces insecurity, beneficence replaces belligerence, respect replaces disrespect, hope replaces despair, and peace replaces war.

Democratic humility operates on the assumption that accomplishing even half of a nation's moral aspirations is better than doing nothing. A good example of democratic humility and the reaction it evoked is seen in a remark by then Secretary of Defense Robert Gates (2009) in response to criticism that he was being "too humble" in his international relationships.

> I think that acknowledging that we have made mistakes is not only factually accurate — I think that it is unusual because so few other governments in the world are willing to admit that, although they make them all the time, and some of them make catastrophic mistakes.
>
> And in speeches myself, I have said that at times we have acted too arrogantly. And I didn't feel that I was being apologetic for America. I just was saying because — I was just saying that that's the way we are in terms of being willing to recognize our own limitations, and when we make a mistake, to correct it, because I think the next time that I always use is, no other country in the world is so self-critical and is so willing to change course when we feel that we've strayed from our values or when we feel like we've been too arrogant.
>
> So I think — I have not seen it as an apology tour at all, but rather a change of tone, a more humble America. But everybody knows we still have a big stick.

Button offers a final caution and hope with regard to putting humility into action as a nation:

> Instead of marking individual pride or vanity as our essential vice, a democratic ethos of humility would put us on guard against the ethical and political dangers of complacency, premature closures, and dogmatism — especially those forms of political dogmatism that foster the illusion of moral completeness and that express a will to mastery or domination. By highlighting the incompleteness and manifold contingencies that enter into our necessary enunciations of what is just, true, or good, democratic humility does not counsel passivity in the face of such judgments but cautions us against the complacency and forgetfulness that can set in once those paths have been taken [p. 861].

Challenges to Virtue Ethics

Virtue ethics is not beyond criticism. A challenge is simply a question, a doubt, a disagreement that may have varying degrees of validity from complete to none. Seriously and objectively considering challenges to one's beliefs is a mark of intellectual honesty and maturity. When the challenges have a ring of truth, they are accepted as an opportunity to strengthen, modify or discard a belief. In effect, the criticisms can also be challenged. Virtue ethics are challenged on three basic points.

1. Virtue ethics may be an interesting theory, but it does not have much use in practice. Two military officers may possess the same degree of the virtue of integrity but strenuously disagree whether high value enemy prisoners should be physically tortured. One officer might state that integrity requires a prisoner to be treated with respect and not be tortured. The other officer would respond that integrity requires respect for the 30 American soldiers who will be killed if the prisoner is not tortured and therefore does not reveal plans to bomb an American stronghold. In other words, eventually, the theories of absolutism or consequentialism will need to be called upon to help solve moral dilemmas.

2. Modern psychology has demonstrated that no phenomenon such as a personal character, disposition, or constitution exists that remains fixed and sturdy like a block of granite throughout life. Personality is quite flexible and can bend in a good or evil direction, often rather easily. The psychological theory of situationalism holds that almost anyone will bend his or her moral virtues or values due to internal or external situations. For example, a soldier may possess the virtue of moral courage in the civilian dimensions of his life, standing up to all those who threaten his core virtues that he has held dear

since early childhood. However, as soon as he puts on a uniform, his moral courage becomes trumped by the value of career success. He goes from the axiom "right is right, and wrong is wrong" in his civilian life to "orders are orders" in his military life, meaning that blind obedience is required.

3. Virtue ethics is an idealistic model worth studying but not useful for people in the real world. For example, virtue ethics is one of the first casualties of war for both soldiers and civilians. A basic objective of any war is to kill and maim as many of the enemy as possible, as well as to destroy the entire enemy infrastructure and land that could aid the enemy. War also entails sending young people not only to act viciously but also to be attacked viciously. Waging war is the antithesis of flourishing for both soldiers and civilians and for both the victors and the defeated.

This is not to say that individual virtuous acts do not occur in war, but viciousness is the overriding theme in war and virtue is the rare exception. Therefore, virtue ethics generates worthwhile discussion and presents a picture of the moral good life, but has a short shelf life in the real world of soldiers and civilians.

As noted above, virtue ethicists have responses to these challenges, which can be found in the relevant literature.

Individual citizens interested in making informed decisions about war can reflect on what place, if any, virtue ethics ought to play in their thinking. Ordinary civilians and soldiers, as well as national political and military leaders, also can monitor their own and each other's actions in the light of the virtues that their nation and military espouse nationally and internationally. A framework for making moral decisions regarding war that would include virtue ethics could be developed using the following questions:

- Is the patriotism my country upholds based on virtue or on reflexive nationalistic emotion? Is my patriotism well thought out, or just part of being "a good American"?
- Does the type of duty my nation espouses reflect a moral virtue related to preserving national and international rights to justice, freedom, and life, or is it merely a value to force soldiers and civilians to obey authority? What is my greater duty — to support my country's constitution or my country's leaders, when there is a conflict?
- Do my political and military leaders possess integrity in speech and action, or do their words and actions contradict each other? Does the integrity promulgated by my nation reflect a moral virtue that assures absolute honesty and trustworthiness, or is it merely a word used to create a sense of confidence in leadership?

- Do my leaders exhibit moral courage in voicing their opinions, or do they hide behind word walls and reflections when confronted with pointed questions?
- Do my political and military leaders demonstrate competence in their discussions and decisions about war, or do they appear to be hesitant, confused, or inept?
- Do my leaders seem capable of admitting confusion, mistakes, and failures, or do they always present themselves as certain, correct, and successful?

While these reflections do not guarantee a sound conscience decision about war, they may create a solid platform for sound thinking in the decision-making process.

A Concluding Narrative

Of all the enterprises on which individuals embark, war most clearly highlights how virtuous and vicious human beings can be. An incident that occurred in the Vietnam War highlights this fact and is addressed here because the war is recent enough for many individuals to remember, yet not so current as to raise political distractions that draw attention away from the moral issues involved.

The following narrative is a classic morality play of war, demonstrating the heights of moral virtue and the depths of moral vice. It is the story of Warrant Officer Hugh Thompson, Jr. (1995–96), a 24-year-old reconnaissance helicopter pilot in the Vietnam War. He and two crewmembers flew over the village of My Lai on March 16, 1968, and saw scores of dead and wounded civilians scattered about the area where United States troops were also present. Because neither Thompson nor his crew had heard enemy gunfire, they landed the helicopter to investigate. It was immediately clear that the U.S. soldiers were killing civilians, men, women, and children, none of whom was of draft age. It was later determined that approximately 400 civilians were killed. When Thompson confronted the lieutenant in charge of the operation about the situation, he was told some variation of "mind your business and get lost." Since Thompson was outranked, he complied. Immediately after that, he and his crew saw U.S. troops chasing civilians and shooting them, so they landed again but this time positioned themselves between the U.S. soldiers and civilians to stop the firing. While his crew held the soldiers at gunpoint, Thompson told the lieutenant, "If you fire on these people when I'm getting them out of the bunker, my people will fire on you." Thompson and his crew called in other helicopters to rescue a number of wounded civilians and fly them to an aid station.

Predictably, Thompson suffered the fate of many moral heroes. When his actions eventually became known, fellow pilots shunned him; dead animals were thrown on his doorstep; and he received many death threats. He was accused of being unpatriotic, and one Congressman declared that Thompson was the only service member who should be punished for My Lai. After My Lai, he was ordered to fly the most dangerous missions, was shot down five times, breaking his back and adding significantly to the post traumatic stress disorder he developed as a result of witnessing the massacre at My Lai.

More than 80 soldiers of all ranks were directly or indirectly involved in the massacre or cover-up (Department of the Army, 1974). Only twelve officers and one enlisted man were charged for various crimes, including murder. Only the lieutenant at the scene and his captain went to trial and only the lieutenant was convicted. A great deal of sympathy existed for the lieutenant, some because he claimed he simply carried out orders or he was the sole scapegoat for the crimes of scores of soldiers of all ranks. The lieutenant served only one weekend in a stockade, three-and-a-half years under house arrest, and was pardoned by President Richard Nixon in 1975.

Thompson died in January 2006 in a Veteran's Hospital after a life of counseling war veterans, continually haunted not only by what he witnessed at My Lai but by the dark cloud that often follows moral heroes throughout their lives. His actions during the Vietnam War include the highest exercise of the virtues: patriotism, duty, responsibility, integrity, moral courage, competence, and humility. Thompson:

- Exhibited the truest form of patriotism by calling attention to war crimes, even when such attention would severely tarnish the image of the United States in the eyes of the world.
- Acted according to the highest demands of duty by disobeying an illegal and immoral order and obeying the duty to honor the military code, the law, and the Constitution. He did the morally right thing, despite strong opposition from some fellow soldiers.
- Manifested integrity in that he witnessed the highest form of injustice in war, the killing of civilians, and reported it, knowing that no soldier who participated in the crime would view his behavior as anything but traitorous.
- Exhibited the highest form of physical courage when he and his crew risked their lives to rescue innocent women, children, and elderly men from slaughter. More importantly, he showed great moral courage when he refused to participate in a cover-up and suffered both personally and professionally for doing so.
- Demonstrated moral competence by sensing the moral implications of

the situation, taking control of the situation, directing other helicopters to the sight and helping treat the wounded.
- Demonstrated humility by defining what he did as simply doing his duty as an American soldier and steadfastly shunning any accolades.

This scene was repeated throughout the Vietnam War, and scenes like it occur in every war, including the current wars in which the United States is involved. Thus, the moral virtues addressed in this chapter will continue to be tested. Sometimes individuals will pass the test successfully and with honor while, at other times, they may fail miserably. However, the failures can be reduced in number and severity only if ordinary civilians, civilian leaders, ordinary soldiers, and military leaders maintain their own sense of virtue and help others to do the same. This goal seems both reasonable and necessary if morality in war is to remain a viable concept.

5

Moral Decision-Making: The Cognitive Dimension

We are all capable of believing things which we know to be untrue, and then, when we are finally proved wrong, impudently twisting the facts so as to show that we were right. Intellectually, it is possible to carry on this process for an indefinite time; the only check on it is that sooner or later a false belief bumps up against solid reality, usually on a battlefield.
— *George Orwell*

An individual's moral position regarding war in general or a specific war is developed from sound or faulty thinking with respect to the elements that comprise war. Contrary to conventional wisdom, while possessing sound moral values is undeniably important in decision-making, it is not the predominant factor. Analogously, love of beauty may be a core value for two artists but how they think, feel, and decide on what constitutes beauty may result in two very different paintings or cause equally respected art critics to judge the same painting as beautiful or ugly.

This chapter addresses the place of cognition in making moral decisions regarding war. This information is relevant for every citizen in a nation — political and military leaders as well as ordinary soldiers and civilians. Because political leaders are the "final deciders" with respect to declaring, waging, and ending wars, it is especially important for them to have a clear and realistic perception of all the factors that lead to success or failure in war. Misunderstandings and miscalculations in one or more of these areas may have catastrophic results.

Military leaders have the responsibility to develop realistic strategies and tactics and to have a sound sense of the military capabilities and commitment of their troops, as well as an accurate perception of the strengths and weaknesses of the enemy. Ordinary soldiers and civilians have the responsibility to arrive at realistic appraisals of the various dimensions of war through study, discussion, and critical thinking. While ordinary citizens and soldiers are not present in the inner sanctums of the war deciders, their voices and votes will resonate in those rooms because, since the Vietnam War, political and military leaders of democratic nations have come to realize the importance of the support or non-support of ordinary citizens in declaring, waging, and ending war. Citizens who provide informed and rational support or non-support for a war can be infinitely more persuasive than those who offer only intuitive kinds of support ("I just think we should protect our country from terrorists, that's all") or non-support ("I'm just tired of all this war, so I'm against it").

It is essential that national leaders and ordinary citizens go into war with both eyes open but, unfortunately, this is rarely the case. More commonly, they go into war with a squint that blocks out the anxiety-producing parts of reality. This tunnel vision makes going to war appear more feasible and necessary than it is in reality. Unfortunately, only when the war is well under way does the tunnel begin to crumble and the previously ignored reality come crashing through. At this time, a litany of laments enters the picture, the theme of which is always an underestimation of the political and military challenges that result when a war is launched: "We underestimated the...

- Length of time the war would last
- Resistance of the enemy soldiers
- Skills of the enemy's military and civilian leadership
- Commitment of the enemies' civilians
- Resourcefulness of the enemy's military
- Animosity of the civilians we fought to liberate
- Number of prisoners and the problems they would cause
- Financial costs of the war and its aftermath
- Number of our troops killed or wounded
- Number of civilian casualties
- Number of repeat deployments of troops
- Number and nature of physical and psychological wounds our troops would receive
- Decreasing civilian support for the war over time
- Skepticism of reasons and intentions for going to war

While war obviously does not lend itself to precise assessments and predictions, many if not most of the "surprises" listed above could have been foreseen and affected the timing of going to war, if not the decision to go to war. To this end, this chapter discusses the factors that cause the distortions that lead to poor decision-making, as well as the nature of realistic, defensive, and responsible thinking and the development of a cognitive worldview toward war with the focus on morality.

Realistic and Defensive Thinking

Realistic thinking will be addressed first because it is at the heart of a sound decision-making process. This section will be followed by a discussion of various kinds of defensive thinking which can short-circuit realistic thinking.

REALISTIC THINKING

Realistic thinking stems from an accurate perception of reality in contrast to a perception distorted by mental gymnastics that bend reality to fit the needs of the perceiver. Realistic thinking seems to be a stand-alone ability that is not significantly correlated with general intelligence, age, education, experience, sophistication, or socioeconomic status. This is borne out by the fact that, since the beginning of wars, political and military decision-makers typically have been perceived as brilliant in their respective fields. Yet, these individuals frequently led their nations into wars based more on political, military, and moral illusions and delusions than on hardcore reality. While centuries of war have led to more effective ways to wage war, they have not resulted in more effective methods for thinking clearly about it.

Initial perceptions are primarily reflexive and not under the conscious control of the observer. Realistic thinking entails having "second thoughts" and hopefully "third thoughts" about an important situation before interpreting and acting upon it. Individuals who think realistically share one central trait — the most compelling and overarching need in their psychological makeup is to perceive reality in its unvarnished state and to make rational decisions based on this perception, whatever the outcome.

Realistic thinking, as presented here, has seven characteristics.

- It distinguishes between facts, possible facts and no facts, and between reasonable theories, unreasonable theories, and merely personal opinions.
- It is disinterested and dispassionate, meaning that understanding the reality of a situation is its sole objective. Accurate interpretations and appropriate emotional responses will take place only after realistic thinking is completed.
- It is not optimistic or pessimistic. Optimism relies on hope and pessimism relies on doubt, each of which is premature in this early phase of cognition and will instantly tilt the perceptual process to one end or the other on the pessimism-optimism scale and away from reality, which lies at the center.
- It does not maximize or minimize reality, making it larger or smaller than it is in its original state.
- It is courageous — it can accept anxiety-inducing reality, as well as anxiety-

reducing reality, so there is no need for defensive mental tactics that artificially ward off threats and distort perceptions.

- It accepts the fact that a lack of clarity is often a part of reality and that it need not be clarified artificially or prematurely to reduce anxiety or confusion.
- It focuses on the present — it keeps the past and the future out of the cognitive process until the present reality is as clear as possible, given the circumstances.

Hereditary predisposition probably contributes to the ability to think realistically, but environmental learning is likely to be as influential, if not more influential. Young children are often more adept at realistic thinking than many adults because children tend to perceive things the way they are, a trait that frequently lands them in trouble.

For example, a 10 year old asks, "Is daddy drunk again?" and his mother responds: "How could you say such a thing! Daddy's just tired." The message learned early is that when authority enters the picture, sometimes it is better not to respond to what you actually see and to "see" what others want you to see. This trait can be lifelong and is particularly dangerous when gathering information regarding decisions about war.

The claim can be made that individuals who possess reality competence would never reach the heights of political and military power because they would threaten too many people and therefore would never be in a position to share their sound thinking with others, especially those in authority. Unfortunately, this claim has some merit, but political and military history demonstrates that at times these individuals can rise to the top and are highly influential in decision-making processes. However, until reality competence becomes an overriding value in the culture of national political and military leadership and all the nation's citizens, faulty thinking may continue to persevere in war and lead to costly consequences.

Defensive Thinking

Defensive thinking occurs when individuals subconsciously use mental gymnastics to distort reality when it significantly raises their anxiety by casting doubt on their hitherto confident perceptions of themselves, others, and the realities in which they live. Anxiety is a general term that includes the experience of threatening thoughts and feelings. Threatening thoughts cast doubt on one's intelligence, courage, worth, competence, wisdom, integrity, popularity, and worth. Threatening feelings include feeling frightened, helpless, confused, angry, guilty, depressed, frustrated, discouraged, and hopeless.

Everyone uses defensive thinking in order to maintain some degree of equilibrium to get through each day. Problems arise only when defensive thinking becomes so prevalent that it distorts realities that must be perceived accurately if an individual is to navigate successfully through critically important straits. A mother who denies that her baby is ill because she cannot admit to herself or others that she has been neglectful puts off seeking medical attention until it is too late. A commander in the field cannot admit to himself or others that he has allowed the enemy to gain the upper hand, so he sees no need to ask for help in strengthening his force protection.

This section addresses how defensive thinking in political and military leaders, as well as civilians and soldiers, can play a significant role in deciding to go to war, choosing how to wage the war, and planning how to end a war. It is based on theories of cognitive science that help explain how ordinarily intelligent, reasonable, and honest individuals can protect themselves from anxiety by misperceiving reality in ways that can negatively influence war decisions. The examples used to concretize the dynamics underlying defensive thinking refer to past wars in contrast to present ones so as not to distract from the central theme of this section. While there are many types of defensive thinking, the following are some of the more common ones that are seen in war related decisions.

Compartmentalization. Compartmentalization is a psychological dynamic that separates conflicting thoughts and feelings into different parts of the mind so that they do not mix with each other and cause friction. An example of compartmentalization occurred in Hitler's Germany when soldiers and agents of all ranks, levels of intelligence, education, religious conviction, and socioeconomic level could imprison, torture, and slaughter "misfits and traitors" during the day and return to their wives and children at night and live ordinary family lives. Compartmentalization creates two problems:

- It allows individuals and nations collectively to make the most destructive decisions and act on them without experiencing much or any conscious anxiety or guilt. Apparently, many of the German soldiers and agents not only had serene consciences but felt righteous about their behavior because they believed they were performing a valuable service for their Fatherland. They felt guilt only when they failed to do a proper job. Therefore, they could continue to act in barbarous ways, feel proud of themselves, and, in fact, boast of their successes to admiring family, friends, and colleagues.
- Anxiety and guilt, which are at least subconsciously and fleetingly experienced, are placed in long-term storage containers. As a result, individuals can continue to function normally, even with a sense of well-being. However,

after a short or long period of fermentation, these feelings often seep out of their compartments and gradually or suddenly flood individuals with anxiety and guilt, which can be a major cause of post-traumatic stress disorder and result in serious, sometimes lifelong consequences for soldiers of all nations and their families.

Dehumanization. Dehumanization is a psychological tactic that fosters the perception that individuals who are different from one's own people, especially if they are perceived as antagonistic, are less than fully human. This defense allows ordinarily intelligent and good people to perceive and treat the enemy in inhumane ways without feeling the least bit guilty. It is the same dynamic that allowed intelligent, god-fearing Americans to treat blacks and Native Americans inhumanely for centuries because they were perceived not as "persons" but as a sub-human if not mere objects to be used or tolerated. Dehumanization of the enemy is present in every war, one side portraying the other as primitive, bellicose, psychopathic, and evil. This viewpoint not only allows each side to treat the other with derision and savagery but to feel righteous about its behavior.

In World War II, the Japanese depicted Americans as white, hairy, fat gorillas that stupidly savaged everything in their path, while Americans depicted the Japanese as squint-eyed, buck-toothed monkeys with thick glasses hanging in trees waiting to spring on American soldiers. In the Vietnam War, some Americans referred to the Vietnamese people as slopes, slants, dinks, and gooks. Interestingly, these pejorative terms were applied not only to the North Vietnamese people who were supposed to be our enemy, but also to the South Vietnamese people who were supposed to be our allies. As one American soldier remarked, "A gook is a gook — that's all you need to know over here." In fact, such racially derogatory terms found their way into informal discussions between Army legal officers who facetiously devised the M.G.R. — the mere gook rule — meaning that military courts were lenient with American soldiers who intentionally killed Vietnamese civilians because they were perceived as being less worthy of life than American soldiers or American civilians. It is of some interest that when soldiers and veterans visit nations with which they were once at war, they are surprised to see how very human — intelligent, kind, attractive, cultured, and creative many of their former adversaries are.

The problem with cognitive short-circuiting is that it creates a break with reality, which never leads to goodness and beauty. When wars are over, many veterans on all sides cannot believe some of the barbarous things they did in battle: "It was like some other force took over my body, and I became a killing machine, totally the opposite of the person I was before the war and want to be now."

Dichotomous thinking. Dichotomous thinking consists of perceiving individuals on a continuum of polar opposites: loyal-disloyal, good-evil, intelligent-stupid, sane-crazy, trustworthy-untrustworthy, competent-incompetent, and so on. Individuals and nations that lack the ability to differentiate degrees and shades of reality take a cognitive shortcut and lump everyone into one of the two polar opposite groups. Such division is not random but based on the deep-seated need to perceive others as safe or threatening. Once this cognitive triaging is done, the perceiver need not invest more time or energy in learning who "those other folks" are with all their complexities, virtues, and vices.

Dichotomous thinking in war takes two forms: international and national. The international form consists of categorizing the enemy as monolithically evil and one's own nation as monolithically good. All the people in the enemy nation are perceived as directly or indirectly complicit, evil, stupid, unstable, psychopathic, or barbaric. A well-accepted sentiment during World War II was that "the only good German is a dead German," a classic symptom of dichotomous thinking. In contrast, all the people in one's own nation are perceived as good, intelligent, sane, moral, democratic and humanistic. When individuals first learn that their soldiers have tortured the enemy, for example, the news is met with confident and complete disbelief: "The story must be false because Americans simply don't act that way."

The problem is that this type of thinking creates a serious distortion of reality. Human beings are very much alike even though their cultures sometimes make them appear to be qualitatively different. Dichotomous thinking on an international level prevents any kind of understanding, compassion, respect or communication with current or potential enemies. The only appropriate response in this case is to be aggressive in the political or military arenas, which only causes the enemy to respond in kind, thus "proving once again" their evil nature.

In reality, the ordinary citizens of an enemy nation likely are not different from those of any other nation and become bellicose only when attacked, no matter what positive motives the attackers have. It is also likely that truly warlike people who rule the nation represent only a small percentage of the population. In this case, the malevolent leaders need to be neutralized, not the great majority of the population.

The national form of dichotomous thinking categorizes the people of one's own nation into two groups: the patriots who support the war and the traitors who are against it. This prevents any kind of meaningful dialogue between the "patriots" and the "traitors." As a result, war is waged on two fronts — internationally and at home, a situation that only spawns more cognitive short-circuiting and leads to even more deplorable decisions and actions, both internationally and domestically.

On the home front, it is likely that those who support a war and those against it are not qualitatively different human beings but simply individuals who perceive the reality of the war very differently. They are not mutual enemies but mutual citizens who want the best for their nation and the world. As long as dichotomous thinking turns them into mutually antagonistic groups, no meaningful and necessary dialogue can take place, which further short-circuits the decision-making of political and military leaders to the serious detriment of the nation as a whole.

Selective attention and inattention. Selective attention and inattention occur on a subconscious level and refer to individuals perceiving and remembering issues that allow them to feel comfortable and failing to perceive or remember issues that would cause them anxiety. Selective attention and inattention with respect to war involves individuals and nations perceiving the positive aspects of their war and failing to perceive the negative ones, even when the negative ones might be more important and obvious.

For example, using selective attention, an individual may focus on the enemy making a hasty and humiliating retreat in the face of overwhelming force, withering firepower, skilled leadership, and our brave troops. This welcome news boosts morale and commitment to the war. However, the individual subconsciously ignores the information that the enemy has forced our troops in another part of the region to make a hasty and humiliating retreat in the face of overwhelming force, withering firepower, skilled leadership, and their brave troops.

This type of thinking allows leaders and followers alike to feel good about their nation and the progress of the war and causes them to grow in confidence and commitment that is not supported by the facts on the ground. The problem is that these very good feelings lead to very bad decisions and lay the groundwork for more failure and unnecessary destruction in the future.

Confirmation bias. Confirmation bias refers to a situation in which individuals and nations develop a theory (bias) and then cognitively seek out information that confirms their theory and ignore information that refutes it. Those who want to go to war gather intelligence in a way that "proves" their position is correct, while those who do not want to go to war gather information that "proves" their position is correct. A realistic perception of the information could "prove" both positions wrong at different times, which is often realized only after the war is over, as happened after the Vietnam

War. Confirmation bias differs from selective attention and inattention in that it is related to forming a theory about a specific issue, for example, an exit strategy, then picking and choosing data that reinforces one's already formed opinion and discounting or ignoring data the refutes the already formed opinion. In contrast, selective attention and inattention is a broader concept that refers to a less than conscious process by which individuals are able to recall issues that make them feel comfortable and forget those that make them anxious.

Critical thinking is an antidote to confirmation bias when it robustly questions all information, whether it does or does not confirm one's biases. The problem is that in times of national threat, a dense pall develops that stifles critical thinking as unpatriotic and politically motivated. Only the individuals with moral courage ask penetrating questions, but they may or may not receive straight answers.

Cognitive dissonance. Cognitive dissonance occurs when the cognitions (thoughts, beliefs, values) of individuals and nations are in direct contradiction to their actual behavior. This ordinarily causes anxiety, sometimes great anxiety, which must be reduced or neutralized. Cognitive dissonance is different from compartmentalization in which individuals do not consciously perceive their actions as evil and, therefore, experience no anxiety or guilt, at least at the time of their actions. There is a flash of conscious anxiety in cognitive dissonance, which can be reduced in one of three ways: by changing the anxiety-causing behavior to match the positive cognition, by changing the positive cognition to match the anxiety-causing behavior, or by minimizing the degree and importance of the inconsistency.

A cognition during the Vietnam War was that the United States wanted to save the lives of the good and decent people of South Vietnam who were being invaded by the communists from the north. The behavior was that the United States in its attacks on the Viet Cong, the communist insurgents in South Vietnam, killed well over 500,000 South Vietnamese civilians by the end of the United States' direct participation in the war. These were the people the United States went to war to protect. The dissonance created by this contradiction created surges of anxiety, primarily guilt, which had to be reduced or neutralized immediately so that the decision-makers and their followers could return to a state of psychological equilibrium and peace. This could be accomplished in one of three ways:

- Reduce the dissonance between the cognition (we are in South Vietnam to save their citizens from Communist oppression) and the actual behavior (killing hundreds of thousands of the people we are supposed to be saving from oppression) by stopping the killing of civilians, or at least substantially reducing it. This action removes or greatly reduces the anxiety or guilt.

• Reduce the dissonance between the cognition (we are in South Vietnam to save their citizens from communist oppression) and the killing of hundreds of thousands by claiming that the people we are killing are, in fact, not "innocent civilians" but actually communist insurgents or their supporters. This move eliminates any reason for feeling anxious or guilty.

• Minimize the importance of the deaths of hundreds of thousands of innocent civilians (we are killing innocent civilians but, unfortunately, some innocent people are killed in war to save the majority of innocent civilians). This move admits the reality of the killing, but discounts its importance, thus reducing any feelings of anxiety or guilt.

Exercising the first option would restore justice to the situation, whereas the second and third options would allow the guilt-producing immoral actions to continue not only with little or no guilt, but quite possibly with a spirit of righteousness.

Attribution theory. Attribution theory refers to how individuals and nations protect themselves and those they support from experiencing a sense of failure when things go wrong. In other words, they place self-protecting perceptual lenses on events so that whatever happens in reality, they come out on the right side of it. When a war is going well, decision-makers use internal attribution. They attribute the current success of the war to their personal competence, wisdom, and courage. When war is going badly, they use external attribution, attributing the failure not to themselves but to others — the politicians, the military, dissonant civilians, or the unjust tactics of the enemy.

This dynamic affords decision-makers and nations the luxury of never doubting the wisdom of their decisions. Therefore, no reason exists for them to reassess the methodology of their decision-making, thus ensuring that the same mistakes will be repeated.

Decision-makers and nations also use attribution when people or nations which they support, including their own, enjoy success or experience failure in war. When their nation is succeeding, they use internal attribution that claims the success is due to the inherent greatness (exceptionalism) of their nation. However, when their nation suffers defeats, external attribution allows them to attribute the defeat to incompetent allies or the illegal or immoral tactics of the enemy.

As a result, decision-makers and nations never have to re-think their decision-making methodology because they are always correct, whether the war is succeeding or failing. This process guarantees continuing failures that demand a high price from soldiers and civilians on all sides of a war.

Pluralistic ignorance. Pluralistic ignorance occurs when individuals perceive everyone else in the room or the government as more informed, intelligent, and sophisticated than they themselves are. These individuals cognitively underrate their abilities to have worthwhile thoughts and overrate the abilities of others. While this appears to reflect humility on their part and respect for the more intelligent people, it is actually a dodge to escape having to make difficult decisions and accepting responsibility for the consequences. This cognitive short-circuit will seldom be found in the most highly placed decision-makers or like-minded people because they perceive themselves as "the smartest guys in the room." It will exist more often in secondary decision-makers or like-minded people, as well as in ordinary soldiers and citizens, especially those who want to escape any responsibility for their leaders' decisions.

As a result, only a small handful of leaders make all the war decisions because the remaining political and military leaders and ordinary citizens take the position: "What do I know about these things? This is why we elect our leaders—they have a lot more knowledge and experience than I do." This position is based on the myth that being intelligent and well-informed is highly correlated with making wise decisions. The history of war clearly demonstrates that "being intelligent" does not necessarily mean possessing wisdom, and "being informed" does not necessarily mean "being correctly informed."

Individuals in high places—political, military, and civilian—may be better informed than the primary decision-makers in one area or another and should have input in the decision-making process. For example, highly respected political science professors may have more knowledge and wisdom on a particular subject than a secretary of state, and well-respected ethicists may have more knowledge and wisdom than a secretary of defense. These individuals should have some input in war decisions, even though they are not included in the inner circle of official decision-makers.

Cognitive overconfidence. Cognitive overconfidence refers to individuals and nations believing that their intelligence is so superior to others that they can accomplish whatever they set out to do, even in situations where others have failed. The overconfidence is a protection against deeper feelings of insecurity and doubt, which leads individuals to overplay their hands and eventually make regrettable decisions. These individuals have an abiding "can do" attitude that knows no limits. They believe that they rarely if ever fail in life because of the previously discussed types of cognitive short-circuiting which protects them from facing the reality of their past failures.

Overconfidence in war is particularly dangerous because it often leads to overestimating one's own competence and underestimating the competence of the enemy, which happened consistently in the Vietnam War. The confident "can do" belief was that the allied armies had superior training, weapons, air power, strategy, leadership, manpower, resources, logistics, and discipline, which was largely but not completely true at the beginning of the war. The companion belief was that the communist insurgents were a rag-tag group of farmers with none of the above resources and who were more interested in farming than fighting. For these reasons, the allied leaders were quite confident that they would eventually outsmart the enemy, which too often was not the case militarily and certainly not politically.

The problem was that the political and military leaders overestimated the commitment of their drafted army, the support of the public, the quality of the military leadership, and the commitment and competence of the South Vietnamese army. They also underestimated the class and race conflicts within their army, the substance abuse problems, the commitment of the North Vietnamese army and public, the quality of the North Vietnamese political and military leadership and their ability to obtain weapons from Russia and China. The result of this cognitive overconfidence was that, after ten years of fighting, the "inferior" side won the war, largely due to cognitive errors related to virtually all facets of the war.

Cognitive perseveration. Cognitive perseveration refers to continuing a behavior long after it has proven to be ineffective and possibly even destructive. Perseveration is the pathological extension of perseverance that can be a virtue until it results in diminishing returns and increasing damage. One basic cause of perseveration is the defense tactic of denial, which is manifested in an inability to admit past mistakes. This denial precludes correcting mistakes and results in the repetition of the same mistakes in battle after battle and war after war.

The practical effects of cognitive perseveration can be seen when military and political leaders plan and launch operations that include the following:

• A proposed strategy that was used by a prior invading army against the enemy and failed miserably
• A proposed strategy that was flawed, so expanding it or sending more troops to execute it is eventually bound to fail
• A proposed strategy that is sound but is carried out by civilian or military leaders who have a history of misapplying and mismanaging even the soundest of plans, despite their exalted public image

Several years after the end of the Vietnam War, Secretary of Defense Robert McNamara admitted that many of the war's strategies and tactics could not succeed because political and military leaders, including McNamara himself, refused to admit that they were "fighting the last war," meaning they did not realize what worked in World War II and Korea could never work in Vietnam for political, military, logistical, geographical, and psychological reasons (McNamara and VanDeMark 1996).

All decisions resulting from these examples could have serious and lasting moral implications. Poor decisions are common in all fields, but the stakes are infinitely higher when they occur in war. A "regrettable decision" in business might cause a small business to fail; a similar mistake in war might cause the loss of many lives, both military and civilian, on both sides. Because defensive thinking is a normal human trait, everyone makes poor decisions based on this dynamic. However, when the same type of cognitive short-circuiting afflicts the same individuals in the same general circumstances time after time, and others stand by and say nothing, this is a moral issue well beyond what can be mitigated by the fog of war.

Unfortunately, people in general and leaders in particular are indisposed to admit they made a poor decision. When an egregiously poor decision causes significant material and moral damage, five lines of defense by the decision-makers are available:

- "No mistakes were made."
- "No individual made mistakes — it was the system that failed."
- "Mistakes were made, but not by me."
- "We made some mistakes."
- "I made some mistakes, but let's not dwell on the past, let's look to the future."

Individuals who are psychologically secure and own their imperfections do not need to hide behind rows of defenses. They can readily admit: "I made a mistake. This is how I was wrong and how I'm going to hold myself accountable for it, and how I am going to try to rectify it, and how I am willing to accept the consequences for it." "The buck stops here" is a much toted claim and boast, but it rarely translates into meaningful behavior, even when deplorable and devastating mistakes have occurred. For example, in the My Lai massacre in Vietnam about 400 innocent civilians were killed in cold blood by American troops. Even though more than 80 soldiers at all levels of the chain of command were directly or indirectly involved, only one soldier, a young lieutenant, was found guilty of anything, and the president later pardoned him.

The subconscious dynamics in defensive thinking can be brought into consciousness through various types of discussion so that realistic thinking,

Responsible Thinking

While defensive thinking refers to individuals deceiving themselves in order to feel more comfortable, responsible (critical) thinking refers to not allowing oneself to be deceived by others.

The term "responsible thinking" is taking the place of "critical thinking" in some circles and for good reasons. One is that critical thinking implies negativity because of the common understanding of the word "critical," as in "He is critical of everything and everybody." The second is that critical thinking has been generally limited to identifying false arguments when issues are debated. However, identifying faulty arguments is only one type of propaganda antidote, so the broader term "responsible thinking" is more appropriate.

Therefore, it becomes the duty of all citizens to responsibly consider war proclamations and ascertain if they appear to be based on reality or myth. This endeavor is critically important if sound moral judgments have a chance of being made because without it, informed moral judgments are impossible.

While the focus of this chapter is on the more inclusive concept of responsible thinking, one of its components, critical thinking, will be addressed occasionally since it is the term most used in the past literature. As Robert Korn (2009) states:

> In reality, critical thinking is of extreme importance for everyone. When things go terribly wrong it is often a result of poor critical thinking. Ethnic hatred is a critical thinking problem. War is a critical thinking problem.... Terrorism is a critical thinking problem.... Most of the greatest problems facing humanity are caused, at least in part, by people's critical thinking failures. The future of humanity depends on making critical thinking a very high priority.

A description of responsible thinking is based on the literal meaning of "responsible"—the ability to respond. Responsible thinking means the ability to respond to statements with active listening, pointed questions, logical analysis, depth interpretation, and an attempt to connect the message implicit in the statement to the underlying philosophy of the individual making it. For example, a national leader states: "I visited the troops last week and was very impressed with their morale, commitment, and fighting skills. They know why they are fighting, and they won't quit unless the people stop supporting them and force them to cut and run." Every leader who supports a war, any war, by any nation, at any time, could make this statement.

The following examples show how individual citizens can apply responsible thinking to this leader's statement.

Active listening: What exactly did the speaker say, and what did he not say? He said he visited some troops; he did not say he interviewed a representative sample of troops.

Pointed questions: How exactly did the speaker obtain this information — was it through casual conversation, or did he interview soldiers in private where there would be less social pressure to give the right answers? How did the speaker assess the troops' morale, commitment, and fighting status? What exactly did the troops say they were willing to die for, and exactly why are they willing to do so? Why is the speaker using emotionally laden language ("cut and run") rather than "retreat," which could be a prudent military tactic?

Depth interpretation: What was the speaker really saying? Was there a hidden agenda that could not be spoken publicly? Was the speaker simply relating a conversation with a few troops that might be heartening to the troops' families back home? Or was the speaker's real message: "Look, this war is going badly, and the public's lack of support will cause us to lose the war and we can't afford that — we can't afford to embarrass the political party underwriting this war (or me, who represents it), or to embarrass our military and the nation in front of the entire world. Whether the war is legal or moral is no longer the point — we're here now and have to focus on the future."

Underlying philosophy: What philosophical or worldview does the speaker seem to have? Is it that when a nation has a just cause for war and wages it justly, it must follow through, even when the war becomes unbearably costly; or is it that when any war, just or unjust, is going badly, the public must do everything possible to win it because the nation cannot risk losing respect nationally and internationally? Are morality and legality relevant considerations at this time, or are they simply encumbrances to be jettisoned to allow the war effort to reach maximum speed?

OBSTACLES TO RESPONSIBLE THINKING

If a war's strategy and its tactics are just, no reason exists to hide information from citizens, except for that which would truly compromise national security. The more information is withheld or faulty information is disseminated, the less support leaders can expect from their citizens. In the worst case, citizens may discover they have been lied to about critical issues regarding the war. This is a clear breach of the social contract and can nullify their obligation to support the nation, even in times of war. This can be particularly problematic if the war is in fact just, but national leaders are not forthright about its important details. In this situation, citizens are not abandoning their nation; the leaders are abandoning their citizens.

Loyalty to authority. Some citizens have a reflexive and unreflective loyalty to those in high places or at least "to the office." This reaction develops from the rubric of "respect for authority," "patriotic duty," "love for one's country," and "national pride," even though history has clearly and continually demonstrated that those in high office — across nations and political ideologies — often lead their nations into catastrophic wars.

Loyalty has a place in politics and war, but it must be carefully nuanced. The basic loyalty of all citizens, including those in high places, should be to the highest values of their nation, which generally explicitly or implicitly include justice, freedom and truth. Loyalty to authority ought not to be automatic, but based on leaders living out these values while planning and prosecuting a war. Loyalty to core virtues can be unconditional; loyalty to authority ought always to be conditional.

Loyalty to one's political party. The reasons that loyalty to one's political party can be an obstacle to responsible thinking are the same as those listed above with respect to those in authority. The practical goal of many, if not most, politicians and political parties is to remain in power. Sometimes, if not frequently, this self-interested motivation consciously or unconsciously trumps the very values the political parties purport to represent.

Unfounded optimism. Some individuals are trusting to a fault. They believe that human beings are basically good and trustworthy. Consequently, they are gullible, naïve, and guileless. They believe most of what they read and hear especially if they have a bond with the message-sender. They are kind and trusting people who tend to assume that everyone else must be the same, just as those who are unkind and untrustworthy tend to assume that all other individuals must be the same. Some individuals are in the middle and are realists who consider the merits of each individual and situation on a case-by-case basis. They realize that both trustworthiness and untrustworthiness are part of every personality, so their attitude is prudently inquiring rather than naively accepting, especially with regard to the critically important matters of war.

Susceptibility to power and scare tactics. Some individuals are overly susceptible to the forces of power and fear, which causes them to abandon reason and blindly turn to their leaders for protection. National leaders who must frighten their constituents into joining their cause are not likely to have a compelling case for war if it requires fear to adopt it.

Close-mindedness. In politics and war, many individuals are unable or unwilling to allow into consciousness ideas that threaten the certainty they enjoy with regard to their beliefs. They only seek information that will reinforce their already formed opinions. To these individuals, the world of politics and war is black or white, right or wrong, while gray falls into a cognitive chasm. Even the most cogent arguments against their position are summarily rejected, while those that support their position are fully embraced, even if they lack the slightest bit of cogency.

Over-identification with one's nation. It can be healthy to identify with one's nation — to take joy in its successes and mourn its failures. It is uplifting, for example, to see the national pride nations manifest and celebrate at international athletic events. However, just as spectators can over-identify with their national team and adopt a belligerent attitude toward rival teams and their supporters, citizens can do the same when it comes to international tensions. They enter into a symbiotic relationship with their nation — when their nation is successful, they personally feel successful, and when the nation fails, they personally feel like failures. When citizens over-identify with their nation (my country right or wrong), they cannot even briefly entertain the possibility that their national leaders may be on the wrong track when it comes to declaring, waging, and ending war.

Obstacles to responsible thinking can be slight or insurmountable, often depending on the individual's level of insecurity. Insecurity has one basic cause — the fear that if one small section of the psychological bunker is breached, eventually the entire bunker will collapse and the individual will be left with no self-identity, self-worth, or self-direction. In extreme cases, individuals would rather die than be found wrong and have to admit it.

Howard Gabennesch (2006) lists some thoughts that directly relate to responsible thinking, including the following:

- Like fish who are unconscious of the water that envelops them, we are often unaware of the constraints imposed on our thinking by the taken-for-granted social forces surrounding us — not to mention the gene-based forces within us.
- We are often ignorant of our ignorance. In addition, the more incompetent we are, the more likely we are to overestimate our competence.
- All good things have costs. Many bad things have benefits.
- Issues frequently appear black-and-white, when in fact they usually consist of grays.
- We typically mistake pieces of the truth for the whole truth.
- Partial truths can be just as misleading as outright lies.
- We are more likely to be misled by people who sincerely believe what they are saying than by liars.
- Self-deception can be an even bigger problem than deception by others.

Sound and responsible thinking are more likely to result in morally responsible decisions and actions regarding war, whereas unsound and irresponsible thinking are more likely to lead to morally irresponsible actions, regardless of the intelligence and virtue of the actors. In other words, individuals can only be as moral as their cognitions will allow. For example, ordinarily religious and moral soldiers may torture a prisoner because their uncritical thinking tells them that torture is not only permissible but also virtuous because their superiors told them it was.

Moral Worldview and War

This final section addresses how cognitions, primarily in the form of beliefs, create a moral worldview that is often translated into practical behavior. A moral worldview of war is a constellation of beliefs about fundamental aspects of reality that ground all perceptions, interpretations, assessments, and actions related to the moral rightness or wrongness of all issues that are part of war.

It is a moral prism for viewing war-related issues. Like all worldviews (political, economic, religious, ecological), moral worldviews held by groups or individuals can be conscious or unconscious, sound or unsound, prosocial or antisocial, explicit or implicit, consistent or inconsistent, idiosyncratic or common, superficial or substantial, well-informed or ill-informed, actionable or inactionable, static or dynamic, open or closed.

Moral worldviews are much more than a cluster of personal opinions about the moral status of war in general or a particular war. Worldviews create perceptual realities which people not only believe but also inhabit. Worldviews are reality for the individuals who possess them. In fact, individuals who vehemently disagree with each other often complain: "I think you and I must live in completely different worlds."

Worldviews can be so deeply rooted and engrained that they comprise a basic, if not the most important, element of the self. Individuals can become willing martyrs for their moral worldviews: saints choose death over renouncing their faith; soldiers choose to sacrifice their lives to save a buddy rather than violate the bond of brotherhood; captured soldiers choose to die rather than divulge secrets; suicide bombers happily blow themselves up in the process of killing a dozen innocent people. People have died in duels, abandoned their religions, quit their jobs, broken off lifelong relationships, gone to jail, and joined or left the military based on their moral worldviews. The point is that strong moral worldviews can have a driving power that propels individuals down very constructive or destructive paths.

Moral worldviews are not simply different ways of looking at the same thing but create entire mental states. Inducing people to change their view of something is sometimes difficult, but changing their realities is virtually impossible. For example, the Vietnam War was perceived as a "noble cause," "a quagmire," and "an imperialist adventure." Each of these quite different worldviews had profound moral (as well as political and military) implications.

When applied to wars, moral worldviews are composed of many elements, some of which are briefly discussed below. These elements are phrased as questions to concretize and personalize them, so that they will be clearer than their abstract, philosophical foundations and, consequently, perhaps lead to some self-reflection and appropriate action. The pronouns "I" and "we" refer to Americans in this case, and "them" refers to the nations and people with whom the United States is in conflict.

- Do I believe justice resides only in us and injustice resides only in them, or do justice and injustice reside in both sides of a war? Does justice really matter in war, or is it merely a restraining element that can cause good nations to lose wars?
- Do I believe it is my responsibility to gather as much information about a war as possible and make my own decisions about the war's justice or injustice, or do I trust our leaders to gather and interpret information, make decisions, take action, and inform us of their decision after the process is complete?
- Do I believe our wars are fought with pure and noble motives — to spread democracy, save the oppressed, make our nation and the world secure, or do I believe that most, if not all, wars are fought for mixed motives: to extend power, increase natural resources, better the economy, flex political muscles, exact revenge, and so on? If all our wars are fought with pure and noble motives, how successful have we been in accomplishing our objectives?
- Do I possess moral certitude or near moral certitude that everything our leaders tell us about war is based on unvarnished truth, or do I believe our leaders tell us the truth when it reinforces their policies, hold it back when the war is progressing poorly, and lie to us when things are so bad we might begin to question their policies?
- Do I believe only two kinds of people exist after the first shot is fired: those who support the war and those who are traitors? Or, do I believe all of us have a moral (and civic) obligation to gather as much information about the war as possible, evaluate it, and then decide if we should or should not support a war?
- Do I believe a war could begin as a noble cause but deteriorate into an ignoble one and thus rightfully lose the support of the people, or do I believe

that once our nation joins a war, we should not cut-and-run, but continue to fight the war to its end, despite any moral or immoral consequences?

- Do I believe our nation ought to obey the international laws of war and torture as we would expect the enemy to do, or do I believe our nation's cause supersedes the laws by which we expect other nations to be bound? Do I believe that if enemy nations violate the laws of war, we are also morally free to violate them? If so, is it also acceptable if our enemy violates the laws as a response to our violation of them?
- Do I believe that "support the troops" means we should stand behind the troops no matter what they do or how just the war is, or do I believe that the best way to support the troops is to support them when they are engaged in moral actions in a moral war, but support their returning home from a war that was or has become unjust and in which our troops are in fact dying in vain?
- Do I believe all human life is equally sacred and worthy of respect, or do I believe some human life should be greatly respected, some less respected, some not respected, and some disrespected? Do I believe how we treat individuals of other nations can have a profound effect on how they perceive us, which may be a contributing cause of the next war, or do I believe that we can diminish and dominate individuals of other nations and expect no consequences in the future?
- Do I believe we always represent good and they always represent evil, or do I believe that good and evil are present on all sides in a war and it is important to understand this and react accordingly?
- Do I believe that individuals in the military, both officers and enlisted people, have a moral duty to obey their well-formed consciences and refuse any order that requires them to violate their consciences in a substantive way, or do I believe that as long as their superiors order them to take a specific action, the moral responsibility for the action rests solely on the superiors?

Thinking seriously about these questions can offer some understanding not only of the theoretical nature of moral worldviews of war but their practical dimensions as well.

Realistic and responsible thinking, along with emotions that interact with these types of thinking, comprise a critically important element in conscience development and decision-making. The more grounded the thinking and the more appropriate the emotions, the more an individual's conscience and decisions are likely to be sound. Over time, the independent segments of the individual's moral attitudes and beliefs coalesce and gradually fashion a sound moral worldview.

On the other hand, the less realistic and responsible the thinking and the more inappropriate the emotions, the more likely it is that the individual's conscience development and decision-making will be impaired. Eventually, the independent segments of the individual's moral attitudes and beliefs coalesce and gradually fashion a distorted moral worldview. Therefore, the more civilians and soldiers can develop an understanding of these concepts as they were addressed in this chapter, the more morally enlightened and empowered they can be when considering and responding to the moral dimensions of war.

6

Propaganda, Deceit and Moral Decisions

> *We must remember that in time of war what is said on the enemy's side of the front is always propaganda, and what is said on our side of the front is truth and righteousness, the cause of humanity and a crusade for peace.*
>
> —*Walter Lippman*

National political and military leaders often claim that ordinary citizens, which includes civilians and soldiers, are not in a position to make informed conscience decisions about war because they are not privy to important information about the war. The irony of this claim lies in the fact that the same leaders who make it are often the same ones who hide information from the public, spread propaganda meant to mislead the public, and deceive the public about important matters—thus ensuring an uninformed public. It is sometimes necessary for political and military leaders to contort truth in times of war, either by lying or by withholding important parts of the truth, but the moral issues remain. Contorting the truth may be the lesser of evils, but it remains an evil, and evil is more likely to beget evil than good in the end.

The objective of this chapter is to address the various ways that national leaders sometimes fail to give ordinary civilians and soldiers the information necessary to make informed moral decisions about war. Knowledge can mean power and, in the case of war, power for ordinary citizens comes from gaining as much knowledge as possible, using it as a basis for making decisions, and putting these decisions into action. To do this effectively, citizens need to learn to protect themselves from the onslaught of misinformation that may be purposely sent their way in times of war and separate truth from partial truth and partial truth from untruth. To this end, this chapter addresses war propaganda and deceit in ways that expand the principles of realistic and responsible thinking discussed in the previous chapter.

Propaganda in War

The term propaganda, as used in this chapter, refers to the communication of information in a manner that distorts reality, the purpose of which is to lead people in the direction of supporting or not supporting a war. However, especially in the early stages of planning and waging war, pro-war propaganda is much more evident than anti-war propaganda. The elements of propaganda, however, are the same in both cases. They include exaggerating or minimizing situations, disseminating false information, conveying only information that supports the desired point of view, and withholding information that fails to support it.

Pope John Paul II's message (1995) on the fiftieth anniversary of the end of World War II addressed this issue: "The perverse techniques of propaganda do not stop at falsifying reality; they also distort information about where the responsibility lies, thus making an informed moral and political judgment extremely difficult. War gives rise to a propaganda which leaves no room for different interpretations, crucial analysis of the causes of conflict and the attribution of real responsibility."

This chapter is not about supporting or not supporting war as an issue in itself. It is not anti-war but anti-propaganda. Those who sincerely believe that a pending or present war is just ought to be against pro-war propaganda as much as those who sincerely believe that the war is unjust. In other words, being dishonest about a good endeavor does not further its cause, but, in fact, often taints and sabotages it.

A Moral Enterprise

Responding to propaganda in war is a moral enterprise. It is the moral duty of each individual citizen (civilian and military) to introduce moral due diligence into the act of gathering and receiving information about war. The basic moral question is: Given the circumstances, does this information seem to be true and compelling. This question acts as a moral x-ray which helps penetrate the deceit and distractions meant to conceal the true nature of war-related issues, thus allowing individuals to advance in their attempts to make informed moral decisions. Therefore, it is important for individual citizens to have the ability to match statements encouraging support for or against war with at least four basic moral benchmarks: honesty, responsibility, accountability, and care. The following types of questions can help illuminate the moral terrain.

- Do the individuals trying to persuade us seem honest — to be telling us the whole and unvarnished truth, or do they seem to be deceptive by distorting or holding back information?
- Do they seem to be responsible — are they responsibly gathering, interpreting, and conveying information and responding openly and honestly to questions, or do they seem to be glossing over important issues and ignoring or deflecting questions?
- Do they seem willing to be professionally, legally, and morally accountable for their beliefs and actions, or will they probably exercise plausible deniability or adopt the "mistakes were made but let's not dwell on the past" mantra and quickly move on with their careers and their lives?
- Do they genuinely seem to care about our personal well-being, the nation's collective well-being, and the safety of the enemy's innocent civilians, or do they seem motivated more by personal, political, or military considerations, prestige, wealth, or advancement?

Persuasion Versus Propaganda

The distinction between persuasion and propaganda is important but not always clear. As defined here, individuals who use persuasion base their message on facts, present both sides of an issue with honesty, then argue for one side over the other by appealing to rational thinking, prudential judgment, and appropriate affect and action. For example, a teacher may state, "There is mounting evidence that second-hand smoke can cause birth defects in pregnant women. However, some researchers disagree with this claim, so we'll present their position first. Then we'd like to tell you why we believe that second-hand smoke can cause birth defects, answer your questions in a forthright way, and let you decide for yourself."

In contrast to persuasion, propaganda tampers with reality — it ignores, exaggerates, or diminishes reality in an attempt to convince an audience of a particular point of view. A teacher may tell her students: "Second-hand smoke causes [not can cause] birth defects in pregnant women — all the experts agree with this now. Even the tobacco companies agree. Have you ever seen the warnings they put on cigarette packages? Here is a picture of a baby born with a birth defect caused by her mother being exposed to second-hand smoke." This example includes several propaganda tactics. It claims certitude, exaggerates support for the claim, makes false claims, and appeals to emotion.

The Use of Propaganda

It is unlikely that any war in history, just or unjust, has been planned or waged without the support of propaganda. Citizens, especially in democratic societies, tend to be naturally reluctant to go to war unless first attacked by another nation. Therefore, war must be sold in much the same way that any product is sold. Propaganda is typically used by both sides in a war, as well as by political parties within each nation, to support or not support a war.

National leaders are generally well-versed in using propaganda because they are politicians who had to become expert at using both persuasion and propaganda to achieve their positions of power. They have been selling their ideas (for better or worse) for most of their lives and often are expert salespeople.

In war, military leaders as well as politicians often employ propaganda. Since 2003, a new concept, "information dominance," has emerged in the United States' (and the United Kingdom's) military as the public relations equivalent of "attacking with overpowering force." Information dominance centers are usually set up near or in the secure regions of enemy nations during war where embedded military and civilian personnel, including news correspondents, craft and release developing information to the world. This information serves several purposes, including communicating accurate, positive information about the progress of a war as well as denying and degrading information from any source, friend or foe, accurate or inaccurate, that threatens the complete dominance of the United States in its efforts to carry out political and military strategies as it deems fit. Regardless of the intentions of the operators of information dominance centers, knowingly disseminating false information not strictly related to national security deceives the citizens of the United States and the world and ultimately precludes them from making correctly informed moral decisions.

Propaganda can be a heredity disease, meaning that brainwashed individuals, including very intelligent and powerful ones, can transmit propaganda like parents can pass down a family illness. Unlike most propagandists who intentionally wrap war in dishonest terms, "genetic propagandists" simply do not realize they are not telling the truth. The use of war propaganda is based on several propositions:

- Citizens are not intelligent enough to make their own decisions about war, so we must help them make the right (our) choice.
- Citizens, especially civilians, cannot handle the truth about war. We have to feed them the information that will be palatable and hold back information they will find distasteful.
- Citizens today are spoiled, selfish, and apathetic, so we have to use scare tactics to force them to face reality.

- The national and international political opposition will be feeding lies to our citizens, so we must neutralize these lies with a more compelling set of lies. We must not lose the battle of the lies.
- Citizens are not inclined to support a war for any reason other than self-defense, so we must tie all our motives for going to war with self-defense, whether or not there is a relationship in reality.

Effectiveness of Propaganda

Propaganda works not so much by changing the substance of the minds of individuals but by adding directionality to the substance already present. For example, most individuals feel some sense of patriotism and want to do the right thing for their nation. Therefore, patriotism must be maintained but directed toward going to war by pro-war individuals and against going to war by anti-war individuals. No nation exhorts its citizens: "Even though you are a moral individual, you must now become immoral and join us in this unjust war." All people who go to war perceive themselves as moral, rational, prudent, courageous, patriotic, humanitarian, and heroic. The same can be said for those who do not support a war.

There are no foolproof signs that an individual is disseminating propaganda, but some possible signs include a rote manner of presenting ideas and communicating them exactly the same way in every statement with the same emotional tone in robot fashion. These individuals hear questions but do not listen to them. They simply alert to key words and play their propaganda tape, never admitting confusion, doubt, or error. They do not perceive themselves as propagandists because "propaganda" has a bad reputation, and they are not bad people; hence, they sincerely wrap themselves in the mantle of political and military educators who simply want to inform ordinary people about the truth of the situation.

Propaganda works, especially in the initial stages of war, for the following reasons:

- Citizens tend to trust their leaders in wartime — "After all, he is the president (prime minister) and has a lot more experience and information than we do."
- Citizens tend to be intellectually lazy, and applying responsible thinking to a complex issue requires motivation, time, and energy that could be better spent on more pressing or enjoyable endeavors.
- Citizens generally have little or no education, training, or role modeling in responsible thinking. They tend to believe almost everything they hear from "people who should know," based on the "What do I know?" proposition.

- Citizens want to believe the best about themselves and their nation, so they tend to reject any information that threatens that belief.

Paradoxically, having a good education may not be a prophylactic against propaganda. Noam Chomsky (1986) states:

> During the Vietnam War, the U.S. propaganda system did its job partially but not entirely. Among educated people, it worked very well. Studies show that among the more educated parts of the population, the government's propaganda about the war is now accepted unquestioningly. One reason that propaganda often works better on the educated than on the uneducated is that educated people read more, so they receive more propaganda.

Little correlation exists between education and immunity from propaganda because most education, even on the graduate level, offers little exposure to responsible (critical) thinking. Responsible thinking, as was discussed in the previous chapter, is a specific skill that requires not so much general intelligence but a specific type of intelligence, as do mechanical, artistic, scientific, and linguistic endeavors. In fact, it is more accurate to state that responsible (critical) thinking must be relearned rather than learned because most young children are natural critical thinkers ("Why?" "Who?" "How?" or "When?"). Because this type of inquisitive thinking is often seen by parents as a nuisance or as a challenge to their authority, they are inclined to discourage if not punish it ("Never mind the questions; just do it!"). Consequently, responsible thinking is generally in short supply when it is most needed.

Propaganda Techniques

Individual citizens have a moral duty to do everything within reason to gather as much accurate information as possible regarding war, so that the moral decision-making process has a sound foundation. By the same principle, national leaders have a moral obligation to transmit the most accurate information possible to their citizens, both civilian and military. Without reasonably thorough and accurate information, the decision-making process is severely compromised and, in fact, may be disabled to the degree that it is impossible to make a truly informed moral decision.

The concept of information gathering and responsible thinking denotes actively pursuing correct information, in contrast to passively accepting dubious or deceitful information. Certainly, in wartime some information must be kept secret for reasons of national security. However, there is a significant difference between national security and political security. It seems fair to state that the vast majority of government-withheld information falls into the latter category. Ironically, it often happens that national leaders unintentionally, release information that is helpful to the enemy but withhold information their citizens have a right to know. National leaders also may dispense war propaganda because they have convinced themselves that if unvarnished reality were presented to their constituents, they would respond in ways the leaders think would be detrimental to the war effort.

Propaganda strategy is always the same — to sell an idea that people would not ordinarily accept as a good one. Therefore, the idea must be clothed in falsehood to become marketable. Propaganda tactics are the means used to disseminate such information. This section addresses two general categories of propaganda techniques: avoidance tactics and tortured reasoning.

Avoidance Tactics

The following tactics are typically used by national leaders to avoid being truthful and thorough with respect to their nation's war policies and practices. Each tactic is exemplified by a scenario to demonstrate how leaders attempt to sidestep and deflect attention from the truth. Each statement is followed by an example of how individual citizens can use responsible thinking to challenge the statement and help them gather information on which to make informed decisions regarding war. Whether or not people in the news media consider themselves "ordinary citizens," this section is particularly applicable to them because they are in a position to ask the questions about matters regularly discussed in the media. Although ordinary citizens rarely can respond directly to their leader's statements, they can make their moral conclusions known to their congressional representatives by contacting them directly, writing letters to editors, contacting the media and participating in political activism.

Parsing language. A national leader reassures the audience: "I have no plans on my desk to go to war — no final decision has yet been reached." This statement is technically correct — the leader does not have actual war plans on his desk. However, in truth, plans to go to war have been discussed extensively and although a final decision to go to war has not been made, it is only a matter of hours, days, or weeks before it will be declared. The statement accomplishes its purpose — it effectively preempts any populist movement against going to war.

The follow-up to the leader's statement might be: "Has the administration discussed going to war at all and, if so, at what point are they in these discussions? Will we be kept up to date on this evolving situation?" These questions will not ensure an honest answer, but they are likely to elicit verbal and non-verbal behavior that can be assessed for its credibility.

Dodging questions. National leaders announce that a war will be declared soon to effect a regime change and free an oppressed people. Citizens may ask, "Why do you believe that simply removing a regime from power will automatically result in freedom for the oppressed people, and why the concern about these people when other, crueler regimes in other nations are oppressing a greater number of people?" The leader welcomes the question: "We believe all people should have the same freedom as we do. As Americans, we have a moral obligation to free oppressed people and, as long as we are in a position to do so, we must do it. Next question." It is clear that the speaker does not have a good answer to the question, or has an answer but does not want to give it because it will dampen the enthusiasm of the people from whom he is trying to win support.

Using "reliable sources." A defector from an enemy nation has top-secret information he wishes to give our national leaders — for a price. Even though defectors, and especially those who are selling information in times of war, are notoriously unreliable, the nation's leader announces, "We have just learned from a high-ranking reliable source that the enemy is planning to capture our soldiers and execute them." The speaker hopes citizens will be outraged at this news and strengthen their resolve to support the war. In fact, citizens would do well to ask questions regarding the credibility of the "reliable source" on which an important decision is being made:

- On what basis do you believe this source is reliable?
- Does he have a history of providing reliable information?
- Have other sources confirmed his information?
- What are his motives for defecting and offering to give up this information?

Unless the leader is willing to present the entire picture, citizens have no obligation to take the information seriously.

Denying mistakes. Leaders make mistakes, sometimes serious ones, in every war. However, they are reluctant to admit even one mistake for fear it will cause citizens to lose confidence in them. A leader, challenged about poor administrative or military decisions that have been made, replies: "Well, some mistakes were made — a few missteps. However, we learned from them and shall move on. It does no good to point fingers and dwell on the past. We have to focus now on supporting our brave troops." Citizens may ask many questions in response to this statement:

- Exactly what mistakes were made?
- Who made the mistakes, and how will those who made them be held accountable for them?

- Why were mistakes made?
- What are the effects of the mistakes?
- What exactly did you learn from the mistakes?
- How exactly will you apply these lessons in the future?

The answers to these questions will demonstrate how willing leaders are to accept accountability for their actions, including mistakes. Based on this information, citizens can decide if the nation can just "move on," or if they need to reconsider the competency and integrity of their leaders.

Assuring trustworthiness. A leader does not want to explain "every little detail" of the war to the public, so she responds: "Trust me on this — we've got it covered. We're absolutely on top of this situation, so you don't have to worry about it." The response from citizens could include, "Why should we trust you — have you given us reasons to trust you in the past?" "What exactly do you have covered, and how are you covering it?" "Why are you reluctant to keep us informed about the situation?" "Where can we get more information if you don't have the time or inclination to give it to us now?" Citizens should keep in mind that individuals with a history of being trustworthy generally do not need to admonish people to trust them — they are already trusted.

Projecting blame. This is the "they started it" justification. A nation's army has been accused of torturing prisoners — throwing them out of helicopters if they refused to give up information. The nation's leader is asked to comment on this report and responds: "Well, I haven't read the report yet, but I doubt our troops would ever do such a thing. But, if they did, the enemy has been doing much worse to our troops."

Citizens can ask:

- Why haven't you read the report since the incident happened a week ago?
- What *did* you hear about the event and, if it is true, can you help us understand what happened?"
- If you don't feel you have enough information now, can you get it and inform us as soon as you get it?
- If the enemy commits illegal and immoral acts, is our nation released from its legal and moral obligations in a just manner? In other words, is it permissible for a nation to commit war crimes as long as it commits fewer than the enemy does?

Employing metaphors. Metaphors are often used to clarify and concretize issues that arise in war. However, this can lead to several problems. Metaphors rarely fit the issue under discussion in any meaningful way, often cloud rather than clarify issues, and distract from the real issue by focusing on the legitimacy of the metaphor rather than on the legitimacy of the issue under discussion.

For example, the "domino theory" was a prime justification for going to war in Vietnam. The metaphor was based on the idea that if one standing domino falls, all the other dominos next to it will fall as well. Therefore, if Vietnam fell to the Communists, the six nations near it would also fall to Communism.

The error in using this metaphor was that the domino theory is based on a principle of physics, not on political, psychological, or moral principles. Unlike dominos, governments and their citizens have their own sets of needs, values, politics, religions, cultures, and resources that can enable them to choose their own political philosophy and the manner in which they wish to practice it. In fact, when the war was over only one of the six nations surrounding Vietnam fell to Communism. In war, metaphors are usually employed to scare citizens rather than to inform them. Citizens can respond: "If you explain the current situation clearly and fully, we will be able to understand it without the use of metaphors."

Appealing to "solid evidence." National leaders often come to the public with "solid evidence" that proves their suspicions regarding enemy activity are correct. A leader states: "We have aerial photographs that show that the enemy is receiving weapons from nations that are supposed to be neutral. This is a serious violation of international law, and we have to take military action against this nation, as well as against the enemy we are already fighting." Citizens can ask the following types of questions:

- Why would these neutral nations choose to support a nation with which we are at war?
- Is there a consensus among analysts that the photographs in fact show weapons being delivered to the enemy from neutral nations?
- Who exactly are these analysts and by whom are they employed?
- Are you in contact with the neutral nations, and, if so, what do they say and, if you are not, why not?
- Exactly what military action do you plan to take against the neutral nation?
- How will the military action affect the deployment of our troops?
- What will be the intended and unintended consequences of attacking a neutral nation?

Appealing to patriotism. This is an emotional and powerful justification for continuing a war that is going badly. After all, if a nation does not support its troops, wars cannot be won, since it is the troops who kill and die in war, not the politicians. A speaker may state, "Whatever you think about the war, we must always support our young men and women who are fighting so valiantly. We cannot abandon our troops as the nation did during the Vietnam War, an act that eventually caused us to lose the war to the Communists."

Because this is such an emotional issue, to challenge it raises even stronger emotions; however, moral principles demand that it be challenged. Morally, a distinction must be made between supporting the troops as individuals and supporting them as soldiers whose job it is to kill as many of the enemy as possible. Citizens who believe a war is unjust can support the troops as fellow citizens, loved ones, and family members, but not support them as soldiers killing and destroying in an unjust war. They can support the troops by trying to end the war, by doing what they can to ensure that soldiers receive the best medical and psychological care, and by doing everything possible to make sure that veterans receive all their benefits in a timely fashion. However, "supporting the troops" does not include continuing to send them into an unjust or no-win situation in which they risk being killed or maimed or risk killing innocent civilians.

Asserting complexity. "The situation is so complex no clear statement can be made at this time." The "fog of war" concept is sometimes used to excuse or mitigate incompetence and war crimes that deserve to be taken seriously and investigated, if for no other reason than to assign accountability and learn from mistakes. There is a valid phenomenon called "the fog of war," which is caused by difficult terrain, deafening noise, unrelenting fatigue, omnipresent fear, confusing orders, infiltration of the enemy, and so on. Mistakenly killing civilians and one's own soldiers in the chaos of combat, as tragic as it is, can be understood. Nevertheless, not every wrong deed in war can be justified by a blanket appeal to "the fog of war." It is necessary to distinguish between when the fog of war is a real phenomenon and when it reflects a smokescreen of propaganda created to hide immoral and illegal actions.

TORTURED REASONING

An important part of responsible thinking is the ability to recognize misinformation due to tortured reasoning that is found frequently in statements that appear to make sense but which, on further analysis, are clearly based on intentional or unintentional tortured reasoning or deceit. The following examples pertain to statements meant to justify going to and waging war.

Appealing to consequences. "Anyone who disagrees with us will be giving aid and comfort to the enemy and weakening the morale of our soldiers who are risking their lives for the very people questioning their dedication." This is a particularly pernicious and anti-democratic tactic that orders the principal stakeholders in war to stifle their own thoughts and feelings about the war — to avoid responsible thinking and moral decision-making and be blindly led to war. The validity of a position on war must rest on its own merits and not be artificially connected to hypothetical consequences that may or may not occur in the distant, unpredictable future.

Discounting dissenters. "It is well known that Jones is a radical socialist so we can discount anything he writes about the war." The statement can be spun in the opposite direction: "Smith is the widow of a solider who died honorably for his country, so she knows what she's talking about when she states we must finish the job before we bring the troops home." The point is not who made the statement but the reasonableness of the statement itself. Ordinarily reasonable individuals can make unreasonable statements, and ordinarily unreasonable individuals can make reasonable statements.

Misrepresenting cause and effect. "The loss of popular support for the Vietnam war caused a premature troop withdrawal and the loss of South Vietnam to the Communists." In war, as in many complex endeavors, a single event rarely causes a single effect. In fact, incompetent leadership, poor foreign policy, faulty military strategies, the poor performance of the South Vietnamese Army, and the dedication and the leadership of the North Vietnamese Army likely were the more substantive causes for the loss of the war and, in turn, were the causes and not the effects of the loss of popular support for the war.

Presenting false conclusions. "Since we are not doing as well as expected in waging this war, we're going to have to send in more troops to increase the ground forces." The difficulty is that this thinking is based on the presupposition that the one and only problem is a lack of troops rather than a lack of competent civilian oversight, ineffective military tactics, or an intractable enemy. Sending more troops may be the answer, but it also may exacerbate the problem and only increase the casualty rate if the true causes of the problem are not properly diagnosed and addressed.

Appealing to pity. "We cannot just sit by and watch while thousands of innocent people, including women and children, are tortured, starved, and slaughtered. We did that before World War II and look what happened to twelve million innocent people." This is a particularly seductive appeal, especially for nations with humanitarian values. However, the appeal to pity alone is not a valid reason to invade nations for at least two reasons. First, wars to stop the oppression of people typically kill more people than were being oppressed in the first place, which only exacerbates the humanitarian problem. Many steps are possible between passively witnessing oppression and waging an all out war to stop it. Second, unless a nation intercedes with armed aggression in *all* nations in which citizens are being oppressed, its motives are legitimately questionable.

Appealing to common sense. "It's just common sense that if we free oppressed people, they will welcome us with open arms." History demonstrates that this is not necessarily true. The process of freeing oppressed people by waging war typically includes destroying their homes, churches, hospitals, and schools as well as killing husbands, wives, children, parents, and grandparents. Many of the freed French in Normandy at the end of World War II felt hostility toward Allied forces who they believed unnecessarily bombarded their region in preparation for the D-Day landings, killing many civilians and destroying towns and farms. Many of the "liberated" residents did not greet Allied soldiers with flags or embraces but with anger and sorrow.

Appealing to emotion. "We must continue to fight this war so that our brave troops who died in it will not have died in vain." This exhortation raises some interesting and complex issues that can only be discussed in summary fashion here. Citizens can question: What defines "dying in vain" and "dying for a worthwhile cause"? Do soldiers who die for an unjust cause in a war their nation wins die in vain? Do soldiers who die in a just cause die worthwhile deaths, even if their nation loses the war? Have American soldiers ever died in vain, and, if so, when did that happen? If they have never died in vain, how is this possible? The basic point is that this issue is far too complex to use as a reason to continue a war that is floundering. If a war is just and worth fighting, this crass appeal to emotion should not be necessary.

Appealing to political, religious, moral values. "As a nation founded on democratic and Judeo-Christian values, we have a moral duty to stop oppression of innocent people wherever it exists." On its face, this appears to be an unassailable position. However, it is assailable on a number of fronts. First, it presupposes that the Judeo-Christian tradition is monolithic when, in fact, Old Testament and New Testament theologies of war and peace differ markedly, just as positions on a war can differ markedly among Christians and among Jews, so their application to freeing oppressed people also will create chaos. History demonstrates that wars do not necessarily free oppressed people but may simply replace one group of oppressors with another. Third, while there may be a universal moral duty to stop oppression, this duty ought to be measured against the overall cost in casualties on all sides, the destruction of life-sustaining resources, the over-extension of one's military, the unintended consequences for the world community, and so on.

Employing rhetorical questions. This tactic makes a statement in the form of a question not meant to be answered or challenged. For example, "What would you do if you lived in a neighborhood where all the families were killing each other? Would you hope the police came in and restored order, or would you throw out the police because you did not want them interfering with neighborhood disputes?" Although several sharp challenges could be made with respect to this statement, including whether it is based on a false forced choice, none is allowed by this hit-and-run tactic.

Arguing from half-truths. "We have the best-trained and best-equipped army and the best equipment in the world, and I can assure you, no one will beat us." The problem with this claim is that a perfect correlation does not exist between a great army and a victorious army because other important factors can be determinative. For example, civilian leadership may micromanage a war in a way that cuts the legs out from "the best army in the world." History is replete with examples of great armies losing wars, including the Roman legions that were soundly beaten by the barbarians, causing the fall of Rome.

Using euphemisms. Soft words can be used to downplay the horror of war, so that it becomes more palatable. The following are soft words and their reality translation:

- The army is making a strategic withdrawal. / The army is being beaten badly and is retreating.
- The bombing resulted in some collateral damage. / Approximately 100 innocent men, women, and children were killed and their village destroyed because of the bombing.
- The army is using enhanced interrogation techniques. / The army is using high levels of torture to extract information from prisoners.
- Three of our soldiers were killed by friendly fire. / Three of our soldiers were victims of fratricide.
- Enemy prisoners were rendered to a friendly nation for interrogation. / Enemy prisoners were sent to a nation that has no qualms about torturing and killing prisoners.

Appealing to testimonials. "Senator Smith is a highly decorated hero who earned the Bronze Star and two Purple Hearts in two wars, so if he says we are fighting the right war, that's good enough for me." This argument is unfair, especially if it uses wounded soldiers to support a war, because it dares anyone to criticize "our brave men and women who have suffered serious casualties for our nation." However, two fundamental problems exist with this thinking. First, there is manifest disagreement about the morality of any war, or at least some of its tactics, among both active duty soldiers and veterans, so the "special knowledge" of the military is not relevant to ultimate moral positions on war. Second, individuals who are or have been in the military, especially if they were wounded, may have a stake in perceiving the war in which they fought and sacrificed as a moral enterprise because to believe otherwise could be psychologically devastating. Therefore, the views of soldiers and veterans should not be automatically suspect or uncritically accepted.

Deceit in War

As Aeschylus (525 B.C.–456 B.C.) wrote: "In war, truth is the first casualty." Sound moral decision-making becomes impossible when the first element in the process (objective reality) is corrupted because it is based on deceit—the conscious distortion of information in order to mislead people. The basic premise of this section is that it is generally immoral for political and military leaders to deceive citizens at any time, but especially in times of war, when the stakes are so high and deceit precludes civilians and soldiers from making correctly informed moral decisions.

Deceit is wrong because American citizens have a moral right to know the truth regarding war, because it is their war. They own the war; they pay, sacrifice, and die for it, which gives them the moral right to the truth so they can make correctly informed moral decisions regarding what is essentially their enterprise.

Secrecy and lying are two basic elements of deceit. Secrecy, as used here, refers to political and military leaders withholding information that citizens and their Congressional representatives, as the primary stakeholders in war, have a right to know. Lying often follows secrecy and refers to leaders making misleading statements to their citizens regarding war.

It is important to distinguish between legitimate and illegitimate deceit. Legitimate deceit in war is generally permitted when it does not breach domestic, international, or moral law and is used solely to maintain the secrecy necessary to carry out legitimate military and paramilitary operations against an enemy. Illegitimate deceit occurs when leaders deceive their own citizens in order to cover up illegal or immoral policies and actions. With this distinction in mind, secret, covert and clandestine operations may be legal or illegal, moral or immoral, depending on who is being deceived and for what reasons.

The United States Senate Select Committee to Study Governmental Operations with Respect to Intelligence Activities (1975–1976), commonly referred to as the Church Committee, held hearings that probed widespread intelligence abuses. In a final report, the committee distinguishes between legitimate and illegitimate deceit:

> Secrecy is essential to covert operations; secrecy can, however, become a source of power, a barrier to serious policy debate within the government, and a means of

circumventing the established checks and procedures of government, The Committee found that secrecy and compartmentation contributed to a temptation on the part of the Executive to result to covert operations in order to avoid bureaucratic, congressional, and public debate.

Whether leaders of other nations use deceit to mislead their citizens more than U.S. leaders deceive their citizens is irrelevant. The moral weight of deceit does not increase or decrease based on the amount of deceit leaders of other nations disseminate. Citizens tend to believe the best of themselves and their leaders and that their leaders (unlike enemy leaders) could never deceive them or act in evil ways. This attitude is seen in what seems to have become mantras in American wars: "If the president says it's legal, it's legal," "American soldiers could not have committed war crimes because Americans don't act that way," and "America is a nation of laws, so it would never break any laws." Even when incontrovertible evidence exists that political leaders, soldiers, or military officers are acting, or have acted, in deceitful ways, it is typically excused as a mistake, a misunderstanding, a miscalculation, a misstep, a poor decision, an anomaly, or an excusable symptom of stress.

Certainly, mistakes, misunderstandings, and poor communication occur, but when they result in evil effects and are repeated time and again by the same people, it is no longer an unfortunate happenstance but willful deceit and a perpetuation of evil. Analogously, due to a misplaced sense of loyalty, parents may excuse their teenagers' continuing delinquent behavior on the basis that their children are simply making some bad decisions. Because of this denial of reality, these teenagers are never held accountable for the destructive behaviors that continue unabated. Similarly, civilians and soldiers who, out of a misplaced sense of patriotism, are incapable of admitting their leaders or soldiers have acted in evil ways do no favor to their leaders or their nation.

The irony of deceit is that politics and wars based on lies generally fail because, like a faulty compass, they lead the nation's civilians and soldiers in the wrong direction, one where optimism camouflages reality until reality springs the ambush. Once the lies begin, more lies must be told to cover up the original ones. In a short period, the lies are woven into the fabric of the war, so that they are even believed by the individuals telling them. This situation enables the deceivers to stare into television cameras with unblinking eyes and assure civilians and soldiers that a war is necessary and is progressing nicely, despite what the "biased media" reports.

One of many examples of both political and military leaders being deceitful with each other and the world at large occurred during the Vietnam War with regard to the invasion and secret bombing of Cambodia. The purpose of the invasion and bombings was to rid Cambodia of North Vietnamese and

Viet Cong soldiers who were fighting for communism in North Vietnam. The bombings were kept secret because the U.S. political and military believed the people of the United States would not support widening the war from Vietnam to its neighboring nations.

These secrets could not have been maintained without the cooperation of the media. The Vietnam War was the first war in which members of the media were embedded with the troops, and many were firsthand observers of the invasion and bombing of Cambodia. Moreover, television was readily available. In fact, the war was often referred to as the "living room war" because families often watched footage of ongoing battles at home.

Not only were the bombings in Cambodia held secret from the American people, their existence was also kept secret from senior government officials, including the secretary of the Air Force, the Air Force chief of staff, and the Office of Strategic Research and Analysis, as well as members of congressional committees charged with recommending appropriations for authorizing and funding war. Only a few sympathetic members of Congress, who had no constitutional authority to approve this extension of war, were quietly informed. The bombings in Cambodia were kept secret for so long that when Congress finally officially learned about them, the damage had been done, and it was too late for any serious discussion or debate, which was the sole reason for the deceit in the first place.

Consequences of Deceit

Deceit leads to several enduring destructive consequences and becomes not an aberration but a ritualized part of war. The moral norm applied seems to be purely pragmatic — if the deceit works to diminish the enemy, it is morally good. In other words, there is nothing wrong with deceiving the American people; it is only wrong if it backfires and the American people (and international community) find out about it.

Deceit rarely accomplishes its desired goals. For example, in the Vietnam War, deceit continually backfired, placing the United States in a politically, militarily, and morally humiliating position. Deceit also turned our supporters in Cambodia into enemies. Finally, the deceit turned the American people's already tepid support of the war into active rebellion against both the war and its political and military sponsors.

Deceit in war places individuals who are privy to the secret operations but have strong moral reservations about them in an impossible situation. If they continue to participate in the illegal or immoral operations, they will feel increasing pangs of conscience. If they bring their concerns to their superiors, they risk censure, if not separation from their careers.

Deceit also leads many civilians and soldiers to replace their loss of faith in the nation's political and military leaders with cynicism, which can be as dangerous to a nation's survival as romanticism and idealism. The term "Vietnam Syndrome" was coined to describe the reluctance of the American people to venture into wars that are not directly related to national self-defense. If Americans lose faith in their leaders, they will not respond to their leaders' call for support even when it is legitimately needed.

By definition, deceit in war precludes the people from making correctly informed conscience decisions about war. Perhaps even worse, the people may make incorrectly formed conscience decisions that may lead to support of what are, in reality, illegal or immoral actions.

Kim Willenson (1987) makes it clear that after all the political and military obfuscation is pierced by truth-seeking analysis, only one true reason exists for most deceit in war:

> Over the years, American secret wars have seldom met their objectives, and there has been a tendency to cope with failure either by making them bigger or by pursuing desperate schemes to try to multiply the leverage of inadequate forces. On both accounts, many of the secret wars have become political embarrassments. In that sense, secret warfare contradicts another dictum from the pen of Clausewitz — that "War is a mere continuation of politics by other means." In Vietnam, secrecy was often used to conceal large-scale warfare not from the enemy but from Americans who might have opposed it [p. 202].

What Can Leaders and Citizens Do?

National leaders, ordinary civilians and soldiers need to be realistic and secure enough to understand that their nation, despite all its political, military and religious virtues and values, is capable of intentionally misleading its citizens in many situations but especially in times of war. National propaganda and deceit are always "well intentioned" but never morally justified, except in cases of true national security. Moreover, political secrets, like family secrets, generally come to light, sooner or later, and call forth profound distrust of the political and military establishment, resulting in pernicious effects that can last for decades.

Massive operations such as the invasion and bombing of Cambodia could not be kept secret in today's world of instant reporting due to satellite transmission and the internet. In addition, secrecy and deceit are not wrong in themselves. At times, even in a just war, it is legally and morally acceptable for political and military leaders to withhold the truth with respect to certain operations from both the enemy and the citizens of the nation. However, whenever secrecy and deceit are used to coverup illegal or immoral activities, they are inimical to the idea of waging a just war.

With this thought in mind, it may be helpful to reflect on how the concepts addressed in this chapter can be brought to the practical plain in a manner that both ordinary citizens and leaders can use to monitor propaganda and deceit. The following section addresses two topics: a code of ethics for national leaders and a responsible thinking format for ordinary citizens.

A Code of Ethics for Leaders

Questions arise as to how seriously political and military leaders take their professional codes of ethics with regard to applying them to telling the truth to the American people. Is information sharing exempt from existing codes of ethics such as honor, duty, truth, integrity, and respect? Is it "a free fire zone" in which it is permissible to "fire at will"—to tell the American people whatever is necessary to further the personal agendas of the leaders? This issue is critically important because the words of political and military leaders can be the direct cause of saving or losing the lives of thousands of soldiers and civilians.

A code of ethics tailored to the dissemination of information regarding war may be helpful. The following points provide an example of such a code.

1. Information ought to be based on objective reality, not on a reality that has been altered to bolster support for or against a war.

2. When the reality at issue is uncertain or continually changing, this caveat ought to be included in all statements.

3. Statements representing the reality should be ideologically pure and not contaminated by tortured reasoning and deceit.

4. Adequate opportunities ought to be provided to question and challenge statements, and all questioners and responders should be treated with respect.

5. Statements that are later shown to be incorrect or no longer correct ought to be corrected and made known to the same audience that received the original information.

6. After an accurate presentation of the reality, it is permissible to try to persuade an audience to think, feel, and act the way the communicator believes would be appropriate under the circumstances.

7. There is only one legitimate purpose for sharing war information with civilians and soldiers—to inform them. It is not to indoctrinate them.

8. Violators of this code should be held accountable for their actions and sanctioned accordingly.

The purpose of this code is positive: To give accurate and truthful information to the most important stakeholders in any war — the nation's citizens, so that they can make well-informed moral decisions to support or not support a war. This concept may not rest well with war salespeople who like selling wars and are good at it. They are likely to perceive any moral code as distressingly naïve and "tying our hands behind our backs." Despite the short-term gains a sales strategy regarding war may provide, its long-term effects may cause serious problems for the nation. When civilians and the military come to realize that they have been "spun" about a war, they will mistrust leaders who tried to sell it and will refuse to support the war, even if it is just, a position that can have disastrous results for the nation in the present and future.

Responsible Thinking Format for Responsible Citizens

It may be helpful to imagine how the incidents discussed in this chapter can help civilians and soldiers ask the right questions of their political and military leaders, if incidents similar to the invasion and bombing of Cambodia were being planned, initiated, or in progress today. While Chapter 5 discusses responsible thinking in general terms, it is of particular importance when it becomes clear that national leaders are contemplating going to war in the near future.

Responsible thinking requires that citizens, both civilian and military, ask pertinent questions when given information regarding war, regardless of the source. These questions can be asked by contacting congressional representatives, joining action groups, or contacting the media, for instance by writing letters to newspaper editors. The following are some of the important questions citizens can ask when leaders try to "sell" going to war:

1. Why exactly do you want us to go to war?
2. Are you going to Congress to ask for a formal declaration of war or, if not, why not?
3. Will the war be legal or illegal by domestic and international standards?
4. How much will the war cost?
5. Where will the money come from and what domestic services will suffer due to the cost of the war?
6. How many military and civilian casualties on both sides can be reasonably expected?
7. How many troops will be deployed on what rotation system and where will these troops come from?

8. How long is the war expected to last?

9. What measures will you employ to protect the lives and property of civilians?

10. Assuming that no war goes exactly as planned, what are some things that could go wrong and what are your contingency plans with respect to those eventualities?

11. What eventually could occur during the war that would cause you to consider terminating it before the long-range goals are met?

12. What measurable outcomes will indicate that the war has been a success?

13. How exactly will you assure us that we will receive the unvarnished truth every step of the way, so we can keep our finger on the political, military, and moral pulse of the war on a day-to-day basis?

14. What concrete plans have you made to restore stability to the defeated nation once the war is over, and what will this require in terms of troop deployment and cost to the nation?

The thought of these questions being asked will elicit a predictable response in certain political and military circles: "War is not like putting on a play where the writers are pretty sure about how and when it will start and end and what the production will cost." This statement is true, but it is equally true that if the planners and managers of a war have few or no answers to these questions, citizens, both civilian and military, have the right to withhold judgment and support until some reality-based answers are presented.

Obviously, there are no foolproof questions to ask. There is no way to prevent political and military leaders from committing the sins of commission and omission described throughout this chapter. However, a combination of piercing questions and relentless follow-up questions can create a framework in which equivocation, obfuscation, and deceit are easier to detect.

Only a few political and military leaders are privy to the daily realities of war and, for better and for worse, they are the sole purveyors of information to the nation and the world. These leaders have two choices: to disseminate truthfully what they learn each day to the public, which is paying for the war in lives and resources, or to present pictures of it that are made more acceptable by tinting, enlarging, reducing and cropping them to meet the leaders' needs.

Leaders cannot realistically expect civilians and soldiers to support a war based solely on a combination of blind trust and automatic obedience. Citizens can learn how to recognize and react to the avoidance tactics, tortured reasoning, and deceit that may be used by political and military leaders to garner support for or against a war. This knowledge will empower citizens to triage information into various categories: true, likely to be true, equivocal, likely to be false, false, or not sufficient detail to make a judgment. Leaders will then be more likely to disseminate truthful information in a forthright manner. As a result, both citizens and leaders will be empowered to work together regarding the moral decisions that confront them on important issues, not the least of which is the declaring and waging of war.

Oliver O'Donovan (2003) describes the effects of moral deliberation by individual citizens making individual conscience decisions:

> A deliberating public would move forward with its military and political representatives from situation to situation, treating each next decision as different from the last one, listening to reasons with an open mind and asking demanding questions about the explanations offered, bearing in mind that there is much it cannot know, but also that there is much *they* [the leaders] cannot know either.... A deliberating public would elicit a more conscientious performance from its representatives, political and military. And a deliberating public would observe much more sharply if the point were reached at which those representatives stepped outside the praxis of judgment and reverted to the lawless extravagances of antagonistic confrontation [p. 17–18].

Individual civilians and soldiers have a moral obligation to make informed decisions regarding war if for no other reason than wars are fought in their name. This moral obligation, in turn, bestows on individual citizens the right to demand and receive all the information necessary to make informed decisions, short of any information that would compromise the security of the nation. When citizens fail to demand this information out of ignorance, laziness, disinterest, or naïveté, as harsh as it sounds, they deserve the wars in which their leaders enmesh them, even if the civilians in enemy nations do not.

There are many ways citizens can cut through the propaganda and deceit that nations, political parties, and the military may employ to circumvent telling the truth to the people who most deserve it. Without accurate information, civilians and soldiers are intellectually unable to make correctly informed moral decisions about war. This leaves them only two options — to make erroneously informed moral decisions about war or no decisions at all, both of which are untenable in a democratic society and detrimental to the nation in times of peace or war.

7

Morality and War: Theoretical Issues

Men who take up arms against one another in public war do not cease on this account to be moral beings, responsible to one another and to God.
— Francis Lieber

All theories have practical consequences and, in war, the consequences of moral, political, and military theories can be serious and often irrevocable. It is ordinarily not helpful to focus solely on practical realities and ignore how those realities come into being in the first place. Simply considering acts of war disconnected from the theories on which they are predicated is not likely to lead to sound decisions regarding the continuance or the discontinuance of those acts. For example, the domino theory constituted a basic reason for going to war against North Vietnam and was espoused by national leaders up to and including the three presidents that sent advisors and troops to Vietnam. This theory held that, like standing dominos, if Vietnam fell to the communists all neighboring nations would fall to communism as well.

Unfortunately, as has been previously noted, this theory was flawed on a number of counts. If the domino theory had been objectively analyzed historically, geopolitically, legally, and morally, it is unlikely that it would have been used to justify going to war in Vietnam.

It is important for citizens, both civilian and military, to have at least a basic understanding of some theoretical principles regarding war so that they can include them in the objective and subjective dimensions that comprise the moral decision-making process discussed in Chapter 1. Many theoretical issues exist regarding justice and war, but the following are particularly relevant to morality and modern warfare: the principle of military necessity, the principle of double effect, and the principles of preemptive and preventive war. Each topic is discussed in terms of its nature and its moral implications for citizens and soldiers seeking to make moral decisions regarding war.

The Principle of Military Necessity

Originally, the majority of international laws were absolute and admitted of no exceptions. The principle of military necessity was introduced to provide exceptions to some of these laws in cases in which an army was unlikely to bring about a successful resolution to an operation unless exceptions to some of the laws were made.

The U.S. Department of Defense (2001) defines military necessity as "The principle whereby a belligerent has the right to apply any measures which are required to bring about the successful conclusion of a military operation and which are not forbidden by the laws of war." In other words, some of these laws, for example rape, remain absolute, while others have exception clauses written into them. As can be seen, no formal guidelines are presented as to what military operations qualify for an exception, which leaves a wide expanse for situational interpretations. Moreover, no distinction is made between just and unjust belligerents, meaning that unjust nations can legally attack just nations in a manner ordinarily prohibited by the laws of war. Therefore, in the case of military necessity exceptions, the only restraint on the method of attack is not found in international law but in a common principle of war, namely the principle of proportionality. Analogously, in order to effect an arrest, police officers are permitted to use force beyond that which can be used by ordinary citizens; but if police officers use disproportionate force, they would be acting unlawfully. Because of the importance of viewing the principle of military necessity from this perspective, three related topics will be discussed: the need for balance, problems with the way in which the laws of war are written, and the principles that allow invoking military necessity.

THE NEED FOR BALANCE

The principle of military necessity requires a balance between the need to win a war with the need to treat civilians in a humane manner. Depending on how the laws of war are written and interpreted, the result may be an equal balance between military necessity and humanitarian values, or the scales may be tipped in one direction or the other. If the situation is viewed as allowing an exception to the laws of war because of dire military necessity, entire cities could be obliterated, as occurred in wars in which carpet bombing was justified. On the other hand, wars fought for the survival of a nation could be lost because of the reluctance to wage all-out war based on humanitarian considerations. Both situations raise serious moral issues.

Jonathan Gibbs (1997) describes the problem:

> Nowhere is the conflict of interest between modern just war theory and modern warfare seen more clearly than in the uneasy relationship between the *jus in bello* criteria of proportionality and discrimination and the realist principle of military necessity. Such conflict would seem to be axiomatic, given the seemingly contrary nature of these two principles.
>
> The former seek to place limits and moral boundaries upon the means to the just ends of war, the latter, when taken as a justification for a policy of politico-military realism, seeks to override these limitations on the basis of the utilitarian axiom that the ends of war justify the necessary means [p. 63–64].

PROBLEMS WITH THE LAWS

Two basic issues can be found in the laws of war, the growth of exceptions and the inherent ambiguity in the laws.

Exceptions. Over the course of history, the laws of war have increased exponentially to keep abreast of the continuous development of more "effective" weapons. During this time, the built-in exceptions to the rules based on military necessity also have expanded. For example, the Rome Statute of the International Criminal Court (1998) includes the following laws (which are paraphrased for the sake of clarity) that admit exceptions for military necessity:

- There shall be no destruction of private property owned by civilians, except...
- There shall be no wanton destruction of cities, towns, villages, except...
- There shall be no forced displacement of civilians, except...
- There shall be no pillaging of property owned by civilians for private or personal use, except...

Given the many exceptions based on military necessity, the laws of war often create more moral and legal confusion than guidance for the treatment of civilians in times of war.

Ambiguity. Many of the laws regarding military necessity are purposefully ambiguous in order to provide latitude for interpretation in specific circumstances. However, the latitude is often so wide that it can diminish the basic intent of the laws. For example, Protocol I (Addition to the Geneva Conventions of August 1949) addresses the protections that should be provided to civilians during war. In paraphrased form, the following statements are made:

- No methods or weapons of attack should be used that cause unnecessary injury or suffering to civilians or combatants.
- Civilians shall not be the object of attack or threats of violence the primary purpose of which are to spread terror among the civilian population.

The statements are ambiguous in that they do not define "unnecessary injury or suffering," and do not indicate if the spread of terror is allowed as a secondary purpose for attacks or threats.

Invoking Military Necessity

While no international laws state when military necessity may be invoked, the general understanding is that it may not be invoked simply because a commander needs the support it provides in a battle. The following are some criteria that ought to be met.

• The military necessity must be highly compelling and not simply a matter of expediency. However, there is disagreement regarding the definition of compelling, such as whether military necessity can be invoked in any battle, or only in a critically important battle, or only in an existential attack that threatens the very existence of the nation.

• The threat must be solely military and not political, moral, or economic. The difficulty arises in determining how clear distinctions can be made between these often interrelated threats.

• No other reasonable military or political alternative to resolving the military threat is possible other than to invoke military necessity and allow an exception to some rules of law. This raises the question: What military and political alternatives were seriously considered before invoking military necessity as a last resort?

• The human and material destructiveness of the necessary military response must be proportionate to the good that is reasonably expected to result from the action. Concerns arise on this issue regarding how the amount of destructiveness will be measured and on what reliable basis the prediction will be made.

• The decision to invoke military necessity must be made by a military authority that understands the principle of military necessity and assumes personal and professional responsibility for the consequences. The problem with meeting this criterion is deciding who qualifies as a "military authority"—the platoon leader facing attack, the commander on the scene or a higher-ranking officer at a command center.

• Under no circumstances does military necessity allow the commission of flagrant war crimes, such as rape, forced labor, biological warfare, poisoning food and water, mutilation or maiming, beating, starving, kidnapping, killing hostages, withholding food and medicine, murder (intentional killing of innocents), massacre, mistreatment of prisoners, looting for personal gain, gratuitous physical and psychological abuse, sexual enslavement, taking hostages, or intentionally attacking civilians.

Moral concerns regarding the principle of military necessity are not limited to civilian moralists but shared by military leaders as well. U.S. Air Force Lt. Col. Kenneth R. Rizer (2001) states his position on the matter.

> "Military necessity" is the principle which justifies measures of regulated force not forbidden by international law which are indispensable for securing the prompt submission of the enemy, with the least possible expenditures of economic and human resources. In simpler terms, military necessity means that if one is justified in going to war, one is justified in doing what is necessary to win. The problem with military necessity is that without another legal principle to balance against it, it essentially allows blanket justification for violations provided a case could be made that the action taken was necessary to win. Even if a particular action is not justified by military necessity, it still must be wanton, or maliciously cruel, to be a violation. Clearing the hurdles of military necessity and wantonness is difficult, making actual prosecution for unlawful bombing unlikely. One could retroactively argue, for example, that the Tokyo firebombing was justified under the Geneva Conventions because of military necessity: it was the only effective way to destroy Japanese industry and win the war. In other words, the very sort of attacks that the Geneva Conventions attempted to prohibit might still be legal under the principle of military necessity.

Because the principle of military necessity is likely to be invoked in all wars and perhaps even be expanded as terroristic attacks and wars increase, civilians and soldiers need to possess at least a rudimentary understanding of the principle in order to become more conscious of their responsibility to judge war-related issues in the light of moral principles.

The Principle of Double Effect

The principle of double effect was introduced by Thomas Aquinas in the 13th century. It was meant to resolve moral dilemmas in which a single act produces both a moral good (just) effect and a moral evil (unjust) effect; hence the term "double effect." Today, different versions of the principle exist, which is common for most theories, especially one that has spanned over seven centuries. The version discussed here is generally representative of those distilled over the years.

The following are four elements of the principle of double effect:

1. The single act, itself, must be morally good or at least morally indifferent (neutral). Soldiers fighting for a just cause plan to liberate ten of their fellow soldiers from an enemy prison camp, which is a morally good act.

2. The individual performing the act must intend only the good effects of the act and not intend the evil side effects, even though they may be foreseen

as likely to occur. Soldiers know that a few noncombatants may be near the prison camp and may be killed if a firefight breaks out as the soldiers approach the camp. In this case, the good effect (freeing 10 soldiers) morally outweighs the incidental evil effect of killing four noncombatants.

3. The individuals performing the act must not use the evil effect directly or indirectly as a means of achieving the desired good effects. The soldiers may not intentionally kill the noncombatants as a direct means of frightening the enemy soldiers into abandoning the prisoners and must make every reasonable effort to protect the noncombatants.

4. The degree of good that derives from the act is commensurate or greater than the degree of evil that derives from the act. The moral good of rescuing the ten prisoners is proportionately greater than the moral evil of incidentally killing four noncombatants.

However, what appears rather simple and clear in these examples can, in practical situations, rapidly become quite complex. According to Aquinas, intention is what drives the principle of double effect. In the rational psychology of his time, intention was an all-or-nothing phenomenon. An individual either intended or did not intend an act. Since then, advances in the fields of law and psychology have added many nuances to the linear "all or nothing" understanding of intention. The law distinguishes between direct and oblique intention, true ignorance and willful blindness, and due diligence and recklessness. These contrasting mental states both clarify and complicate an enlightened understanding of intention. The following discussion addresses the contributions of psychology to the understanding of intention.

INTENTION AND PSYCHOLOGY

The traditional and current understanding of intention as it is often used in the moral literature presupposes two propositions: all intention is conscious, and all intention is a function of the intellect. Modern psychology has long demonstrated that both these presuppositions are mistaken.

Intentions can be conscious, subconscious, or unconscious. Individuals can think they are acting for only one (good) reason but, in fact, may be acting for one or more bad (evil) reasons. Both the individual intentions of national leaders and the collective intentions of a nation can be consciously perceived by their owners as good but, in fact, be evil on deeper levels of self-awareness. For example, a nation's leaders may consciously believe they are going to war for only one (good) reason — to spread democracy. However, their actions belie the accuracy of this perception when their nation undercuts democratic activities initiated by the defeated nation that would weaken the power of the victorious nation. If the only intention underwriting the war was to spread democracy, but the victorious nation does not allow democracy to develop, what other less conscious and perhaps less moral intention can legitimately be considered?

A second psychological factor with regard to the concept of intention is described by G.E.M. Anscombe (1961), who addresses how easy it is to abuse the principle of double effect because intention is extremely vulnerable to tinkering — to talking oneself and others into the belief that one's intentions are pure.

> At the same time, the principle [of double effect] has been repeatedly abused from the seventeenth century up till now. The causes lie in the history of philosophy. From the seventeenth century till now what may be called Cartesian psychology has dominated the thought of philosophers and theologians. According to this psychology, an intention was an interior act of the mind which could be produced at will. Now if intention is at all important — as it is — in determining the goodness or badness of an action, then, on this theory of what intention is, a marvelous way offered itself of making any action lawful. You only had to "direct your intention" in a suitable way. In practice, this means making a little speech to yourself: "What I mean to be doing is..." [p. 56].

It is likely true that no individual or group of individuals who ever intentionally massacred noncombatants had conscious evil intentions or told themselves and others: "What we plan to do — or are doing — is intrinsically and extrinsically profoundly evil, but we must do it to do it anyway in order to meet our evil objectives."

In the everyday world, intentions are rarely one-dimensional, as in the claim that the reason people get married is that they deeply love each other. This statement represents the "just cause" not only for getting married but also for marrying a particular individual. But individuals also can marry because they are lonely, lack a purpose in life, want to escape a bad family situation, are bored, need to feel loved, want guilt-free sex, want to have children, and need to be taken care of. While these intentions sound positive or at least benign at first glance, on closer examination, each less than completely conscious intention could be problematic and may be a good reason for not getting married. In other words, what appears at first to be "just cause" for getting married based on a single intention can collapse under the weight of critical thinking that illuminates other less altruistic intentions which likely will lead to bad (evil) effects as the marriage progresses.

The same is true when considering intentions for nations going to war, which are typically layered and multidimensional. The top layer — the declared intention — is usually the same — self-defense or the defense of humanitarian virtues. The lower, less conscious layers consist of external and internal intentions. External intentions may be to acquire natural resources, territory, power, or ideological control, or to punish a nation for its past practices and contemptuous attitudes. Internal intentions may include the nation's need to feed the military-industrial complex, deflect attention from domestic problems, retain domestic political power, bolster a flagging economy or increase patriotic fervor. As in the marriage analogy, each less than conscious intention could be problematic and eviscerate just cause, depending on the circumstances.

A second way that modern psychology's understanding of intention differs from the scholastic, pre-enlightened understanding is that intention is not solely an act of the intellect but has a strong affective (emotional) component. Keeping with the analogy of marriage, the affective component projects the cognitive (intellectual) thought ("I'd like to get married") into action: "I'm so in love — I am going to get married as soon as possible." The same is true for deciding to go to war. Nations do not go to war solely because they simply think it is necessary but because they also feel it is necessary. Thinking without feeling is unlikely to lead to marriage or war.

This concept of intention is important for both theoretical and practical reasons. Kimberly Kessler Ferzan (2007) applies the concept of intention to the law and holding defendants responsible for their crimes: "Some theorists argue that intentions simply mask political judgments. We now see why this appears to be so. If we can simply jump back and forth between the narrow view of intention as motivational significance and the broader holistic view, then judges and juries are not bound by rules, but by other inappropriate value judgments" (p. 1188).

To put it simply, when the declared cause for attacking a nation is to "spread democracy," this only starts a discussion as to the justice of the cause; it does not end it. When this occurs, how do "the judges and juries"— the citizens of the nation — know what other layers of intention and affect are operative, perhaps in a way that eviscerates just cause? Ferzan continues:

> My argument is that intentions cannot be relied upon to distinguish reasons from side effects because intentions are broader than previously assumed. If intentions are not what we presuppose them to be, we must question whether we can still rely on them to set normative boundaries.... We have been led astray by viewing intentions as one-dimensional, ignoring the robust nature of our thought.... Because intentions are broader than motivational significance, they are not the windows to human agency [p. 1189, 1190].

Several important conclusions can be drawn from this discussion of the psychological aspects of the concept of intention as it relates to the principle of double effect. Those most relevant to war are:

- Intentions come in layers, and all layers must be ferreted out by citizens, the media, and national leaders, so that the operative intentions, both pure and impure, are known by all stakeholders, and decisions can be made on that basis.
- Less than conscious intentions are likely to be nefarious or they would be completely conscious, declared as such, and used to bolster the argument for going to war or embarking on some other war-related action.
- Emotions play a critical factor in decisions regarding going to war because they are the booster rockets that propel intention into action. When just intention is declared, its justice should evoke a sufficient degree of appropriate emotion to launch a just war. Emotions that must be artificially created and stoked suggest that the conscious, declared intentions are not sufficiently strong to evoke emotions that will generate action by the stakeholders.

As this section demonstrates, the concept of intention is more complicated than is generally believed. When the legal elements of intention are coupled with its psychological aspects, it becomes clear that intention as a critical element in the principle of double effect requires more examination than it is generally afforded.

Challenges to the Principle of Double Effect

The principle of double effect is challenged with regard to two basic issues: Is the principle itself cogent, and if it is, is it being applied consistently across situations? The following challenges have arisen over the years, some of which support the principle of double effect but counsel caution in its use, while others hold that the principle lacks integrity. These concerns are phrased in a manner that reflects the differing viewpoints.

1. The principle of double effect cannot be rightly applied in any or all military interventions, wars, and economic sanctions. This view holds that the principle of double effect may only be applied by just nations acting on behalf of just causes and employing just tactics. Analogously, bank robbers who lack both just cause and just tactics may not rightly appeal to the principle of double effect to justify their actions ("We had to kill the security guard to avoid having to kill the tellers and customers who might otherwise try to interfere with our reaching our objective. In fact, we actually saved lives by killing the security guard.") Before the principle of double effect may rightly be applied to practical situations such as war, just war principles or some other principles of justice ought to be clearly established and reestablished throughout military and political actions.

2. Any theory of morality that is so controversial, even among noted ethicists, philosophers, and theologians, ought not to be applied in practical life and death situations. While continuing the debate is important in the halls of academe, the principle of double effect is not ready to be applied in cases of war and war-related issues, such as economic sanctions and the treatment of prisoners.

Mitchell R. Thomas (2005) discusses the problems with applying the principle of double effect to real life situations. He distinguishes between using the principle of double effect as an instrument that generates debate and aims to explain behavior, in contrast to using it as a finely tuned instrument to justify behavior. Thomas and those he references are concerned that employing the principle in practice is what has caused it to devolve from "double effect" into "double think" and "double speak." He writes:

> All the theorizing that is done works well when it is applied in a controlled intellectual exercise, away from the grittiness of the real world. However, once any theoretical model is applied in practical situations, problems will arise. I don't think that this militates against theorizing and theory in general, but we must be careful not to get so caught up in the theory that we forget what is at stake: being able to meet real practical situations that call for a practical moral response [p. 20].

When a very complicated principle (double effect) is applied to a very complicated endeavor (war), it is difficult to attain that a successful resolution to these very complex problems.

3. Good intentions as they relate to the principle of double effect cannot simply be "good"; they must be reasonably informed, as well. Good intentions often are based more on a "hope and a prayer" than on sound reality. Truly good intentions are based as much as possible on good intelligence, foresight, robust debate, and empirical objectivity. Perhaps the most common symptom of "good intentions" are negative unintended consequences, many or all of which would have been predicted had good intentions not induced a state of impaired consciousness and decision-making.

4. What exactly are good intentions? The argument can be made that they are largely offered as a mitigating factor for making bad decisions. When decisions turn out well, people do not claim, "Well, at least my intentions were good." Simply claiming that the deaths of twenty noncombatants caused by bombing a target in a populated area were "unintended" is not sufficient to justify these deaths. The claim of "unintentional killing of noncombatants" is likely to be legitimate in a case in which just aggressors who bomb a factory are unaware that noncombatants are hiding in it. However, if the just aggressors know that noncombatants are residing in the factory but think bombing

it is the only way to neutralize the enemy threat, the situation raises questions regarding the validity of the "unintentionality" claim. Legitimate mitigating claims might be made to justify the bombing, but making the claim that the civilian deaths were spawned from good intentions would not be one of them.

5. The principle of double effect is likely to be used in a way that gives more moral worth to the soldiers of one's nation than to the noncombatants of the enemy nation. This result violates the moral (and theological) proposition that all human life has equal worth. When calculating cost-benefit ratios, which are an inherent part of double effect calculations, the implicit if not explicit assumption is that a rank order exists relative to the moral importance of human beings in wartime. In order of descending "moral worth" are the citizens of the just nation, the soldiers of the just nation, the citizens of the enemy nation, and the soldiers of the enemy nation. Therefore, in cost-benefit analyses each group is given a different weight. For example, in order to complete an important mission successfully, the situation may arise in which either ten soldiers of the just nation or twenty noncombatants of the enemy nation are likely to be killed. The commander employing the principle of double effect is unlikely to allow ten of his soldiers to be killed rather than allow twenty noncombatants to be killed. In this situation, an appeal could be made to the principle of partialism (It is morally acceptable to protect "our people" more than "their people.") However, the question remains: At what point does the ratio between the deaths of "our soldiers" and the deaths of "their noncombatants" reach a disproportionate ratio that challenges the principles of justice?

While ordinary civilians and soldiers, by definition, may never directly apply the principle of double effect in war decisions, they are in a position during times of war to gather information regarding evolving events and the decisions political and military leaders are making in reaction to those events. Although the concept of double effect is rarely mentioned outside of the seminar rooms of political and military ethicists, it is applied in war whenever the question arises: "The good we are trying to do will likely include some negative consequences. How do we deal with that problem?" Therefore, ordinary citizens can become familiar with the principle of double effect, judge whether it is a sound principle, and, if it is, determine whether it is being applied appropriately or inappropriately.

Principles of Preemptive and Preventive Force

In modern warfare, launching preemptive or preventive force against nations perceived as threats is one of the more controversial issues. Since the 9/11 attacks on the United States, these two concepts have entered the common parlance of political, military, legal, and moral discussions and debates. These concepts are not new — they have been developed and discussed for centuries. They reemerge now because more nations have developed weapons of mass destruction and are willing to use them as a first-strike attack. Therefore, this topic is of the utmost importance. Colin S. Gray (2007) states:

> Far from providing mere footnotes to history, those who have spoken and debated about preemption and prevention have sought to address matters of the gravest significance. There is not much that can compete in importance with decisions for war or peace.... The policy and strategic issues of preemption and prevention are here to stay, whether Americans like it or not.... Clear yet sophisticated thinking on preemption and prevention, or the reverse, can have the profoundest significance for international order and American security [p. 4, 5].

The following sections attempt to clarify these concepts and their relationship to just war principles.

Preemptive Force

The U.S. Department of Defense defines preemptive attack as one "initiated on the basis of incontrovertible evidence that an attack is imminent." The international legal standard for what constitutes an imminent attack is that the threat is "instant, overwhelming, leaving no choice of means and no moment for deliberation."

The Department of Defense definition clearly states that incontrovertible evidence ought to exist and that an attack ought to be imminent. This is official U.S. policy. "Incontrovertible" means not legitimately open to question or doubt because the evidence is so clearly compelling. This standard of proof is comparable to the legal standard of proof in U.S. criminal law — a jury must possess certainty beyond a reasonable doubt and to a moral certitude that the evidence indicates the defendants committed the crime of which they are accused. This standard is higher than the standards of proof in civil cases. In some civil courts, clear and convincing evidence is necessary to conclude responsibility for an act, which means that the defendants "most probably" (but not certainly) are responsible for the act of which they are accused. In other civil courts, a preponderance of evidence, which means it is over fifty percent likely that the defendant committed the act, is all that is necessary to conclude the defendant is responsible for the act.

"Imminent" means about to take place, without delay, or on the way to completion. As a result, three important options are created.

- If national leaders follow the letter and spirit of U.S. policy, they must have incontrovertible evidence that an attack is underway.

- National leaders may officially modify their nation's official policy and craft a new, exceptionless policy that is more nuanced and, they believe, is more realistic.
- National leaders may simply ignore the official policy and make up their own *ad hoc* policies as different situations arise. A major problem with this option is that when nations disobey their own policies they place themselves in deep legal and sometimes deep moral waters. Moreover, national leaders who disobey their own policies are not in a strong position to criticize other nations that disobey their own policies, or to reprimand their own politicians, military leaders, and soldiers who disobey their nation's policies.

Preemptive force is a first-strike action aimed at a specific enemy target, such as a nuclear facility, or a strike meant to do massive damage to an enemy nation's military and civilian population and infrastructure. This strike is meant to neutralize any and all imminent threats.

A nation planning preemptive force ought to know with a reasonable degree of certainty that the suspect nation:

- Has the weapons to cause massive, catastrophic destruction
- Has the technical knowledge and skills to launch these weapons
- Has the explicitly or implicitly stated intention to launch an attack on a specific nation
- Leaves the attacking nation no other reasonable recourse but to launch a first strike
- Plans to launch an imminent attack, which means in a few hours or days

The use of preemptive force resembles a situation in which a belligerent neighbor:

- Has purchased a gun and bullets
- Knows how to use them
- Clearly indicates he is on the way to kill his innocent neighbor
- Begins to walk, loaded gun in hand, toward the innocent neighbor's house
- Does not allow sufficient time for the neighbor to call police or to escape

In this case, the claim of self-defense would likely be legally and morally acceptable.

Preventive Force

The Department of Defense defines a preventive war as one "initiated in the belief that military conflict, while not imminent, is inevitable, and that to delay would involve great risk." Whether purposeful or not, this definition is weaker and broader than that for preemptive attack. It does not require "incontrovertible evidence" that a military conflict is inevitable, does not define the degree of national threat an enemy nation poses, and does not define how great the risk must be. Based on this definition, a belief based on no substantive and consensual intelligence could permit launching an attack, which could mean launching a war based on a threat of "military conflict" such as an unfriendly nation purchasing weapons that could be used for its own defense or to attack another nation.

In the use of preventive force, which also is a first-strike attack, the suspect nation is believed to be gathering weapons that may or may not cause significant destruction, may or may not yet have the technical skill to launch the weapons, is bellicose toward the potential target nation, but does not pose an *imminent* threat of attack.

In contrast to preemptive force, a preventive first strike resembles a situation in which a belligerent neighbor:

- Plans to purchase bullets and a gun but has not yet done so, or
- Has purchased the gun but not the bullets, or
- Has purchased the gun and bullets but does not know how to use them, or
- Has learned to use the gun, or
- Threatens to shoot the innocent neighbor if the right circumstances arise.

Before the right circumstances can arise, the innocent neighbor invades the belligerent neighbor's property and shoots him, severely wounding or killing him. The case is much more problematic than that given as a domestic example for preemptive force. In this case, several neighbors on each block could launch preventive attacks against an equal number of neighbors based on the hunch that the "right circumstances" are about to arise or have arisen.

Shared Concerns of Preemptive and Preventive Force

While preemptive and preventive strikes pose separate concerns, they also share some common ones. How do nations declare, wage, and end wars on individual terrorists, terrorist groups, and rogue states? How is this done politically, legally, morally and militarily?

If "war" is armed aggression between two or more nations, how does a *nation* fight terrorists who are anonymous individuals moving freely among the general population with no external identifiable attributes? This is a difficult military question; it is an even more difficult moral question. How does a nation identify terrorists in another nation and separate them from their innocent neighbors? Is there such a thing as innocent families and friends of terrorists—which families are aiding and abetting their terrorist family members, friends, and neighbors, and which want nothing to do with them? What exactly is a "rogue state," and who are its citizens? In a city of one million people, how many are "rogues"—one thousand, ten thousand, a half-million? Even if a half-million terrorists exist in the nation of one million people, 500,000 noncombatants remain—men, women, children, doctors, lawyers, farmers. Where do these noncombatants fit in the target selection process?

A serious concern arises when a nation that rightfully or wrongfully feels threatened by another nation unilaterally determines the nature and extent of the threat. The nation that feels threatened acts like a detective, prosecutor, judge, jury and executioner, roles that are replete with conflicts of interest.

Unilateral decision-making is susceptible to several types of cognitive and affective methodological errors such as groupthink, selective perception, and confirmation bias. Those who are carefully chosen to participate in the highest levels of decision-making—the president, the president's cabinet, and political, military and legal consultants—are likely to gather as the team that will protect the nation against all threats, external and internal. Members of teams are chosen not only for their knowledge and experience, but also for their ability to be team players—they have similar backgrounds, personalities, politics, values, and worldviews. In other words, they typically are not a random or representative sample of policy experts but a select, self-sorting sample well in tune with each other. For this reason, a multilateral approach to diagnosing the nature and degree of threat is necessary, just as physicians consult with other independent specialists in difficult cases. Nations that reject multilateral investigations and consultations raise a question as to their true competence and motives for launching a preemptive or preventive attack.

With respect to rogue states, it is necessary to determine what constitutes "a rogue state" that can be declared a proper target for preemptive or preventive attacks. The U.S. government adopted a national security strategy in 2002 (see Bush 2002) that defines rogue states as those which

• brutalize their own people and squander their national resources for the personal gain of the rulers;
• display no regard for international law, threaten their neighbors, and callously violate international treaties to which they are a party;
• acquire weapons of mass destruction, along with other advanced military technology, to be used as threats to achieve their aggressive designs;
• sponsor terrorism around the globe; and
• reject basic human values and hate the United States and everything for which it stands (p. 12).

Although the United States adopted a new national security strategy in 2006, it does not modify any of the elements regarding rogue states in the 2002 strategy. The following discussion addresses each of these elements in sequence, as to whether all or just one of the elements of the definition need to be met to legitimize a preemptive or preventive strike and to determine the degree to which the elements must be met.

First, it is necessary to decide to what extent brutality must be present in a rogue state to justify an aggressive response. National leaders who brutalize their dissidents and squander their national resources for personal gain have always existed and will continue to exist. In fact, the United States has supported such nations and their leaders in the recent past. Undoubtedly, these crimes against humanity should be addressed by the international community, but absent a direct and serious threat to a specific nation, these crimes in themselves do not justify a unilateral armed response by a nation.

Concerning the second part of the definition of a rogue state, some nations display little or no regard for international law, threaten their neighbors, and callously violate international treaties. However, many nations, both friendly and unfriendly, have violated international law and international treaties, especially before and during a war. This fact in itself does not make them legitimate targets for preemptive or preventive strikes.

With respect to the third element of the definition, many nations have acquired or are attempting to acquire weapons of mass destruction, along with advanced military technology to achieve their aggressive designs. However, the possession of weapons of mass destruction does not necessarily mean a nation is contemplating aggression and is not in itself a legitimate reason for launching a preemptive or preventive attack.

The fourth element, sponsoring terrorism around the globe, is the one most closely related to national self-defense, but it still lacks the specificity necessary to be perceived as a legitimate cause for launching a preemptive or preventive strike. What defines "sponsoring" and "terrorism"? Does it mean that all the nation's citizens are complicit in the sponsorship of terrorism, or does it mean a small governing regime and its henchmen are primarily responsible for the nation's links to terrorism? This question raises a related one: If the vast majority of citizens are unaware of their nation's connection with terrorism, or are aware of it but profoundly opposed it and are helpless in the face of it, how are they factored into a preemptive or preventive attack, especially if it is launched with bombs and missiles?

The final element of the definition — that the rogue nation rejects basic human values and hates the United States and everything for which it stands — is the weakest of the five criteria for a number of reasons. Even within the United States, vehement disagreement exists regarding what constitutes "basic human values" as a philosophical concept and "basic American values" as a political concept. Is a nation open to legitimate attack simply because it hates other nations or their values? In the world of nations, many of them would meet this standard, including the United States.

The final question to be considered is whether any or all of these criteria meet the just war standard of just cause. Without just cause, all actions that follow are unjust, but even with just cause, not all the acts that follow are necessarily just.

Section V of the U.S. National Security Strategy ends with the following statement:

> The United States will not use force in all cases to preempt emerging threats, nor should nations use preemption as a pretext for aggression. Yet in an age where the enemies of civilization openly and actively seek the world's most destructive technologies, the United States cannot remain idle while dangers gather. We will always proceed deliberately, weighing the consequences of our actions. To support preemptive options, we will:
>
> • build better, more integrated intelligence capabilities to provide timely, accurate information on threats, wherever they may emerge;
> • coordinate closely with allies to form a common assessment of the most dangerous threats; and
> • continue to transform our military forces to ensure our ability to conduct rapid and precise operations to achieve decisive results.
>
> The purpose of our actions will always be to eliminate a specific threat to the United States or our allies and friends. The reasons for our actions will be clear, the force measured, and the cause just [p. 14–15].

These criteria for a rogue state are not the passing thoughts of some individual in government. They are an integral part of a critically important national security statement, which is presented as an actionable statement—a warning to the world of what is in store if any nation falls within the rubric of this definition of a rogue state. For this reason, all citizens must understand and take seriously the strategy's directive that the United States "will always proceed deliberately, weighing the consequences of our actions."

Contrasting Perspectives

Equally informed and reasonable individuals can disagree on the use of preemptive and preventive force, just as they can with regard to many issues regarding morality and war. For example, some people believe both can be immoral and illegal; others view only preemptive war as possibly moral and legal; and still others believe both types of attack can be moral and legal. The following sections demonstrate contrasting views of preventive war.

Argument for preventive force. Whitley Kaufman (2005) supports the concept of preventive force and bases his argument on the principle of natural law and natural right, which permits nations to protect themselves and their citizens against unjust harm. He views launching preventive first strikes as not only a right but also a duty, and claims that this right is so compelling that the burden of proof should be on those who oppose preventive attacks. However, as Kaufman cautions, preventive strikes cannot be used unless certainty or near certainty is present at every turn. He refers to Vitoria's admonition that one should not kill an individual for a sin he has yet to commit because many other measures short of killing exist for preventing future harm (p. 26). Kaufman states his concern about the abuse of the concept of preventive force:

> The literature is full of warnings about the important limitations on the preventive use of force. Grotius, for example, warned that while there is a right to anticipate and prevent danger, it cannot be that "any degree of fear" is a "ground for killing another to prevent his supposed intention." Citing Xenophon, he cautioned against those who have "committed the most enormous cruelties against those who neither designed, nor wished them any harm." Samuel Pufendorf equally worried about those who resort to force before there is clear evidence of a malevolent intention: "Before I can actually assault another under color of my own defense, I must have tokens and arguments amounting to a moral certainty, that he entertains a grudge against me, and has a full design of doing me a mischief, so that unless I prevent him, I shall immediately feel his stroke." Gentili insisted, "A just cause for fear is demanded; suspicion is not enough." Vattel averred that one must be careful not to act on doubtful suspicions of future threats, lest one become the aggressor [p. 26].

Kaufman supports the concept that only one justification exists for preventive attack — the "manifest evidence of a wrongful design," meaning that the fear of threat, no matter how great, must be based on one element: a threat that is clear, intended, specific, actionable, incontrovertible, and directed toward a specific nation. Kaufman continues:

> There is no doubt that the phenomenon of terrorism requires vigorous, early, and effective preventive intervention — this is especially true today as terrorists seek access to weapons of mass destruction. As we have seen, however, the just war tradition fully endorses such preventive use of force, so long as it is necessary, proportionate, and so on. At the same time, it does make a sharp distinction between war in self-defense against an actual or imminent threat (that is, preemptive war), and preventive war, against a potential future or emerging threat. The former is a right of each individual state. The latter belongs to the central authority vested with a monopoly on international force — that is the Security Council [p. 37].

Kaufman summarizes his position by stating that while the United Nations Security Council is an imperfect body, he believes it provides the best option at this time for adjudicating the legality if not the morality of a preventive attack and that it can be strengthened to become a competent and trusted mediator.

Argument against preventive force. In arguing against preventive attack, Air Force Major Steven R. Prebeck (1993) discusses three errors in thinking:

> The first is the belief that a preventive attack is a quick solution to remove a threat. In fact, the removal of a specific threat does not remove an attacked country's entire military capability. Because of this, after launching preventive attack, the attacker must expect to remain in the area and stop possible retribution attacks against countries that may have cooperated in the attack...
>
> The second error is the assumption that a preventive attack will be decisive. The United States demonstrated in Desert Storm a tremendous capability to conduct precision warfare.... However, coalition air forces were not totally successful. While it is true that Iraq's nuclear program was set back through the bombing campaign, the continued identification and destruction of more nuclear facilities by UN inspectors suggests underestimation of the extent of Iraq's nuclear program and an inability to set it back as far as the Persian Gulf War allies intended.
>
> The final fallacy associated with preventive attack is one of omission — the failure to realize the political ramifications of a conflict between a major power and a lesser power. Conducting a preventive attack, especially by a superpower, against a third world nation means weighing the military gain against the possibility of UN condemnation, trade restrictions, and loss of regional interest. To ensure support for an attack in the world community, a clear threat must be identified, clear goals for the operation must be declared, and a coalition must be established among neighboring countries. Failure in accomplishing these actions will make the attacker appear to be the world's bully instead of the protector and promoter of democracy [p. 4–5].

From a moral perspective, which may be different at times from a legal perspective, it seems that, all variables remaining the same, preemptive force is permissible under the doctrine of self-defense. Nations have an inherent right and duty to protect their citizens against imminent attacks by other nations. In fact, the argument has been made that it would be immoral for nations to wait until they have been actually attacked and thousands, if not millions, of their citizens killed before taking action.

With respect to preventive force, the moral issue becomes less clear. While the principle of self-defense still may be applicable, concerns arise in two areas. First, how narrowly or broadly will the concept of self-defense be defined? The narrow definition would be that self-defense is justified only in cases of imminent and massive attacks, while the broader definition could include any possible and future threat to self-defense, no matter how oblique and distant. For example, based on the domino theory, a communist dictator in a small, distant nation could be considered a threat to democratic nations in the region, and therefore could be the target of a preventive attack.

The second concern is: What amount of force can be used in the preventive attack based on the principle of proportionality? The moral cost-benefit assessment must calculate the amount of damage the enemy nation would inflict if, at some point in the distant future, it would attack the target nation. How does the nation contemplating a preventive attack apply the principle of discrimination? How many noncombatants will be killed for a sin they have yet to commit? The fact that the moral issues involved with preventive attacks are quite complicated and require virtually perfect military intelligence does not necessarily negate the possibility that preventive attacks can be permissible in very controlled and rare circumstances.

Every act of war, whether it relates to deciding whether to declare war, how to wage war, and when and how to end war is based on the use or abuse of some political, military, or moral theory, and often a combination of all three. Most wars will include the invocation of military necessity, especially if they are long and hard-fought. Double effect is frequently present in war because urban warfare, which will increase as terrorism increases, presents an endless series of operations in which civilian casualties are foreseen and anticipated as the side effect of accomplishing a substantial good. In addition, whatever wars lie in the near and distant future, they either will be preventive or preemptive wars likely to generate a good deal of discussion and debate.

Depending on the interpretation of these theoretical principles, they can be norms to restrict violence appropriately or justifications to override the conventional laws of war inappropriately, thus increasing violence unnecessarily. It is important for individual citizens, civilians and soldiers to acquire a basic knowledge of these principles and the cautions that pertain to them in order to have a greater understanding and appreciation for the moral complexities that arise on a daily basis in war. The following chapter addresses several of the complex war-related actions that evoke robust discussions and debates with respect to their moral implications.

8

Morality and War: Practical Issues

Justice and power must be brought together, so that whatever is just may be powerful, and whatever is powerful, may be just.

— Blaise Pascal

This chapter focuses on some practical issues regarding war that have profound moral implications. The topics discussed are complex and do not lend themselves to facile moral judgments. They can evoke discomforting thoughts and feelings as they portray the "war is hell" dimension most individuals would rather not consider. However, moral judgments cannot be made until the moral fog of war is penetrated and the reality is allowed to enter awareness as much as possible.

The topics addressed are modern terrorism, unmanned aerial vehicles, cluster munitions, economic sanctions and depleted uranium, all of which raise moral questions and concerns. Each topic presents a unique set of challenges with regard to the concept of noncombatant immunity, which includes the *in bello* principles of proportionality and discrimination.

Terrorism: Practical Considerations

Many issues in the practical world ordinarily do not have the concept of morality explicitly attached to them. The topics of health care, social security, and economic crises are rarely presented as moral issues, yet they are among the most pressing moral issues of the day because they affect the welfare of the citizenry in numerous ways. Similarly, the topics addressed in this chapter are typically perceived as political, military, legal, and economic issues rather than as moral issues. With this in mind, the following elements of terrorism ought to be understood before moral judgments can be considered.

While war was viewed through a periscope or a bombsight during World War II, the view of conventional and terroristic war today is through a kaleidoscope — contrasting shapes, colors, and configurations which change in split seconds. Yesterday's deadly enemy is today's close ally. Good and evil are no longer fixed entities but dynamic, defined and redefined by both the secular and religious worlds. The same act of war and act of torture is deemed good or evil, depending on which soldier, civilian, politician, philosopher or theologian is making the call. This section addresses some of these issues in an effort to expose "the devil" that resides in the details.

Understanding terrorism is complicated for several reasons:

• No universal definition of terrorism exists; the literature has over 100 definitions.

• Important differences in the definition are present not only among nations but within the same nation. The United States has several definitions; for example, the Department of Defense, the Federal Bureau of Investigation, and the State Department all have their own definitions of terrorism.

• Some individuals believe it is fatuous to debate the definition of terrorism because when nations suffer a terrorist attack, no definition is necessary — they are well aware of what terrorism is. However, the definition is important from moral and legal perspectives because it creates specific latitudes and restrictions as to how domestic and international law and security measures are carried out; for example, deciding whether terrorists should be tried in military tribunals or civilian criminal courts has both moral and legal ramifications.

• Those who construct definitions often shape them according to their own political agendas. If there were an international definition of terrorism, many nations would be in violation of it on a regular basis.

Noam Chomsky (2003) discusses some problems with current definitions of terrorism:

> Searching for the most valid and complete definitions of terrorism today is unlikely to lead to anything useful because the old definitions are problematic. For example, the U.S. Army Manual defines terrorism as "the calculated use of violence or threat of violence to attain goals that are political, religious, or ideological in nature ... through intimidation, coercion, or instilling fear." The British government's definition is similar: "Terrorism is the use, or threat, or action which is violent, damaging or disrupting, and is intended to influence the government or intimidate the public and is for the purpose of advancing a political, religious, or ideological cause." However, since no nation is willing to define itself as terrorist or its acts terroristic acts, even though their tactics clearly fall within their own definitions of terror, they now do not use the term "terrorism" but use "counterterrorism," "counterinsurgency," or "low intensity conflict" [p. 188–189].

In the midst of all these complications, most of which are man-made, Jean-Marc Sorel (2003) considers the various factors related to defining terrorism and arrives at one he believes to be reasonably empirical and tamper-proof:

> Although it is clear that no perfect definition could be given, an attempt might be made along the following lines: International terrorism is an illicit act (irrespective of its perpetrator or its purpose) which creates a disturbance in the public order as defined by the international community, by using serious and indiscriminate violence (in whatever form, whether against people or public or private property) in order to generate an atmosphere of terror with the aim of influencing political action [p. 371].

The definition has five basic elements:

- It is an illicit act (not sanctioned by law, mores, or custom).
- The political nature of the nation or group that commits the act does not define terrorism — the intention and the act itself are the basic defining factors. In other words, the fact that an ordinarily "just" nation commits the act does not mitigate or absolve it. Terrorism is terrorism, whoever causes it.
- It creates a massive disturbance — gross instability, fear, disorder, and upheaval.
- It employs serious and indiscriminate violence upon innocent individuals and their property.
- The upheaval creates an intensely fearful atmosphere whose purpose is to bring about some desired change in the political situation, whether or not this change is perceived as desirable or undesirable by objective observers.

By this definition, terrorism never can be moral or legal because it includes indiscriminate, disproportionate, and directly or indirectly, intentional attacks on innocent civilians to further a political cause. In other words, when acts of terrorism occur, no legitimate distinction can be made between "our friends, the freedom fighters," and "our enemies, the terrorists," or "our friends whom we would ordinarily refer to as terrorists but won't because they are currently helping us achieve our goals."

CHALLENGES TO UNDERSTANDING TERRORISM

The overarching challenge in understanding terrorism is derived from the fact that the phrase "the war against international terrorism" is problematic in several ways, including the following:

General moral issues. The word "war" sets in motion a number of domestic and international laws that affect how nations morally respond to terrorism. For example, it makes a significant difference if captured terrorists must be treated as "prisoners of war," "common criminals," or "rogue assassins" because each designation calls for various degrees of moral attention. This distinction affects the type of due process proceedings that are required, the methods of interrogation that are permitted, and the available legal sanctions, including summary execution, all of which are not only legal but serious moral issues. All of these serious moral issues affect not only the terrorists and the nations that have been subject to terrorist attack, but also the world that is observing how nations, especially democratic ones, address the problem.

Humanitarianism. According to international law and just war principles, only armed aggression between nations can be characterized as war. As a result, nations that are viewed correctly or incorrectly as "sponsors of terrorism" can be attacked by aerial bombardment and surface weapons. These attacks, no matter how "surgical" they are, typically kill civilians and destroy their property, which raises moral concerns.

Some individuals believe "the war on international terrorism" is a metaphorical war, like "the war on poverty" or the "war against drugs." These individuals believe terrorism is a law enforcement matter that should be handled by international courts and law enforcement agencies. This position would make terrorism, among other things, a problem that involves the entire international community. As a result, no one nation would be required to lose thousands of lives and billions of dollars waging pitched battles against terrorists. However, as appealing as this may sound, it has its own problems. For example, who would be members of this law enforcement agency; what would be their powers; who would finance it; who would act as prosecutors and defense attorneys; what kind of international court would adjudicate the cases; where would the guilty parties be imprisoned; who would finance their prosecution and incarceration? Each of these questions has important moral ramifications.

A basic challenge of terrorism is that it violates all the political, military, and legal principles upon which conventional wars are predicated. The following are some examples of terrorism's uniqueness:

- Its directly intended objectives are to murder innocent civilians for political or religious reasons and to destroy the morale of other innocent civilians through violence so that they will pressure their leaders to yield to the demands of the terrorists.
- It not only ignores but also disdains moral and international laws that are perceived by the terrorists as instruments for enforcing the very evil they are trying to destroy.
- It has no respect for sovereign nations, believing that evil transcends all geographical and political boundaries.

• It has no fear of divine retribution because it sees itself as doing God's (Allah's) work.
• It does not fear human retribution which precludes the principle of reciprocity, the "Golden Rule," from acting as a restraint.
• It has neither shame nor guilt, so these emotions cannot be used as instruments for shaping behavior.
• It not only does not fear death but also happily welcomes it as a pending reward, so threats of violence against it have only a reinforcing effect.
• It may be state-sponsored but has no allegiance to any state and becomes autonomous when necessary.

Specific moral issues. War has always been an inherent threat to the just war principles of proportionality and discrimination, which require that only the amount of force needed to accomplish necessary and legitimate military objectives is permitted and all reasonable care must be taken to protect the physical and material welfare of civilians. These principles apply both to conventional wars and those against terrorists, each of which presents a unique set of challenges. One important difference between the two types of war is that in conventional war, the combatants generally wear uniforms designating what nation they represent, and each nation generally travels in mass movements of troops, weapons and supplies. These elements were present in World War II, for example, and made it easier to identify and seek out the enemy, which at least allowed for the possibility of proportionality and discrimination.

The Vietnam War was a hybrid war in which national and regional armies fought each other, with the United States and North Vietnamese armies generally wearing uniforms and employing mass troop and materiel movements. However, the Viet Cong, the South Vietnamese Communist insurgents, fought like terrorists do today — in small, non-descript groups, carrying their weapons and supplies on their backs, blending in with the civilian populace and frequently fighting from the midst of populated villages.

Today, terrorist groups involved in wars are more tribe-bound than nation-bound and fight not only against aggressor nations but against other tribes as well. The United States and its allies are fighting a war against several sets of combatants who are also fighting against each other. In a war against terror, the principle of discrimination is especially challenged because it is difficult to distinguish between combatants and noncombatants when engaged in both ground and air operations, and the principle of proportionality is challenged, especially in aerial bombing.

A nation's greatest temptation in reacting to armed attacks and especially sneak attacks is to "take off the gloves," seek revenge, render "pay back in spades," or bomb the enemy back to the Stone Age. While such sentiments are emotionally understandable and satisfying, they are likely to generate serious violations of the moral and legal principles of proportionality and discrimination.

A related temptation is to over-define the enemy — the "shoot a cannon to kill a fly" syndrome, in which every individual in the sponsoring nation is assumed to be an enemy combatant or sympathizer when in reality, there may be as many, if not more, noncombatants as combatants in any field of fire. This response represents a two-pronged attack on the principles of proportionality and discrimination. The schoolyard justification for responding in ways that violate just war principles ("They started it!") places the aggrieved nation in the same unjust category as the enemy. As a result, the question changes from "Which is the just nation?" to "Which nation is more unjust — more evil — at any point in time?" In addition to creating a serious moral problem, this response gives priceless fodder to the enemy. In other words, bringing terrorists to justice using unjust methods is an ethical double standard of the worst kind, which rightly elicits skepticism if not scorn from friendly nations as well as hostile ones.

The proposition that the killing of innocents is the worst act any military can commit is universally accepted, except in the world of terrorists. It does not make any difference if the killing is unavoidable, unintentional, regrettable, or financially compensated. It is well known that armies can win all the battles but lose the war — the war for the hearts and minds of not only the civilians caught in the midst of war but also the hearts and minds of those back home.

This lesson was supposed to have been learned in the Vietnam War. It is quite possible that the killing of one civilian — a wife, mother, husband, child, grandparent, or close friend — will undo all the good accomplished by flushing terrorists out of a town or village, even when it costs the lives of several American troops. Glib comments such as, "Well, civilians die in all wars — it's regrettable but it happens," is a statement that is as ill advised as it is true — not at all in keeping with the spirit of just war principles. While the killing of a civilian may be the lesser of evils, it still remains a profound moral evil and ought never to be dismissed simply as unintended and regrettable.

In the interests of empathy, no one who experienced the death of a loved one in a crossfire between bank robbers and police would feel any less badly, angry, and unforgiving simply because the death of the loved one was caused by "the forces of justice" and is lamented as "unintended and regrettable." The grief and anger would not be limited to the immediate family but would spread to the friends, neighborhood, and city in which the victims lived. All the good and courageous work that a 30,000-member police department does for years can be significantly diminished by the killing of one innocent civilian by one police officer.

The victims of terrorist acts typically perceive themselves as morally justified in retaliating with not only greater force, but at a level that fits most definitions of terrorism. Yet, victim nations never consider their reactions as terrorist in nature because, in their minds, they are not terrorists, only their attackers are. Larry Derfner (2008) addresses this point in the *Jerusalem Post*:

> I supported Israel's unstated policy of punishing the civilian population in Lebanon during the war two summers ago [2006] because I saw no other way to rein in Hizbullah, no other means of bringing pressure on these fanatics to leave us alone.
> But unlike most of the Israelis at all levels who want the IDF [Israeli Defense Forces] to make ordinary Gazans suffer and die, believing that this will force Hamas and Islamic Jihad to stop their terrorism against us, I recognize that such a policy is itself terrorism. Deliberately targeting civilians for a political purpose is textbook terrorism...
> But even though Israel, on balance, has a lot less to apologize for than the Palestinians do in the matter of terrorism, Israel should be a lot more cautious than it's being these days about hurting and killing Palestinian civilians as a strategy for changing their leaders' warlike ways. If we're going to be so outspoken in condemning terror, we ought to think a lot longer before engaging in it ourselves.

A political and military response to terroristic attacks is likely to be necessary, but it ought to be well planned not only politically and militarily but morally as well. The fact that a good deal of time is taken to carefully plan a response does not necessarily mean that the planning was well-informed, honestly debated, morally grounded, or took into account all the intended and unintended political, cultural, and international consequences. Analogously, the fact that students study long and hard for a final examination does not necessarily mean that they studied the correct material or studied it properly.

Unmanned Aerial Vehicles

Unmanned aerial vehicles (UAVs), which also are called unmanned aircraft systems (UAS) and drones, are the most modern, technically advanced weapons in the world. The purpose of this section is to describe the nature of UAVs, how they work, their effects, and the moral implications that arise from their deployment. Based on an understanding of this material, individuals can make at least preliminary judgments about the morality of these weapons and decide how best to translate their judgment into action.

Because UAVs have been used by the United States in at least five nations in combat support and targeted killing roles, they have engendered a good deal of discussion and, in many circles, controversy. Their main uses in war are surveillance, target acquisition, and striking targets with ordnance. Their main purposes are to save the lives of U.S. soldiers, to take the lives of enemy soldiers and high value leaders, and to reduce the number of civilian casualties that less precise attacks might cause.

UAVs first appeared in the Persian Gulf War (2003) when thirteen were deployed for intelligence purposes. By 2010, over 1,000 UAVs were deployed in the Iraq War. They logged approximately 500,000 flight hours over a nation that is approximately the size of California in both geography and population.

UAVs have been used by the United States to fight the Taliban and Al-Qaeda in Iraq, Afghanistan and Pakistan and, on occasion, they have been deployed in Yemen, Somalia, Kosovo and Libya. There are over ten types of UAVs, some of which are used only for reconnaissance and others for both reconnaissance and combat. One of the newer combat types is the MQ-9 Reaper, which is a hunter-killer system. It is designed to travel up to 450 mph on 15-hour flights reaching 50,000 feet in altitude. It can carry a variety of weapons, including two 500-pound laser-guided "smart bombs" and 14 Hellfire missiles. Each Reaper costs approximately $11 million.

UAVs flew 185,000 hours over Afghanistan and Iraq in 2009 and approximately 300,000 hours in 2010. UAVs are operated remotely by a team of controllers ("pilots"), some of whom are located on the ground in the secure sections of combat areas. However, the vast majority of controllers are located in Nevada, California, Arizona, and Virginia. These controllers sit at banks of computers and see what the UAVs see as they fly over enemy territory. The controllers gather the data that the vehicle transmits, analyze it, and, in combat situations, fire the weapons at enemy targets. The elapsed time between the vehicle recording video, relaying it to the control centers, and the controllers responding with weapons activation is from three to six seconds.

The United States now has 7,000 UAVs, which cost approximately $5 billion a year. Three views exist regarding the use of UAVs:

Positive: UAVs reduce American as well as civilian casualties in the nation being attacked and are cost effective. Therefore, their use is not only appropriate, but necessary.

Negative: UAVs make going to and waging war easier, which can lead to declaring and waging wars that are unnecessary, indiscriminate, and disproportionate with regard to civilian casualties.

Undecided: UAVs are in the infancy stages of development and deployment, so it remains to be seen if their long-range cost-benefit ratio is on the side of cost or benefit on and beyond the battlefield.

Capabilities of Unmanned Aerial Vehicles

UAVs are highly effective and relatively inexpensive weapons of war. They have a high number of capabilities:

- They can fire missiles and drop bombs in carefully targeted areas without risking the lives of pilots.
- They can "see" combatants planting improvised explosives devices (IEDs) or setting ambushes and notify the commanders on the ground before they send troops into the dangerous areas.
- They can identify and track high-value enemy leaders and attack them and their dwellings.
- They can fly at an altitude of 50,000 feet, making it difficult, if not impossible, for ground weapons to destroy them.
- They are infinitely cheaper than traditional aircraft, costing $10 million to 15 million compared to $350 million for a jet aircraft.
- They can participate in force protection in that they can aid troops pinned down in firefights.
- They can carry small bombs or 500-pound bombs, depending on the mission.

More than any other weapons system, UAVs are precise in their targeting, present no risk to their controllers, and are highly cost effective. However, they are not free from moral concerns.

Moral Issues

Several moral issues are evident in the deployment of UAVs. Again, the presence of concerns does not imply that UAVs ought never to be used, only that if they are used, moral principles should be included in the spectrum of considerations related to their use.

The first moral issue is the number of civilian casualties caused by UAVs. Civilian casualties in war are always difficult to predict. This is especially true in Muslim nations in which the dead are buried as soon as possible for religious reasons. One report on the casualty rates of UAVs is a longitudinal study by the New American Foundation, an independent group that studied the number of reported casualties in Pakistan from 2004 to July 15, 2010. Based on information compiled from several sources, the report by Peter Bergen and Katherine Tiedemann (2010) states: "Our study shows that the 114 reported drone strikes in northwest Pakistan from 2004 to 2010 have killed approximately between 830 and 1,362 individuals, of whom around 550 to 850 were described as militants in reliable press accounts. Thus, the true civilian fatality rate since 2004 according to our analysis is approximately 32 percent" (p. 3).

The report indicates that in 2009, 502 people were killed in drone strikes, 382 of which were described as militants, for an average civilian fatality rate of 24 percent. Whether this lower rate indicates a new trend remains to be seen.

A more recent report was published in August 2011 by the Bureau of Investigative Journalism, a British non-profit organization based at City University, London (Woods 2011). The report states that, since 2004, there have been 291 UAV attacks in Pakistan. In these attacks, 385 to 775 civilians have been killed, including more than 160 children.

A significant issue arises, however, in that CIA officials strongly disagree with the report's conclusions regarding the large number of civilian deaths. For example, the CIA claims that between May 2010 and August 2011, UAVs have killed more than 600 militants, and not a single civilian casualty has been reported. However, as Woods (2011) reports, the Bureau of Investigative Journalism states that while "civilian casualties do seem to have declined in the past year," the bureau still found "credible evidence" of at least 45 non-combatants killed. As Scott Shane (2011) states: "The civilian toll of the C.I.A.'s drone campaign, which is widely credited with disrupting Al Qaeda and its allies in Pakistan's tribal area, has been in bitter dispute since the strikes were accelerated in 2008. Accounts of strike after strike from official and unofficial sources are so at odds that they often seem to describe different events."

A second moral consideration relates to the fact that deploying UAVs makes going to war easier in three ways. First, the "last resort" just war principle may be given short shrift. Instead of the serious and lengthy political, military, and legal deliberations that ought to precede a last resort war, the deliberation to launch a UAV on a sovereign nation may take only hours or days. Second, a UAV strike on a sovereign nation will not have the appearance of going to war, but merely appear to be "just another strike on some terrorist group or another." Third, it is a safer and more economical way to wage war. There are no American casualties and the price is minuscule compared to other types of air attacks. Individuals tend not to become intellectually interested or emotionally invested in weapons of war unless or until they exact a significant loss of life of one's own soldiers and cost an exorbitant amount of money. This "citizen disconnect" has serious moral implications because disconnected citizens have little or no knowledge of the war and therefore are in no position to make informed moral decisions regarding it. As R.W. Singer (2009) writes, "The increasing use of robotics may be motivated by saving lives, but by doing so, it does affect the way the public views and perceives war. In turn, it will also affect wars' processes and outcomes, perhaps even transforming that public into the equivalent of sports fans watching war, rather than citizens sharing in its importance" (p. 318).

A third moral consideration relates to the response of the civilian and military population of the nation being attacked by UAVs. The assumption is that those who were injured or who lost loved ones in the attack will become paralyzed with fear and dread and capitulate to the attacking nation. This type of thinking continues in warfare despite the fact that ancient and modern wars largely demonstrate that the exact opposite occurs. Whatever good has come from UAVs strikes killing militants in Pakistan, a large portion of the civilian population, including national leaders, has told the United States to cease and desist any further use of UAVs, a demand that is not likely to be met.

A fourth issue is the proliferation of UAVs across the world. UAVs are relatively simple to construct because they are based primarily on the same principles as remote-control model airplanes. They are also cheap to construct compared to traditional fighter planes and bombers. Approximately 45 nations, including Iran, Russia, and China, either own or are developing UAVs. In fact, American companies have sold UAVs to nations that, in turn, have sold them to other nations known to be hostile to the United States. Iran is now using UAVs to patrol its borders as a defense strategy. Therefore, as UAVs proliferate around the world, including in "friends now, enemies later" nations, the United States may well be caught in never-ending wars to attack nations and groups who may become direct threats to U.S. security.

A fifth consideration arises when UAV attacks are intended to be covert and, consequently, military and political leaders must lie to their citizens when asked about them, as is the case in Pakistan. The reason for the secrecy is that Pakistan is a sovereign nation and ally of the United States and the UAV attacks are being carried out not by the U.S. military but by the Central Intelligence Agency (CIA), which is a civilian organization. The United States does not want its own citizens, much less the world, to know it is allowing American civilians to invade a sovereign, allied nation, an action that has serious moral and legal ramifications.

As is the case with most "covert" operations, the entire world knows about them because they are covered daily in the world's media. In fact, the New American Foundation study mentioned previously indicates that their statistics on the effect of these operations must be gathered from accounts obtained from reliable media organizations with deep-reporting capabilities in Pakistan. Because the U.S. government does not provide information on these attacks, the American people are left to find other sources for the information necessary to make informed moral decisions on the attacks.

The final issue regarding UAVs relates to their use in "targeted killings" (assassinations) of suspected militants. This situation raises a highly complex moral and legal issue. Domestic law is unclear and variable on the issue of assassinations, and international law is, for all practical purposes, silent on the topic. However, the issue requires serious discussion and debate because it is likely that as long as UAVs exist, they will be used for targeted killings. Unfortunately, it is unlikely morality will be a serious consideration in the continuing development and deployment of UAVs. Brett H. McGurk (2010), referencing the use of UAVs, writes: "The technology is here to stay, and it is being deployed to kill designated enemies of the United States and its allies. What are the legal and ethical implications of this trend? And, what rules govern killing by pilotless drones in some of the most remote regions of the world? Surprisingly, we seem to have no idea."

Because this is the case, it is important for individuals and groups who deeply care about these issues to learn as much as possible about UAVs and develop well-informed consciences so that they can add their voice to the debate.

Cluster Munitions

"Cluster bombs" and "cluster munitions" are air- and surface-delivered dispensers containing explosive submunitions. Aerial bombing and ground launching from howitzers and rocket launchers are the two main methods of deploying cluster munitions, which are rigged to explode as they approach the ground or an object (tank, bunker, or building). Generally, the submunitions contained in bombs are referred to as bomblets and those in surface munitions as grenades.

Over 200 models of cluster munitions exist, making it impossible to offer anything more detailed than a broad description of them. The bomblets differ markedly in size and shape; for example, they can be in the shape of a D battery, soda can, softball, or tennis ball. Cluster munitions also differ markedly in range, firepower, accuracy and radius of destruction ("footprint"), which varies from 50 to 1500 feet. The footprints are caused by the explosion of bomblets housed in the canisters.

Cluster bombs can contain as few bomblets as three and as many as 2000.

Their purpose is to kill and wound the enemy, penetrate armor and cement, and set fires to ensure force protection for ground troops. The bomblets have a dud rate (the rate at which they fail to explode on contact) of from five to 30 percent. The dud rate is determined by factors such as the type of bomb, the speed and altitude at which the aircraft is flying, the wind, the accuracy of the bombing system, and so on. Duds can remain on the ground in plain view or hidden in buildings and ground cover. They also may lie buried 10 feet into the ground, depending on the size and weight of the bomblet and the altitude from which it was dropped. It has been estimated that about 40 percent of duds on the ground are hazardous and will explode if handled, stepped on, kicked, or struck with construction or farming implements.

Cluster munitions are very effective against the enemy because of their relatively large "kill area." For example, precision-guided ground (non-cluster) munitions would hit one tank in a twenty-tank convoy, whereas a cluster munition could hit all twenty in the same strike, likely saving the lives of many U.S. and coalition soldiers. In ground warfare, cluster munitions are mostly used as a counter-attack defense to repel terrorist attacks and are rarely used as a first-strike weapon. When they are used, all reasonable steps should be taken to avoid civilian casualties.

Fifteen nations have deployed cluster munitions, 36 nations and territories have been attacked by them, 34 nations have produced them, and 85 nations have stockpiled them. The United States has deployed cluster bombs or other cluster munitions on eight countries: Vietnam, Laos, Cambodia, Kuwait, Afghanistan, Iraq, Pakistan and probably Libya.

Handicap International (2007) studied the use and effects of cluster bombs in 24 nations and regions. The following information is from its study.

With respect to the recent deployment of cluster munitions, the United States has used cluster munitions in three wars and a number of aggressive interventions. During the Persian Gulf War (August 1990–February 1991), the United States dropped 61,000 cluster bombs containing 20 million bomblets. From 1991 to May 2007, unexploded duds have killed 1,600 civilians and injured 2,500. In Afghanistan (2001) 1,228 cluster bombs containing 248,056 bomblets were dropped. Between October 2001 and November 2002, 127 civilians were killed by them, 70 percent of whom were under the age of 18.

In the Iraq War (2003), 13,000 cluster bombs containing nearly 2 million bomblets were dropped and left approximately 1.2 million unexploded duds. The United States claimed for several years that it did not deploy cluster bombs after 2003. However, in response to a Freedom of Information Act request, the Air Force confirmed that 63 cluster bombs containing 12,726 bomblets were dropped on Iraq between May 1, 2003, and August 1, 2006.

Handicap International (May 2007) also studied the number of individuals killed by cluster munitions. As previously stated, it is impossible to make reasonably accurate estimates of casualties in war zones, even after the war is over. For this reason, statistical ranges are generally given which represent the estimates made by individuals and agencies. With respect to Afghanistan the range of estimated casualties from cluster munitions is 2,814 to 4,132; for Iraq it is 2,287 to 5,500, and for Kuwait only one estimate is given — 4000. When these casualty figures are broken down demographically, it appears that civilians are the victims in 98 percent of the cases and often among the poorest in the population.

After a six-month investigation, Amnesty International issued a report on June 7, 2010, claiming that sound evidence exists that the United States dropped cluster bombs in Yemen during a "covert operation" against an Al Qaeda training camp on December 17, 2009. The evidence includes witnesses, weapon fragments, and a clear, close-up photograph taken immediately after the attack of an unexploded cruise missile, along with its unexploded bomblets. The missile markings clearly indicate it was manufactured in Kansas in 1992 and is a type of missile deployed only by U.S. forces. Both the United States and Yemen deny such attacks took place because each has its own reasons for keeping them quiet. The U.S. Department of Defense (DoD) affirmed in June 2008 that it planned to continue to deploy cluster munitions:

> The DoD policy above is intended to minimize the potential unintended harm to civilians and civilian infrastructure of U.S. cluster munitions employment to the extent possible. DoD recognizes that blanket elimination of cluster munitions is unacceptable due not only to negative military consequences but also due to potential negative consequences for civilians. Large-scale use of unitary weapons, as the only alternative to achieve military objectives, could result, in some cases, in unacceptable collateral damage and explosive remnants of war (ERW) issues. Combatant Commanders will continue to ensure that employment of cluster munitions is consistent with the law of armed conflict and applicable international agreements in order to minimize their impact on civilian populations and infrastructure.

Moral Issues

This section focuses only on aerial cluster bombing because ground-launched cluster munitions are more difficult to quantify and likely cause less radical damage than cluster bombs. Two basic issues are related to dropping cluster bombs — the immediate civilian casualties and the long-range civilian casualties.

Assuming that the wars under discussion are morally just, the two most relevant *in bello* principles are proportionality and discrimination: Are the destructive effects of the bombs proportional to the just military necessity, and do they adequately discriminate between combatants and civilians?

Four positions are possible on these issues.

- The civilian casualties caused by the cluster bombs are proportionate and discriminating with respect to both the actual bombings and the long-term effects.
- The casualties are proportionate and discriminating with respect to the actual bombings but not days or decades after the actual attack.
- The casualties are proportionate and discriminating neither at the time of nor after the attack, which creates a serious moral issue.
- It does not matter if the civilian casualties are proportionate or discriminating, as long as they are necessary to win a battle or a war.

The use of cluster bombs (and all cluster munitions) challenges both the moral and legal principles of proportionality and discrimination. Proportionality enters the picture at two points — at the actual time of the bombing and the days and decades after the bombing when cluster duds explode and kill and maim civilians.

The major point of disagreement lies not so much with the principle of proportionality being applied to the actual cluster bombing but with the after-action casualties. Until recently, there has been resistance to including destructive after-effects of a weapon's discharge in the pre-attack proportionate analysis. Currently, a growing body of moral and legal literature argues that *all* destructive effects of a weapon's discharge ought to be included in the analysis. A legal analogy is that individuals who shoot a victim several times in the stomach are responsible not only for the immediate medical damage, but also for the infections that may result from the wounds and kill the victim a month later. A document from Human Rights Watch (Broad, Corsi, and Kamhi 2008) summarizes the point:

> This study of the positions of international bodies, states, and legal scholars regarding IHL [International Humanitarian Law] shows that most in the international community now believe that the proportionality principle requires consideration of the after effects of a weapon, such as a cluster munition, or an attack. Such an approach is particularly important with regard to cluster munitions because their footprint and inevitable duds make civilian victims, even after hostilities, virtually guaranteed [p. 12].

The use of cluster bombs (and other cluster munitions) similarly challenges the moral and legal principle of discrimination. The question is: Do cluster bombs adequately discriminate between combatants and civilians at the time of the attack and after the attack?

The size of the cluster bomb attack's footprints raises this question. Bombardiers dropping a conventional bomb, especially a laser-guided "smart bomb," can be reasonably certain that the relatively tight diameter of destruction will not include known civilians, even though such judgments are never perfect. However, when cluster bombs explode, footprints are left around and across an area equivalent to one to five football fields, and a challenge to the principle of discrimination often occurs. Bomblets don't discriminate between combatants and civilians as they streak through a wide radius of destruction. It is helpful to keep in mind that bombardiers do not drop one cluster bomb for each attack but a string of them that can number five or ten bombs at each drop from an aircraft traveling at 400 mph.

The second challenge of cluster bombs to the principle of discrimination arises after the bombings have occurred. From five to twenty percent of the bomblets dropped by cluster bombs are duds that are deposited on the ground, in the ground, inside walls, roofs, homes, barns, vehicles, schools, and hospitals. Many of these bomblets are volatile and can be activated by sound waves and ground vibrations, as well as by being handled or stepped on. These exploding duds cannot discriminate between combatants and civilians and, in fact, years after the conflict, civilians will be the only casualties.

As is true of most important issues in war and life, divergent opinions exist regarding the morality and legality of cluster bombs in their current state. Air Force Major Thomas J. Hertel (2001) believes cluster bombs are an acceptable weapon of war as long as ordinary moral and legal precautions are taken. He writes:

> Military planners must evaluate whether the use of cluster munitions will cause collateral damage on a case-by-case basis. Like every other target analysis, technical experts, with input from military lawyers, should consider, among other things, the lawfulness and military value of the target, as well as the feasibility, based on aircraft capabilities and enemy air defenses, to accurately strike the proposed target. By doing so, commanders fulfill their legal and ethical obligations [p. 267].

On the other side of the issue, T.A. Cavanaugh (2006) believes that while cluster bombs in theory may not be intrinsically immoral (or illegal) weapons, in practice, cluster bombs in their current form do not pass the proportionality and discrimination tests because of their gross imprecision, especially with respect to duds which explode long after the initial attack. He states:

> Acceptance of the status quo suggests a callous indifference to unnecessary human suffering, a violent cynicism with respect to military ethics, and a lack of imagination as to how currently available technology can better the human condition. As said of Napoleon's behavior on one occasion, "*C'est plus qu'un crime, c'est une faute*"; it is more than wrong, it is stupid. To develop, manufacture, or use cluster

submunitions that result in such numerous avoidable civilian casualties is unjust and foolish; for both reasons it must stop [p. 144].

Economic Sanctions

Economic sanctions clearly present a moral issue because their primary purpose is to place a degree of hardship on citizens in the targeted nation to the degree that they will rebel against their leaders and compel them to comply with the wishes of the targeting nation. A generally overlooked question is: How will a half-starved, disorganized, untrained, and probably small group of ill-equipped civilians overpower a well-trained and equipped terrorist group or terrorist state, kill or imprison these individuals, and take charge of running their country? Paradoxically, this would encourage a group of civilian rebels to take aggressive action in violation of *jus ad bellum* just war principles, such as legitimate authority and the likelihood of success.

Although economic sanctions have been imposed since ancient times by many nations, they take on a special interest in a time of terrorism for two reasons. First, the most recent sanctions by the United States have been levied against nations perceived as a threat to the security of the United States: Iran, Afghanistan, and Iraq. Second, this fact and the fact that the morale of civilians is the primary target of sanctions raise moral questions that call for serious thought and discussion.

Another purpose of sanctions is to punish nations perceived as threats for resisting diplomatic efforts to make desired political and military changes and to force their citizens to apply pressure on their leaders to make the changes. This section addresses the moral dimension of sanctions, areas of concern with regard to sanctions, and their use in a time of terrorism.

CONCERNS REGARDING SANCTIONS

A number of political, legal, economic, and moral issues are related to sanctions. In order to make an informed assessment of the morality of sanctions, it is helpful to be aware of the following areas of concern.

The vast majority of individuals who are grievously harmed by sanctions are innocent men, women, and children, especially those under the age of five. Robert F. McGee (1988) addresses this issue when he states:

> Not only do sanctions punish the innocent civilian population, they often punish people who are already being victimized by their own government. Thus, sanctions are a double evil. The people of Cuba, Iraq and North Korea are prime examples, but not the only ones. Just like the mentality of the American army during the

Vietnam War — we have to destroy the village in order to save it — sanctions aim at destroying or greatly weakening an economy in order to save the people from the government that is oppressing them.

In general, the leaders of the sanctioned nation are left untouched by sanctions because their influence, access, and wealth allow them to maintain their standard of living and, in many instances, enhance it. In most cases, these leaders welcome sanctions because they increase the leaders' power over a weakened populace that relies on its leaders for help. These leaders use sanctions and the suffering they create as proof that the sanctioning nations are evil and must be resisted at all costs.

Sanctions usually have a paradoxical effect that is not in the least paradoxical to people with a rudimentary understanding of social psychology. Not only do sanctions fail to motivate a nation's citizens to pressure leaders into complying with the sanctioning nation's demands, sanctions also may motivate citizens to become more nationalistic and entrenched against the sanctioning nation. This reaction is similar to that seen in World War II when the German area bombing of England strengthened the resolve of the English people to defeat Germany.

Sanctions often punish the nations doing the sanctioning as well as the target nations. For example, when the United States imposes sanctions, as it has done over 200 times since 1916, U.S. companies are placed at a significant disadvantage because the sanctioned nations often shift their business to highly competitive firms in non-sanctioning nations. Sanctions also hurt U.S. allies who are not permitted to continue lucrative trade agreements with U.S. sanctioned nations.

In 1998, Jeffrey J. Schott addressed the U.S. Senate Committee on International Relations:

> Recent research by my colleagues at the Institute for International Economics calculated the impact of U.S. sanctions on trade, jobs, and wages in the United States. They found that U.S. exports to the 26 countries subject to U.S. sanctions in 1995 were $15 to $19 billion lower than they would have been in the absence of the sanctions.... The longer these sanctions remain in force, the greater the cumulative cost for U.S. workers.
>
> Simply imposing costs on the target country may satisfy a thirst for retribution, but it does not necessarily achieve U.S. foreign policy goals. Sanctions are blunt policy tools that are easily circumvented. Targeted regimes often adapt to sanctions, even if their people suffer. Meanwhile, ongoing sanctions become increasingly burdensome to U.S. firms and workers.

In contemporary times, most sanctions are perceived by the international community as causing wanton human and material destruction. In 2004, the United Nations voted 179–4 to oppose the United States' embargo on Cuba.

The United States, Israel, Palau, and the Marshall Islands voted to retain the embargo and Micronesia abstained. The vote was not meant to be an endorsement of Cuban policies but a sign that after thirteen years, the sanctions showed no sign of being effective in changing Cuba's human rights policy and that perhaps more positive measures ("carrots") should be attempted.

Unlike war, sanctions often fall beneath the radar when it comes to congressional and citizen oversight because they attract much less attention, do not carry a financial cost to the government, and do not cause the deaths of American military. Joy Gordon (1999) describes the low profile of sanctions:

> To the extent that we see sanctions as a means of peacekeeping and international governance, sanctions effectively escape ethical analysis — we do not judge them by the same standards we judge other kinds of harm done to innocents. Yet, concretely, the hunger, sickness, and poverty that are ostensibly inflicted for benign purposes affect individuals no differently than hunger, sickness, and poverty inflicted out of malevolence. To describe sanctions as a means of "peacekeeping" or "enforcing human right" is an ideological move, which, from the perspective of concrete personal experiences, is simply counterfactual.

The moral aspect of sanctions is heightened because their pernicious effects are known in advance since sanction plans include predictions as to how many people will be adversely affected by the sanctions. For example, a 1991 U.S. Defense Intelligence Agency document illustrates awareness that sanctions against Iraq would lead to the inevitable destruction of the Iraqi water system, resulting in a devastating humanitarian crisis. In other words, unlike bombing strikes which cause collateral damage, sanctions cause calculated damage in the attempt to force innocent civilians to move against their leaders.

Although the prevention of war is a third purpose of sanctions, they have been referred to as a way station to war because war often follows sanctions, initiated by the sanctioning or the sanctioned nation. One reason given for the Japanese attack on Pearl Harbor is that United States' sanctions were threatening the survival of Japan. This is not necessarily a criticism of the validity of those sanctions but demonstrates that sanctions are not a strong prophylactic against war.

Smart Sanctions

Comprehensive sanctions, in contrast to specifically targeted sanctions, were ineffective in Afghanistan and Iraq and received almost universal criticism by the international community because the oppressed population of the sanctioned nations became further oppressed because of the sanctions. As a result, the United Nations Security Council and some concerned nations developed a plan for "smart sanctions," presumably in contrast to the "dumb sanctions" of the past. Daniel W. Drezner (2003) describes the purpose of smart sanctions:

> Smart sanctions are designed to raise the target regime's costs of noncompliance while avoiding the general suffering that comprehensive sanctions often create. Like precision-guided munitions, smart sanctions target responsible parties while minimizing collateral damage. Examples include asset freezes, travel bans, and arms embargoes — measures that stand in stark contrast to the comprehensive trade ban against Iraq [p. 107].

Smart sanctions have the following five elements:

• *Targeted sanctions* are aimed at leaders of the sanctioned nation and supposedly will have little or no negative effect on civilian populations.

• *Humanitarian exemption* allows for the modification of sanctions in cases of a future natural disaster, outbreak of insurgency, uncontrollable epidemics, and other unexpected crises.

• *Automatic suspension clauses* allow originally imposed sanctions to be suspended in the face of unforeseen situations, such as the onset of natural disasters, unexpected indirect effects of sanctions, or civil or international wars breaking out.

• *Periodic monitoring* of sanctions means that the sanctioning authorities conscientiously monitor the effects of the sanctions in order to shift their focus, decrease sanctions, or initiate the exemption clause before the ground reality reaches a critical stage.

• *Follow-up assessment of long-term effects* means that the domino effect of sanctions, even after they are lifted, can reach into areas and cause destruction that would not only unfairly affect the citizens of the target nation but also possibly put neighboring nations or the world at large in jeopardy.

Unfortunately, smart sanctions aimed at national leaders or specific groups do not have concrete boundaries that prevent their effects from spreading to the rest of the population. For example, the freezing of financial assets eventually may force the government to close down government-operated hospitals, clinics, schools, and other public services, and flight bans can disrupt the shipment of food, cold-storage medications, and the importation of health care personnel.

The harsh reality is that whether sanctions are smart or comprehensive, they cannot be crafted to prevent large segments of a population from being punished for the sins of a few. After a careful analysis of economic sanctions and humanitarian safeguards, Robin Geiss (2005) concludes:

> Economic sanctions — even when targeted and designed in a "smart" way — are liable to cause severe human rights violations due to their complexity and the fact

that unforeseen factors may greatly enhance their adverse side effects. The humanitarian safeguards presently employed, namely, exemption clauses and time limits, do not provide adequate protection for the fundamental right to life in all circumstances [p. 198].

By this point in the history of sanctions, all national leaders are aware of every kind of sanction that could be imposed against them. As a result, they have ample time to stock up on commodities necessary for their own survival. They can stock up on food, medicine, arms, aircraft, industrial and farm equipment, gas and petroleum, and they can hide their financial assets. When this occurs, the leaders will not be affected by the sanctions and will be perceived by their people and other sympathetic nations as having outsmarted the sanctioning authorities. Drezner (2003) states: "Even as the sanctions become smarter, so will the targets" (p. 109).

Research does indicate that sanctions work, in one way or another, at one time or another, about one-third of the time. However, sanctions in the absence of other "carrot and stick" proposals rarely work as planned.

Consequences of Sanctions

When a nation destroys or impedes another nation's means of obtaining nourishing food, potable water, and fresh medicine, the innocent civilians of the target nation will suffer medical and psychological illnesses that can be life threatening, especially for children who are naturally immune-compromised due to their physical and psychological immaturity.

The United States and the United Nations Security Council imposed comprehensive sanctions on Iraq as soon as it invaded Kuwait on August 2, 1990. The objective of the sanctions was to force Iraq to withdraw from Kuwait. However, after the Persian Gulf War, the sanctions were still maintained, the justification being to force Iraq to disarm and discontinue its plans to develop nuclear weapons.

A study of the effects of sanctions in Iraq by Richard Garfield (1999) consisted of a statistical analysis that re-examined four of the better-known child mortality studies and examined parts of approximately 75 relevant studies. His estimate of "excess deaths of children under five," meaning the number of deaths above the norm for pre-sanction years, between August 1991 and March 1998, was 106,000. Garfield updated the figure to 350,000 through 2002. He believes the majority of these deaths were caused by contaminated water, poor food quality, inadequate breast feeding and weaning due to the mother's malnutrition, and inadequate medical services and supplies.

Garfield's numbers are considered conservative because they are significantly lower than other studies. For example, the United Nations Food and Agriculture Organization (FAO) reported in December 1995 that more than one million Iraqis died, 567,000 of them children, as a direct consequence of economic sanctions.

The international protests against the sanctions led Denis Halliday to resign his position as U.N. Humanitarian Coordinator in Iraq in October 1998. In a 2001 television presentation, he states:

> You've got ten years of sanctions ... where there is massive malnutrition amongst children in particular, including chronic malnutrition, which leaves permanent damage, mental and physical damage, to this sort of "sanctions generation" that we in the United Nations have created.
>
> We cannot have the United Nations, the guardian of well-being, sustaining a regime of embargo or sanctions on a people that impacts only on the people, not on the decision-makers, not on the government. And more than impacts, it kills the people.... We are, in my view, guilty through the Security Council of committing genocide in Iraq.

Economic sanctions clearly raise moral questions because they are aimed directly at civilians and may cause them great physical and psychological harm. In addition, civilians cannot escape sanctions because they are rarely in a position to rebel successfully against their leaders. Thus, sanctions are rarely successful in accomplishing their goals. Once again, however, this does not necessarily mean they should never be employed because the totality of the circumstances must be considered before a final moral judgment can be made.

Depleted Uranium

Uranium is a dense, weakly radioactive metallic element that exists naturally in the environment (in rocks, soil, and water) and in human beings, animals, and mammals. Depleted uranium is a waste product of the uranium enrichment process and is forty to sixty percent less radioactive than natural uranium. Because depleted uranium is cheap, easily warehoused and transported, and is significantly denser than ordinary armor, various militaries have used it during and since the Persian Gulf War.

The main civilian use of depleted uranium is as a counterweight on commercial aircraft and to shield patients and health care workers from the radioactive effects of radiography cameras. While the shields themselves possess depleted uranium, it is considered to be within the limits of safety whereas the amount of radioactivity emitted from the radiography camera is substantially higher.

The military use of depleted uranium includes armor plating on personnel carriers and tanks. Due to the protection of depleted uranium, no U.S. tank was penetrated by enemy fire in the Persian Gulf War, even at very close range. Depleted uranium is also used for armor piercing ammunition (bullets and bombs) and nuclear weapons. When depleted uranium shells strike tanks or other vehicles, they self-sharpen as they penetrate the lighter metal of the vehicles and pulverize them and their occupants. Not only is depleted uranium much tougher than ordinary armor plating, it is also much less expensive. In the Persian Gulf War, 320 tons of depleted uranium were deployed by the U.S. and British militaries, and in the Iraq War 1,700 tons of depleted uranium were used.

The health concerns regarding depleted uranium revolve around its chemical toxicity and radioactive properties. With respect to chemical toxicity, the concern is primarily about internal rather than external exposure. The three main pathways to internal exposure are inhalation, ingestion, and embedded fragments as would occur in war. The oxide dust produced when depleted uranium munitions burn is easily inhaled into the lungs and retained for some time. From the lungs, the particles are deposited in the lymph nodes, bones, brain, and testes. The dust can travel over a half-mile and may travel further in arid, desert climates.

The use of depleted uranium in munitions is highly controversial and emotions run high on both sides of the question: Does depleted uranium cause adverse health outcomes in soldiers exposed to it? When the answers to this question are drenched in emotionalism, they often have their own toxic effects on the brain, causing illogical thinking and selective perception.

In 2008, the Institute of Medicine was commissioned by the Department of Veterans Affairs to establish a committee to review the research on exposure to depleted uranium and human health outcomes that was reported from 2000 to 2008. The Institute of Medicine was established in 1970 as a component of the National Academy of Sciences. It works outside the framework of government to ensure scientifically sound analysis and unbiased, evidence-based information to those who seek its expertise. In this case, the charge of the committee was to "make determinations on the strength of the evidence of associations between exposure to depleted uranium and human health outcomes." The committee extensively searched the scientific literature, placing in their database approximately 1,000 articles that addressed health outcomes of human beings who were exposed to uranium. The committee summarized its findings:

> On the basis of the available literature, the committee concluded that there is *inadequate or insufficient evidence to determine whether an association exists* between uranium exposure and all the health outcomes examined: lung cancer, leukemia,

lymphoma (Hodgkin lymphoma and non–Hodgkin lymphoma), bone cancer, renal cancer, bladder cancer, brain and other nervous system cancers, stomach cancer, prostatic cancer, testicular cancer, nonmalignant renal disease, nonmalignant respiratory disease, neurologic effects, reproductive and developmental effects, and several other health outcomes (cardiovascular effects, genotoxicity, hematologic effects, immunologic effects, and skeletal effects) [p. 4].

The fact that no hard or compelling evidence demonstrates an association between exposure to depleted uranium and adverse health outcomes in human beings does not mean that an association, correlational or causal, does not exist. It will take several if not many years to shed a clear light on that issue. However, very few informed individuals believe that there is no possibility that an association does exist. The military admits this concern at least implicitly by consistently updating clinical protocols for assessing active duty soldiers and veterans who have been exposed to depleted uranium. The question arises, however, as to whether that is a sufficient protection not only for U.S. troops but also for noncombatants in nations that have depleted uranium in the atmosphere, ground, and water.

The moral issue related to depleted uranium is somewhat more complex than that attached to the issues addressed above. While a great deal of anecdotal data suggests that exposure to depleted uranium may have serious and often chronic side effects on individuals exposed to it, no sound empirical evidence presently demonstrates a direct cause-effect relationship between depleted uranium and the health problems that have been attributed to it. This situation presents a good example of an issue in which moral judgments must be made in the absence of clear empirical data. All that can be done in these types of situations is to learn as much as possible about the issue and make tentative moral decisions based on that information. However, that does not end the issue. For example, even if research demonstrates clearly that depleted uranium causes negative health outcomes, it only raises another question: Is whatever harm depleted uranium causes to human beings and the environment still less than the harm that would be done to our troops and our nation if we discontinued its use? Until this research is completed, the moral and medical questions are likely to be strenuously debated, and the empirical question is likely to remain largely unanswered. In the meantime, because of the superior "protection power" and "kill power" of depleted uranium, its ease of storage and transportation, its relatively low cost and the absence of empirical evidence that clearly demonstrates it causes negative health effects, the military is unlikely to relinquish its use.

In a real sense, this chapter can be viewed as a final examination for the entire book because it focuses on some particularly difficult moral issues that are often a common part of war. It is important to know these issues exist, to understand their nature, and to realize that no nation is exempt from these practices and their accompanying moral implications. It should render no comfort to the citizens of any nation that whatever immoral and illegal acts "we" participate in, they may be far less immoral and illegal than the acts "they" commit. No principle of ethics, law, or religion recognizes this kind of thinking as a justifying, in contrast to a mitigating, factor.

One especially pernicious "solution" to the moral dilemmas inherent in the actions and weapons addressed above occurs when national leaders deceive their citizens either by indicating that these actions and weapons are not being deployed or, if they are, there is no reason for moral, physical, or psychological concern. If leaders truly believe the actions and weapons are justified morally and legally, there is no legitimate reason for deceit. If the actions and weapons cannot be justified morally or legally, they should not be deployed.

As this chapter illustrates, no comfortable relationship exists between war and morality. In the end, individuals can educate themselves by trying to understand some basic ethical methodologies and their relationship to the weapons and actions that are a common part of modern war. The topics discussed in this chapter reflect the concept that nothing is simple in war or morality and when they coalesce in one action, the situation becomes exponentially more complex. However, this reality does not create a reason to surrender to the complexity. Rather it is a call for citizens to take a hard look at the issues, to create a moral framework for making decisions about war, and to develop the courage to act on their decisions.

Bibliography

Agresto, J. (2007). *Mugged by reality: The liberation of Iraq and the failure of good intentions.* New York, NY: Encounter Books.
Anscombe, G.E.M. (1961). War and murder. In W. Stein (ed). *Nuclear weapons: A Catholic response* (pp. 43–62). London, England: Burns and Oates.
Aquinas, T. (1981). *The Summa Theologica of St. Thomas Aquinas.* Notre Dame, IN: Christian Classics.
Ash, E. (2001). Purple virtues: A leadership cure for unhealthy rivalry. *Aerospace Power Journal* 15 (2), 32–39.
Bainton, R.H. (1960). *Christian attitudes toward war and peace: A historical survey and critical re-evaluation.* Nashville, TN: Abingdon.
Bergen, P., and K. Tiedemann (2010). *The year of the drone: An analysis of U.S. drone strikes in Pakistan, 2004–2010.* Washington, DC: The New America Foundation. Retrieved from http://vcnv.org/files/NAF_YearOfTheDrone.pdf.
Bess, M. (2008). *Choices under fire: Moral dimensions of World War II.* New York, NY: Vintage Books.
Blight, J.G., and J.M. Lang (2005). *The fog of war: Lessons from the life of Robert S. McNamara.* Lanham, MD: Rowman and Littlefield.
Broad, E., J. Corsi, and A. Kamhi (2008, February 7). *Cluster munitions and the proportionality test.* Memorandum to delegates of the Convention on Conventional Weapons. New York, NY: Human Rights Watch. Retrieved from http://www.hrw.org/news/2008/04/07/cluster-munitions-and-proportionality-test.
Bush, G.W. (2002). *The National Security Strategy of the United States of America.* Washington, DC: Office of the President. Retrieved from http://georgewbushwhitehouse.archives.gov/nsc/nss/2002/.
Button, M. (2005). "A monkish kind of virtue"? For and against humility. *Political Theory* 33, 840–868.
Cavanaugh, T.A. (2006). *Double-effect reasoning: Doing good and avoiding evil.* New York, NY: Oxford University Press.
Challans, T.L. (2007). *Awakening warrior: Revolution in the ethics of warfare.* Albany, NY: State University of New York Press.
Chomsky, N. (1986). *Propaganda, American-style.* Interview conducted by David Barsamian of KGNU Radio, Boulder, Colorado. Retrieved July 5, 2009, from http://www.zpub.com/un/chomsky.html.
Chomsky, N. (2003). *Hegemony or survival: America's quest for global dominance.* New York, NY: Metropolitan Books.
Christopher, P. (1999). *The ethics of war and peace: An introduction to legal and moral issues* (2nd ed.). Upper Saddle River, NJ: Prentice Hall.
Coates, A.J. (1997). *The ethics of war.* New York, NY: Manchester University Press, distributed by Palgrave.
Cole, D. (2002). *When God says war is right: The Christian's perspective on when and how to fight.* Colorado Springs, CO: Waterbrook Press.

Cook, M.L. (2004). *The moral warrior: Ethics and service in the U.S. military.* Albany, NY: State University of New York Press.

Combs, C.C. (2000). *Terrorism in the twenty-first century* (2nd ed.). Upper Saddle River, NJ: Prentice Hall.

Committee on Gulf War and Health, Institute of Medicine (2008). *Gulf war and health: Updated literature review of depleted uranium.* Washington, DC: National Academies Press.

Davies, K. (2008, October 29). Humility is the forgotten virtue. *Seattle Post-Intelligencer.* Retrieved from http://www.seattlepi.com/opinion/385532_humility30.html.

Defense: Bombing cover-up (1973, July 30). *Time.* Retrieved from http://www.time.com/time/magazine/article/0,9171,907615,00.html.

Defense Health Board Task Force on Mental Health (2007). *An achievable vision: Report of the Department of Defense Task Force on Mental Health* (Accession Number: ADA469411). Falls Church, VA: Defense Health Board.

Department of the Army (1974). *Report of the Department of the Army review of the preliminary investigations into the My Lai incident* (Vol. 1) (Also known as the Peers Inquiry). Washington, DC: Department of the Army.

Department of the Army (1986). *The bedrock of our profession: Army white paper 1986* (DA Pamphlet 600–68). Washington, DC: Department of the Army.

Department of the Army (2010). *Army health promotion, risk reduction and suicide prevention: Report 2010* (DA Pamphlet 600–24). Washington, DC: Department of the Army.

Department of Defense (2008). *Supplemental information and clinical guidance for DoD depleted uranium (DU) medical management program.* Washington, DC: Department of Defense. Retrieved October 12, 2009, from http://www.pdhealth.mil/downloads/OIF_med_mgmt_supp.pdf.

Derfner, L. (2008, March 12). Rattling the cage: Terrorism, theirs and ours. *The Jerusalem Post.* Retrieved from http://www.jpost.com/Opinion/Columnists/Article.aspx?id=94794.

Dinneen, J.A. (1971). Freedom of conscience in philosophical perspective. In W.C. Bier (ed.), *Conscience: Its freedom and limitations* (pp. 101–106). New York, NY: Fordham University Press.

DiSilverio, L., and S. Laushine (2002). *Divided loyalties: Civil-military relations at risk.* Paper submitted for partial fulfillment of requirements for graduation, Air War College, Air University. Retrieved from http://www.au.af.mil/au/awc/awcgate/awc/laushine.pdf.

Doty, J., and D. Herdes (2000). Humility as a leadership virtue. *Military Review* 80 (5), 89–90.

Drezner, D.W. (2003). How smart are smart sanctions? *International Studies Review* 5 (1), 107–110.

Eisenhower Study Group (2011). *Costs of War.* A project from the Watson Institute for International Studies, Brown University, Providence, RI. Retrieved from http://costsofwar.org/.

Elshtain, J.B. (2003). *Just war against terror.* New York: Basic Books.

Erb, S. (2005). *Machiavelli and power politics.* Paper presented at the University of Maine at Farmington, October 26. Retrieved October 13, 2010 from http://hua.umf.maine.edu/Reading_Revolutions/Machiavelli.html.

Fahey, J.J. (2005). *War and the Christian perspective: Where do you stand?* Maryknoll, NY: Orbis Books.

Feith, D.J. (2008). *War and decision: Inside the Pentagon at the dawn of the war on terrorism.* New York, NY: Harper Books.

Felice, W.F. (2009). *How do I save my honor? War, moral integrity, and principled resignation.* Lanham, MD: Rowman and Littlefield.

Ferzan, K.K. (2007). Beyond intention. *Cardoza Law Review* 29 (3), 1147–1191.

Gabennesch, H. (2006). Critical thinking: what is it good for? (In fact, what is it?) *Skeptical Inquirer* 30 (2). Retrieved from http://www.csicop.org/si/show/critical_thinking_what_is_it_good_for_in_fact_what_is_it/.

Garfield, R. (1999). *Morbidity and mortality among Iraqi children from 1990 through 1998: Assessing the impact of the Gulf War and economic sanctions.* Retrieved April 4, 2010 from http://www.casi.org.uk/info/garfield/dr-garfield.html.

Gates, R. (2009). Interview on CNN's *Fareed Zakaria GPS,* May 3. Retrieved June 30, 2010 from http://transcripts.cnn.com/Transcripts/0905/03/fzgps.01.html.

Geiss, R. (2005). Humanitarian safeguards in economic sanctions regimes: A call for automatic suspension clauses, periodic monitoring, and follow-up assessment of long-term effects. *Harvard Human Rights Journal* 18, 167–200.

Gendler, E.E. (1968). War and the Jewish tradition. In Finn, J. (ed.) *A conflict of loyalties: The case for selective conscientious objection* (pp. 78–102). New York, NY: Pegasus.

Gibbs, J.C. (1997). *Noncombatant immunity and military necessity: Ethical conflict in the just war ethics of William V. O'Brien and Paul Ramsey* (Document ADA 325546). Washington, DC: Defense Technical Information Center.

Gordon, J. (1999). Economic sanctions, just war doctrine, and the "fearful spectacle of the civilian dead." *Cross Currents* 49 (3), 387–400.

Gray, C.S. (2007). *The implications of preemptive and preventive war doctrines: A reconsideration* (monograph). Washington, DC: Strategic Studies Institute. Retrieved from http://www.strategicstudiesinstitute.army.mil/Pubs/display.cfm?pubID=789.

Griswold, D. (2005). *Four decades of failure: The U.S. embargo against Cuba*. Speech presented at the James A. Baker III Institute Program on Cuba and the United States in the 21st Century, October 12, Rice University, Houston, TX. Retrieved April 24, 2010, from http://www.freetrade.org/node/433.

Halliday, D. (2001, January 16). Statement after the airing of the CNN Special Report: *The unfinished war: A decade since Desert Storm*. Retrieved February 22, 2010 from http://www.cnn.com/COMMUNITY/transcripts/2001/01/16/halliday/.

Hartle, A.E. (2004). *Moral issues in military decision making* (2nd ed., revised). Lawrence, KS: University Press of Kansas.

Hauerwas, S. (2001). *Just war tradition and the new war on terrorism*. Panel discussion sponsored by the Pew Forum on Religion and Public Health at the National Press Club, Washington, DC, October 5. Retrieved October 15, 2010, from http://pewforum.org/events/?EventID=15.

Hedges, C. and L. Al-Arian (2008). *Collateral damage: America's war against Iraqi civilians*. New York, NY: Nation Books.

Hertel, T.J. (2001). On the chopping block: Cluster munitions and the law of war. *The Air Force Law Review* 51, 229–258.

Holmes, A.F. (eds.) (2005). *War and Christian ethics: Classic and contemporary readings on the morality of war* (2nd ed.). Grand Rapids, MI: Baker Academic.

Hynes, H.P., and S. Ibragimov (2003). *Depleted uranium: Questions and answers on its use in war*. Boston, MA: Boston University School of Public Health. Retrieved September 22, 2010, from http://www.iicph.org/du_qa.

Irons, P. (1983). *Justice at war: The story of the Japanese American internment cases*. Berkeley, CA: University of California Press.

John Paul II (1995). *The gospel of life*. Boston, MA: Pauline Books and Media.

John Paul II (1995, May 16). *Message on the fiftieth anniversary of the end of the Second World War*. Retrieved July 4, 2010, from http://www.ewtn.com/library/papaldoc/jp2wwii.htm.

John Paul II (2005). *Memory and identity: Conversations at the dawn of a millennium*. Rome, Italy: Rizzoli.

Johnson, J.T. (1999). *Morality and contemporary warfare*. New Haven, CT: Yale University Press.

Kaufman, W. (2005) What's wrong with preventive war? The moral and legal basis for the preventive use of force. *Ethics and International Affairs* 19 (3), 23–38.

King, M.L., Jr. (1967). *Where do we go from here: chaos or community?* New York, NY: HarperCollins.

Kirk, K.E. (1999). *Conscience and its problems: An introduction to casuistry*. Louisville, KY: Westminster John Knox Press.

Korn, R. (2009). *How does responsible thinking differ from critical thinking?* Retrieved April 24, 2010, from http://www.truthpizza.org/critdiff.htm.

LeShan, L. (2002). *The psychology of war: Comprehending its mystique and its madness*. New York, NY: Helios Press.

Lieber, F. (1863). *Instructions for the government of armies of the United States in the field*. Retrieved April 24, 2010, from http://www.icrc.org/IHL.NSF/WebPrint/110-FULL?OpenDocument.

Machiavelli, N. (2005). *The Prince (Wooten Edition)*. Indianapolis, IN: Hacket.

Maguire, D.C. (2007). *The horrors we bless: Rethinking the just-war legacy*. Minneapolis, MN: Fortress Press.

Mansfield, A.J., J.S. Kaufman, S.W. Marshall, B.N. Gaynes, J.P. Morrissey, and C.C. Engel (2010). Deployment and the use of mental health services among U.S. Army wives. *New England Journal of Medicine* 362 (2), 101–109.

Margerum, W.H. (1983). Integrity: The military professional and society. *Air University Review* 34 (6) 78–84.

McGee, R.W. (1998). MFN status, trade embargoes, sanctions, and blockades: An examination of some overlooked property, contract, and other human rights issues. *Dumont Institute Working Paper No. 98.1*. Dumont, NJ: The Dumont Institute for Public Policy Research.

McGurk, B.H. (2010). Lawyers: A predator drone's Achilles heel? *Harvard National Security Journal* (posted March 11). Retrieved, August 10, 2011, from http://harvardnsj.com/2010/03/lawyers-a-predator-drone%E2%80%99s-achilles-heal/.

McMaster, H.R. (1997). *Dereliction of duty: Lyndon Johnson, Robert McNamara, the Joint Chiefs of Staff, and the lies that led to Vietnam*. New York: HarperPerennial.

McNamara, R.S., and B. VanDeMark (1996). *In retrospect: The tragedy and lessons of Vietnam*. New York, NY: Vintage Books.

Miller, R.B. (2009). Just war, civic virtue, and democratic social criticism: Augustinian reflections. *The Journal of Religion* 89 (1), 1–30.

Miller, W.I. (2000). *The mystery of courage*. Cambridge, MA: Harvard University Press.

Morgenthau, H.J. (1965, April 18). We are deluding ourselves in Vietnam. *New York Times Magazine*, 87.

Morgenthau, H.J. (1967). To intervene or not to intervene. *Foreign Affairs* 45 (3), 424–436.

Morgenthau, H.J. (1978). *Politics among nations: The struggle for power and peace* (5th ed., revised). New York, NY: Alfred A. Knopf.

Murray, J.C. (1964). *We hold these truths: Catholic reflections on the American proposition*. Garden City, NY: Image Books.

Muskopf, J. (2006). *Integrity failures: A strategic leader problem* (AD-A449-640). USAWC Strategy Research Project. Carlisle Barracks, PA: U.S. Army War College.

Nardin, T. (1996). *The ethics of war and peace: Religious and secular perspectives*. Princeton, NJ: Princeton University Press.

Niebuhr, R. (1943). *The nature and destiny of man*. New York, NY: Scribner.

O'Donovan, O. (2003). *The just war revisited*. New York, NY: Cambridge University Press.

Orend, B. (2006). *The morality of war*. Peterborough, ON: Broadview Press.

Patterson, E. (2007) *Jus post bellum* and international conflict: Order, justice, and reconciliation. In Brough, M.W., J.W. Lango, and H. van der Linden (eds.). *Rethinking the just war tradition* (pp. 35–52). New York, NY: State University of New York Press.

Prebeck, S.R. (1993). *Preventive attack in the 1990s?* Thesis presented to the faculty of the School of Advanced Airpower Studies, Maxwell Air Force Base, for completion of graduation requirements, Academic year 1992–1993. Retrieved July 1, 2010, from http://www.comw.org/qdr/fulltext/9305prebeck.pdf.

Price, J.F. (2006). *Moral competence for the joint warfighter: The missing element in defense transformation* (ADA480321). Master's thesis. Norfolk Virginia: National Defense University Joint Advanced Warfighting School. Retrieved from http://handle.dtic.mil/100.2/ADA480321.

Ramsey, P. (2002). *The just war: Force and political responsibility*. London, England: Rowman and Littlefield.

Reilly, R. (2003). Conscience, citizenship, and global responsibilities. *Buddhist-Christian Studies* 23, 117–131.

Rizer, K.R. (2001). Bombing dual-use targets: legal, ethical, and doctrinal perspectives. *Air and Space Power Chronicles*, document created May 1, 2001. Retrieved May 24, 2010, from http://www.airpower.maxwell.af.mil/airchronicles/cc/Rizer.html.

Robbins, J.S. (2004, August 18). Holiday in Cambodia. *National Review Online*. Retrieved April 22, 2010, from www.nationalreview.com/robbins/robbins200408180835.asp.

Rohr, J.A. (1971). *Prophets without honor: Public policy and the selective conscientious objector*. Nashville, TN: Abington Press.

Saberian, M.R. (2004). The flaming sword: Napalm and its effects. *Gaines Junction: An Interdisciplinary Journal of History*. College Station, TX: Phi Alpha Theta, Texas A&M University.

Schott, J.J. (1998, June 3). *U.S. economic sanctions: Good intentions, bad execution*. Statement before the Committee on International Relations, U.S. House of Representatives. Retrieved March 24, 2010, from http://www.iie.com/publications/papers/paper.cfm?ResearchID=314.
Secretary of Defense (2008, June 19). Memorandum on DoD policy on cluster munitions and unintended harm to civilians. Washington, DC: Department of Defense. Retrieved from http://www.defense.gov/news/d20080709cmpolicy.pdf.
Shadle, M.A. (2011). *The origins of war: A Catholic perspective*. Washington, DC: Georgetown University Press.
Shane, Scott (2011, August 11). C.I.A. is disputed on civilian toll in drone strikes. *New York Times*.
Shawcross, W. (1979). *Sideshow: Kissinger, Nixon and the destruction of Cambodia*. New York, NY: Simon and Schuster.
Shay, J. (1994). *Achilles in Vietnam: Combat trauma and the undoing of character*. New York, NY: Scribner.
Singer, P.W. (2009). *Wired for war*. New York, NY: Penguin Press.
Slim, H. (2008). *Killing civilians*. New York, NY: Columbia University Press.
Sorel, J.M. (2003). Some questions about the definition of terrorism and the fight against its financing. *European Journal of International Law* 14 (2) 365–378.
Standish, J (2001). *Just war tradition and the new war on terrorism*. Panel discussion sponsored by the Pew Forum on Religion and Public Health at the National Press Club, Washington, DC, October 5. Retrieved October 15, 2010, from http://pewforum.org/events/?EventID=15.
Steinhoff, U. (2007). *On the ethics of war and terrorism*. London, England: Oxford University Press.
Stooksbury, W. (2002). *Ethics for the Marine lieutenant*. Annapolis, MD: Center for the Study of Professional Military Ethics, U.S. Naval Academy.
Taylor, T. (1970). *Nuremberg and Vietnam: An American tragedy*. Chicago, IL: Quadrangle Books.
Temes, P.S. (2003). *The just war: An American reflection on the morality of war in our time*. Chicago, IL: Ivan R. Dee.
Thomas, M.R. (2005). *The intentions/foresight distinction in the doctrine of double effect: From theoretical impasses and double-think to practical applications in bioethics*. Unpublished master's dissertation, Louisiana State University and Agricultural and Mechanical College. Retrieved from http://etd.lsu.edu/docs/available/etd-01232005-164221/.
Thompson, H., and R. Ridenhour (1995–96). Vietnam testimony: Two veterans recount their roles at My Lai. Transcripts of statements by Thompson and Ridenhour at a conference at Tulane University in 1994. *Louisiana Cultural Vistas* (Louisiana Endowment for the Humanities), Winter, 22–29.
Toner, J.H. (2005). *Morals under the gun: The cardinal virtues, military ethics, and American society*. Lexington, KY: University Press of Kentucky.
U.S. Army Center for Health Promotion and Preventive Medicine. *Depleted Uranium — Individual*. Retrieved October 29, 2009 from http://chppm-www.apgea.army.mil/documents/fact/65-050-0503.pdf.
U.S. Defense Intelligence Agency (1991, January 22). *Iraq water treatment vulnerabilities* (File: 950901_511rept_91.txt). Retrieved November 28, 2009, from http://www.gulflink.osd.mil/declassdocs/dia/19950901/950901_511rept_91.html.
U.S. Senate Select Committee (1975–76). *Report of the United States Senate Select Committee to Study Governmental Operations with Respect to Intelligence Activities* (also known as the Church Committee). Washington, DC: U.S. Government Printing Office. Retrieved July 23, 2010, from http://pwl.netcom.com/~ncoic/cia_info.htm.
VonClausewitz, C. (2007). *On war*. London, England: Oxford University Press.
Wakin, M.M. (ed.) (1986). *War, morality, and the military profession* (2nd ed.). Boulder, CO: Westview Press.
Walzer, M. (1977). *Just and unjust wars: A moral argument, with historical illustrations* (4th ed.). New York, NY: Basic Books.
Walzer, M. (2004). *Arguing about war*. New Haven, CT: Yale University Press.
Weigel, G. (2003). Moral clarity in a time of war. *First Things*, 129, January, 20–27.

Welch, M. (2002). The politics of dead children: Have sanctions against Iraq murdered millions? *Reason Online*, March 2002. Retrieved October 22, 2010: http://www.reason.com/news/printer/28346.html.

Wheeler, N.J. (2001). Protecting Afghan civilians from the hell of war. *Social Science Research Council After September 11 Essay Forum*. Retrieved from http://essays.ssrc.org/sept11/essays/wheeler_text_only.htm

Willenson, K. (1987). *The bad war: An oral history of the Vietnam War*. New York: New American Library.

Woods, Chris (2011, August 10). Drone war exposed: The complete picture of CIA strikes in Pakistan. *The Bureau of Investigative Journalism (Online)*. Retrieved August 26, 2011: http://www.thebureauinvestigates.com/2011/08/10/most-complete-picture-yet-of-cia-drone-strikes/.

Yoder, J.H. (2001). *When war is unjust: being honest in just-war thinking* (2nd ed.). Eugene, OR: Wipf and Stock.

Zahn, G.C. (1962) *German Catholics and Hitler's wars: A study in social control*. New York, NY: Sheed and Ward.

Zimbardo, P. (2007). *The Lucifer effect: Understanding how good people turn evil*. New York, NY: Random House.

Zinn, H. (2001). *On war*. New York, NY: Seven Stories Press.

Zinn, H. (2003, April 12). A kinder, gentler patriotism. Long Island, NY, *Newsday*, opinion page. Retrieved from http://www.newsday.com/a-kinder-gentler-patriotism-1.316229.

Index

Aeschylus 139
Anscombe, G.E. M. 81, 153
Aquinas, Thomas 15, 16, 82, 95, 96, 151, 152
Aristotle 6, 15, 80, 81
Ash, Eric 82
Augustine, St. 95–96
avoidance tactics 131–135, 145

balance of power 71, 78
Bentham, Jeremy 20
Bergen, Peter 175
Broad, C.D. 18
Broad, E., J. Corsi, and A. Hamhi 181
Bureau of Investigative Journalism 176
Button, Mark 97, 99

Carr, E.H. 68
Casey, George 87
categorical imperatives 18–20
Cavanaugh, T.A. 182–183
Chomsky, Noam 130, 168
Church Committee 139–140
Cicero 15, 37
cluster munitions 9, 49, 167, 178–183
cognition 104–124
cognitive dissonance 112–113
cognitive overconfidence 114–115
cognitive perseveration 115–116
collective guilt 7
compartmentalization 95, 108–109, 112
competence 9, 80, 83, 92–95, 101, 102, 107, 113, 115, 120, 161
competent authority 38–40; *see also* legitimate authority
confirmation bias 111–112, 161
conscience of the laws 6, 63, 66
conscience: autonomy 29; critical analysis 27–28; examination of 31–32; influence of ideology 29–30; nature 11–14, 24–25; unconscious factors 28–9
conscientious objection 62–66
consequentialism 15, 20–23, 81, 99

courage 7, 8, 9, 25, 80, 83, 90–92, 99, 100, 101, 102
Cousins, Norman 11
Cuba 46, 72, 183, 184–185

Davies, Kate 96
deceit 9, 139–142
decision-making process *see* moral decision-making process
defensive thinking 9, 105, 107–117
dehumanization 107–108
deontology 15, 17–20, 22–23
depleted uranium 9, 167, 188–190
Derfner, Larry 173
dichotomous thinking 110–111
Dinneen, John 25
discrimination 19, 47, 62, 149, 166, 167, 171, 172, 180–183
DiSilverio, I. and S. Laushine 84–85
domino theory 134, 147, 165
double effect 9, 147, 151–157, 166
Drezner, Daniel W. 186, 187
duty, virtue of 9, 80, 84–88, 102

economic sanctions 9, 183–188
Eichmann, Adolf 26
Eisenhower Study Group 3
Elshtain, Jean Bethke 5
Erb, Scott 74, 75
exceptionalism 18, 95, 97, 113

Felice, William F. 8–9
Ferzan, Kimberly Kessler 154
Finnis, John 15
flourishing (*eudaimonia*) 81, 100
Foot, Philippa 15
Fried, Charles 18

Gabennesch, H. 120–121
Gandhi, Mahatma 59, 61
Garfield, Richard 187–188
Gates, Robert 98
Geiss, Robin 186–187

199

Index

Gendler, Everett E. 36
Geneva Conventions 33, 149, 151
Gibbs, Jonathan 149
Gordon, Joy 185
Gray, Colin S. 158
Grisez, Germain 15
Grotius, Hugo 15, 16, 164

Halliday, Denis 188
Handicap International 179, 180
Hare, R.M. 20
Hartle, Anthony E. 85
Hauerwas, Stanley 61
Heraclitus 15
Hertel, Thomas J. 182
Hobbes, Thomas 68
hubris 83, 96–98
Human Rights Watch 181
humility 9, 80, 83, 95–99, 102, 103, 114

impartialism 20–21
individualism 6, 96
individuality 6, 12
information dominance 128
Institute of Medicine 189–190
integrity 9, 80, 82, 83, 88–90, 96, 99, 100, 102, 107, 133, 143
intention and intentionality 13, 17–18, 20, 22, 34, 35, 38–40, 47–48, 55, 82, 105, 152–155, 158; *see also* right intention
International Criminal Court 149
Iraq War 174, 179, 189

John Paul II 83, 126
Jones, James L. 91
jus ad bellum 22, 34, 37, 38–46, 54, 183
jus in bello 34, 37, 43, 46–49, 149
jus post bellum 34, 37, 43, 49–54
just cause 38, 40–42
just war principles 2, 9, 19, 33–58, 59, 61, 66, 68, 77–79, 81, 86, 145, 155, 158, 170–172, 183; *see also jus ad bellum*; *jus in bello*; *jus post bellum*; just cause

Kamm, Frances 18
Kant, Immanuel 18–19, 49
Kaufman, Whitley 164–165
Kennan, George F. 68
King, Martin Luther, Jr. 67–8
Kirk, Kenneth 28
Kissinger, Henry 59, 68, 79
Korean War 36, 67
Korn, R. 117

last resort 22, 34, 38, 45–46, 51, 62, 75, 150, 176
legitimate authority 16, 38–40, 183; *see also* competent authority

Lieber, Francis 147
Lippman, Walter 125

Machiavelli, Niccolò 68, 73–75
Maguire, Daniel C. 56, 57
Mansfield, A.J., *et al* 87–88
Margerum, W.H. 88
McGee, Robert F. 183–184
McGurk, Brett H. 178
McNamara, Robert 115–116
military necessity 9, 147, 148–151, 166, 181
Mill, John Stuart 20
Miller, Richard B. 33
Miller, William Ian 90
Moore, G.E. 20
moral decision-making process 9, 23–27, 31, 32, 45, 90, 106, 107, 114, 130, 147
moral worldview 9, 15, 105, 118, 121–124, 161
Morgenthau, Hans 68, 72, 73
Murray, John Courtney 37
Muskopf, James A. 89

Nagel, Thomas 18
nationalism 6, 34, 79, 83
natural law theory 15–17
neorealism 68, 75–76
New American Foundation 175–176, 177
Niebuhr, Reinhold 68, 73
noncombatant immunity 46, 47–49; *see also* discrimination
Nuremberg Trials 33, 85

O'Donovan, Oliver 146
Orend, B. 22
Orwell, George 104

pacifism 2, 9, 58, 59–68, 78, 79, 90
partialism 20, 21, 157
Pascal, Blaise 167
paternalism 6, 7
patriotism, virtue of 9, 22, 80, 83–84, 100, 102, 129, 134–135
Patterson, Eric 54
Persian Gulf War 53, 165, 174, 179, 187, 188, 189
pluralistic ignorance 114
Prebeck, Steven R. 165
preemptive attack or force 9, 24, 40, 147, 157–159, 160–166, 184
presumption against war 34, 55
presumption for war 34, 54
preventive attack or force 9, 40, 147, 157, 159–163, 164–166
probability of success 22, 38, 44–45
propaganda 9, 58, 117, 125–135, 142, 143, 146
proportionality 19, 22, 38, 43–44, 46–47, 57, 62, 148, 149, 166, 167, 171–172, 180–182

Index

Ramsey, Paul 37
rationalization 28, 39
realism 2, 9, 59, 68–79, 149; classical 68–73, 79; prudence in 70; Machiavellian 73–75, challenges to 78–79; *see also* neorealism
realistic thinking 9, 105, 106–107
Reilly, Richard 66
responsible thinking 9, 105, 118–121, 144–146
right intention 22, 34, 38, 42–43, 50–52, 77; *see also* intention and intentionality
Rizer, Kenneth 151
rogue states 160, 161–163
Rohr, John A. 7–8
Romero, Oscar 67
Ross, W.D. 18

sanctions 20, 46, 170, 183–185; *see also* economic sanctions; smart sanctions
Scanlon, Thomas 18
Schott, Jeffrey J. 184
selective attention or perception 111–112
situationalism 21, 99
smart sanctions 185–187
Sorel, Jean-Marc 169
Standish, James 55
Steinhoff, Uwe 57
Suarez, Francisco 38

terrorism 9, 51, 76, 117, 161, 162, 164, 167–173
Thomas, Mitchell R. 156
Thompson, Hugh 101–103
Thucydides 68
Tiedemann, Katherine 175–176
tortured reasoning 131, 135–139, 143, 145

United Nations 33, 71, 75, 184, 188
United Nations Security Council 164–165, 185, 187
universalism 20, 21
universalizability 18, 21
unmanned aerial vehicles (UAVs) 9, 173–178
U.S. Defense Intelligence Agency 185
U.S. Department of Defense 148, 158, 159–160, 168, 180
U.S. National Security Strategy 161, 163

Vietnam War 5, 6, 36, 45, 48, 64, 72, 79, 101, 102–103, 105, 109, 112, 115, 122, 130, 135–136, 140–141, 171–172, 184
virtue ethics 2, 9, 15, 59, 79, 80–103
Vitoria 7, 164
Von Clausewitz, Carl 68

Walzer, Michael 48
Watson Institute for International Studies 3
Weigel, George 37
Wheeler, Nicholas 52–53
Willenson, Kim 142
World Court 33, 71, 75
World War II 7, 24, 26, 36, 37, 49, 51, 56, 61, 66, 67, 70, 109, 110, 116, 126, 137, 139, 168, 171, 184

Yoder, John Howard 35

Zahn, Gordon C. 56
Zinn, Howard 83–84

www.ingramcontent.com/pod-product-compliance
Ingram Content Group UK Ltd.
Pitfield, Milton Keynes, MK11 3LW, UK
UKHW041919140426
5217IPUK00013B/223